# I CAN DO THAT! **WOODWORKING PROJECTS**

## 3RD EDITION

**EDITED BY DAVID THIEL & SCOTT FRANCIS**

**POPULAR WOODWORKING BOOKS**

# Table of Contents

SEATING

**1**   Skansen Bench . . . 50

**2**   Hall Bench . . . 52

**3**   Simple Side Chair . . . 56

**4**   Patio Chair . . . 64

**5**   Mud Room Bench. . . 70

**6**   Folding Stool. . . 74


TABLES

**7**   Round Taboret . . . 78

**8**   Victorian Side Table . . . 82

**9**   Coffee Table . . . 84

**10**   Factory Cart Coffee Table . . . 90

**11**   Tapered-leg Table. . . 92

**12**   Game Table. . . 94

**13**   Tiered End Table . . . 100

**14**   Contemporary Coffee Table . . . 104

**15**   Contemporary Side Table . . . 107


STORAGE

**16**   Pirate Chest. . . 110

**17**   Storage Bench . . . 112

**18**   Country Tool & Toy Chest . . . 114

**19**   Mitered CD/DVD Rack . . . 116

**20**   Canted Wall Box . . . 118

**21**   Pleasant Hill Firewood Box . . . 120

**22**   Painted Cupboard . . . 122

**23**   Gent's Chest . . . 130

**24**   Shaker Carry Box . . . 133

Yes You Can Do It! . . . 4

Rules for Using the Tools . . . 6

Techniques . . . 42

Materials & Hardware . . . 45

Suppliers . . . 203

Index . . . 204

SHELVING

**25**  Egg Crate Shelves . . . 136

**26**  Whale Tail Shelves . . . 141

**27**  Stacking Bookcases . . . 144

**28**  Contemporary Shelves . . . 146

**29**  Simplified Stickley Bookcase . . . 148

**30**  Shaker Shelves . . . 150

**31**  Library Magazine Rack . . . 154

**32**  Corner Shelf . . . 156

**33**  Open Bookcase . . . 158

**34**  Contemporary Bookshelves . . . 164

**35**  Shaker Shelf . . . 166

**36**  Hanging Shelves . . . 172

MISCELLANEOUS

**37**  Message Center . . . 175

**38**  Tool Rack . . . 178

**39**  Step Stool . . . 180

**40**  Fish Sticks Trivet . . . 182

**41**  Knife Block . . . 184

**42**  Shaker-inspired Step Stool . . . 186

**43**  Low-profile Serving Tray . . . 188

**44**  Recycling Station . . . 190

**45**  Bi-fold Shutters . . . 192

**46**  Magazine Rack . . . 194

**47**  Lap Desk . . . 196

**48**  Weekend Pot Rack . . . 199

# Yes You Can Do It!

When you get started in woodworking there are many paths to follow, forks in the road, dead-ends and short-cuts. It's a journey that our forebears would make with the help of a living, breathing guide: a master, a grandfather, a shop teacher.

Sadly, the guides are fewer in number today. And so you are left with people like me to help. Like the making of meat by-products, it's not a pretty sight. Getting your woodworking instruction from books, magazines, television and the occasional class is a slow way to learn a complex task. In fact, many woodworkers spend a long time (years!) simply accumulating machines and tools before they ever build a single piece of furniture. And when they do begin to build, they inevitably discover that they actually need different machines and tools to make what they really want to make.

So they buy more tools and machines.

I want you to know something important that doesn't get said much: There is another way to begin building furniture. You don't need a table saw, a workbench or even a shop. You don't need to spend $1,000 to build your first birdhouse. You can go to the home center in the morning and start building something the same day.

I'm not talking about building junk, either. The difference between a nice-looking set of bookshelves and a rude assemblage of 2×4s isn't a table saw. The difference is cleverness, sound design and just a wee bit of patience.

To build nice furniture you need a handful of decent tools that you won't outgrow. This book will help you select the right tools that strike a balance between price and function. You need to use these tools correctly; we'll show you how to use them to build furniture (something you rarely find in the instruction manual). You need a place to work; a drive-way, garage or corner of the basement will do nicely. You need good materials; we'll show you how to get everything you need from the local home center. And you need plans and ideas for things to build that look nice and can be con-structed with these tools, methods and materials.

In *Popular Woodworking* magazine we publish a column

called "I Can Do That" because we want readers to say that (out loud or in their heads) when they read the maga-zine (and now this book). We've offered many of the plans used in the magazine and have added another ten, built specifically for this book and for you.

Eventually, we think you'll outgrow the manual part of this book (and on the web at www.icandothatextras.com) as your skills improve. I bet you will want a table saw someday. And a drill press. And a smoothing plane. When that day comes, however, you'll also have a house full of well-proportioned, well-built proj-ects under your belt. You will be ready for those awesome tools, and the learning curve will be mercifully short.

If all this sounds like something that a bunch of ideal-ists cooked up at a corporate strategy meeting, you're wrong. Though I had some carpentry training from my father and grandfather, I started building furniture on my back porch in Lexington, Kentucky, with a very similar set of tools. Probably the only major difference is that I had a circular saw instead of a miter saw (I didn't know those existed yet). I built a lot of stuff with my simple setup — some stuff we still have today and some stuff that was long ago abandoned at the curb or given away.

So this, dear reader, is a valid path.

My only regret in following it is that I wish I'd had this book (or a master) to make the journey easier.

— Christopher Schwarz
*Contributing Editor, Popular Woodworking Magazine*

# Rules for Using the Tools

BY CHRISTOPHER SCHWARZ AND THE POPULAR WOODWORKING MAGAZINE STAFF

"The pioneers cleared the forests from Jamestown to the Mississippi with fewer tools than are stored in the modern garage."

— *unknown, attributed to Dwayne Laws*

I'm not an emotional guy. I don't get nostalgic about high school, my first car or my first dog, Scampy. I don't much hug family members at holiday gatherings. But I do have the deepest respect and affection for my tools. The care you give tools will gush readily into the things you build with them. None of the tools in the following kit are disposable; if you take good care of them, they will be around for many years of service.

## STOP RUST

Here are some basic tips for caring for all tools. Don't you dare let them rust. Rust spreads like a cancer in ferrous materials (iron and steel) and can make your measuring and cutting tools difficult to use. There are a lot of products out there to prevent and remove rust, but the best thing going cannot be found on the shelf: a small can of vigilance.

When you are done with a tool, wipe down the metal surfaces — especially the cutting surface — with a rag that has been soaked with WD-40. Always keep the rag nearby (mine is seven years old) and renew it with a squirt of WD-40 when it gets dry. Wiping your tool down does two things: First, it removes dust from the tool. Dust can carry salt. Salt attracts water. The combination of salt and

moisture will start breaking down your iron and steel tools.

Second, the WD-40 helps prevent rust by forming a thin protective barrier, albeit one that must be constantly renewed to be effective. Other people will disparage WD-40 (I once did). Ignore them. We tested all the rust preventative products on the market one spring weekend. We applied the products to a cast-iron plate and left the plate outside in the dewy grass for a couple of days. The area treated with WD-40 came out of the test looking the best. WD-40 is cheap. It's readily available. It won't stain your work. Spray some on a piece of wood and watch what happens. Once it dries, there's nothing to see.

## LEARN TO SEE

All of your tools require tweaking and maintenance. They might work perfectly right out of the box; they might not. It all depends on who made the tool and what sort of day they were having when your tool came down the assembly line — whether the assembler was a robot or a person.

You need to learn to set up your tools so they do what they were intended to do — cut square, bore straight holes, measure accurately. Once you set them up, you need to check on them every once in

a while. Trust, but verify. It's a fact: Tools lose their settings after regular use.

In fact, one of the biggest challenges in woodworking is training your eye to see the right things. You need to learn to see if the cut is square. You need to see if your square is square. Have you ever heard the old expression "tried and true?" It is an expression that applies to your tools as well as your work. When you make a cut you should test it to make sure it's the cut you wanted — this is called *trying* your work. If the cut is correct it is said to be *true*. Likewise with your tools, you must try them to ensure they are cutting true. We're going to show you how to test all of your tools (and joints) so they are true. It's not hard, and it pays off big-time.

## BUYING QUALITY

You can spend a ridiculous sum on any tool — ridiculously huge and ridiculously small. Jigsaws can cost $35 to $500. Awls can cost $2 to $180. I wouldn't recommend you buy the tool on either extreme of the spectrum. It would be easy for us to say simply: "Buy the best you can afford." But that's a cop-out. If money is tight, you shouldn't buy the $35 jigsaw. You should wait and save a bit more cash. If you're a wealthy heiress, you shouldn't buy the $180 scratch awl just because you can afford it (save your money for some real jewelry).

What's important is to buy tools that do what they are supposed to do. Tools that hold their settings. Tools that are easy to maintain and adjust. Tools that are reasonably durable. Tools that are safe. We are going to explain what is important about each tool, and what is not. We might not be able to offer brand-name advice or model numbers because those change from month to month and from city to city (no lie; ask me about that fact over a beer sometime). But we can help you narrow your choices considerably.

All of the tools on our list can be purchased from a home center or a hardware store. There is no specialty stuff on the list to search the world for.

## MEASURING TOOLS

You want to buy both of your measuring tools — a 12" combination square and a 16' tape measure — at the same time so you can check the scale on one to make sure it matches the other. They are unlikely to disagree, but if they do, you'll be chasing your tail for a long time before you figure out what the problem

In general, we recommend a metal-bodied combination square. These are, usually, more durable and accurate.

is. To buy these tools, take with you to the store a mechanical pencil and a scrap of wood that is at least 6" square and has one straight edge.

## 12" COMBINATION SQUARE

This is the tool that will lay out your joints and cuts, and check all your work to ensure your cuts are accurate. The home center should have a few different brands available with some variation in price. Here's what's important:

First, the square must be square. The ruler and head must meet at 90° or the tool is worthless. There are ways to tweak a faulty square, but we don't recommend them. It's not something you should have to do. This is why you brought the wood and the pencil along with you — they will

help you sort through the pile of combination squares to find the most accurate one in the bunch. Don't be embarrassed to do this in the store; they should be embarrassed that you have to do this.

First, take the ruler and press one edge against the straight edge of your board to confirm that the edge is straight. Generally you don't want to see any light peeking out between the ruler and the wood. If your wood is out of whack, wander over to the lumber section to look for an offcut to borrow. Usually there's a barrel by the panel saw or radial arm saw where they cut down big stock into small stock for customers.

With the square reassembled, press the head of the combination square

The ruler from your combination square can confirm if the edge of the board is straight. Off-the-rack lumber will usually have at least one decent edge.

Accuracy is important here. Keep the square registered securely against the wood as you scribe the line. If anything feels like it shifted during scribing, make another line. Use a mechanical pencil to ensure your line is consistent in width.

Now flip the square over and show the ruler to the line. If your square is true and your line consistent, then the line and the ruler should be perfectly parallel. If the line and the ruler don't match up, try the operation again before you reject the square — it's easy to trip yourself up when checking your square.

against the straight edge of the board and use your fingers to hold the ruler down and steady against the face of the board. With a pencil, scribe a thin line along the edge of the ruler. Make it as thin and consistent as possible. If the square moves or the line changes thickness, simply move the square and try again.

Now flip the square over so the other face of the ruler is flat against the face of your board and hold the head of the square against the edge. Push the square up to your perfect line; this is called "showing the line to the square." If the edge of the ruler is perfectly parallel to your pencil line, you have found a square that is indeed square. Congratulations. If the line is slightly off, try the test again. If it's off in the same way, put the square back for another sucker, er — shopper.

Now look at the ruler itself. It must be readable. Look for fine dimension marks. Better-quality squares will have them engraved in the metal rather than printed on. Ideally, you want the ruler to have different scales on each edge. The best combination squares will have one scale in 8ths of an inch, another in 16ths, 32nds and 64ths. You can get away without the 64ths. The 32nds are helpful in most cases. The 16ths are non-negotiable and necessary.

Remove the square from its head by loosening the nut below the ruler. The ruler should be easy to remove and replace. You'll be doing this quite a bit. Now tighten up the nut and make sure

the ruler locks firmly in place. It should stay put when you tug on it.

Check out the rest of the square. Is there a bubble level in the head? Yes? No? It doesn't much matter; it's mostly worthless in such a small tool. Is there a removable scribe/scratch awl in the head? Again, pretty worthless in my book. I seem to lose mine right away, but never miss it. It's too small to use anyway.

Treat your combination square like it is a holy relic. If it gets knocked to the floor, curse yourself and then test it immediately. If it's out of true, get in your car and head back to the hardware store. Throw away the old head but keep the ruler — it's still useful. Never slide the ruler needlessly through the head (I've seen some people who do this like it's a nervous tic). This activity wears the area where the head meets the ruler. I've had squares that went out-of-true after only a couple hundred full-length motions through the head. If that happens to you, buy a better brand of square next time.

## 16' TAPE MEASURE

First, why not buy a 50' tape measure like all the contractors have on *This Old House*? My dad always mocks my 16' tape measure. Let me tell you, the big tape measures are a pain for furniture work. They curl up more and are hard to lay flat on the work. They weigh a lot. They are bulky. They rarely have the right scales on them.

A 16' tape measure is just the right size for furniture and cabinet work. I sometimes use a 12' tape, but it isn't appreciably smaller or cheaper than the 16' tapes, which are pretty easy to find. The first thing to do when buying a tape measure is to pull the tape out and look at the scale. It's nice to have 16ths on the entire length and 32nds along the first 12" or so.

The hook should move in and out. The distance it moves should be equal to the thickness of the hook itself. Tweak the hook with pliers until the tape consistently measures inside and outside measurements.

After comparing about 15 brands, I like the Lufkin scales. They have fine graduations and avoid the ridiculous gimmickry on some scales (some measure in 10ths of an inch!). Note the 32nds at the bottom and the 16ths at the top.

Now compare the scale on your combination square with the scale on the tape measure. They should match up. Line them up on the 1" mark and check the dimension lines between 1" and 2". The tape itself is important. You want the lines to be as fine as possible and you want the tape to lay as flat as possible on the work (this makes it easy to mark and measure accurately).

There also is a thing called *standout* with tape measures, this is how far out the tape will extend before it bends and droops. For building furniture, this is not a big deal — a mere 36" to 48" of standout is no problem in the shop. (Know, however, that you can never visit a home-building site with this sissy tool.)

A 12' or 16' tape measure is a good size for building furniture and dealing with household projects. When you start building houses, then you can step up to the big-boy tapes.

Always check your tape measure against your combination square to ensure that the graduations are similarly fine and actually line up. Manufacturers of tape measures and combination squares swear that inaccurate scales cannot occur. I, however, have found occasional discrepancies.

Now check the tab, sometimes called the hook, on the end of the tape measure. It should move a little bit. How much? Exactly as much as the thickness of the tip of the hook. If the hook is 1/32" thick, the hook should slide forward and back 1/32". Some people foolishly glue (or weld) the hook so it doesn't move. This prevents you from taking accurate measurements on either the inside or outside of your work. When you measure the inside of a box, the hook is pushed in so the outside face of the hook is zero. When you measure the outside of a piece, the hook is pushed out so that the inside face of the hook is zero.

You can tweak the hook a bit with pliers back at home in order to make the tape measure accurate for inside and outside measurements. For now, find one where the hook looks like it moves enough to be accurate.

There are other features on a tape measure that are personal. A clip for the belt is necessary. The locking mechanism should be easy to activate and release — but not too easy. I've always fumbled with the tape measures that release by pressing a plate on the underside of the tool. I constantly retract the tape by mistake. Also — and this might sound funny — I like to have a brightly colored tape measure. The color makes it easy to find when you set it down.

## STYLES OF SAWS

We had some long discussions about which kind of portable saws should be in this tool kit. The circular saw seemed a natural part of the tool kit, but it has some limitations when dealing with smaller work, and it won't cut miters that are good enough for picture frames (I'm sure someone can do it; but we can't). Plus, it can be difficult to find saw blades that have enough teeth to make a furniture-grade cut. Circular saws are best suited for the job site.

In the end, we settled on a jigsaw for rip cuts and curves, and a 10" miter saw for crosscuts and miters. The jigsaw has the disadvantage that you need to clean up your rip cuts with a block plane. But its advantages far outweigh that disadvantage. (Plus, learning to use a block plane is an essential furniture-building skill; more on that later). The jigsaw cuts curves beautifully and it is safe, powerful and inexpensive. Plus, with a little practice, you'll find that you need very little clean-up of your sawn edges. We'll show you how to achieve this (the trick is the blade you buy and your left thumb).

The miter saw is a great crosscutting tool for fine and rough work when it is properly tweaked. It will make airtight crosscuts, perfect miters and even break down stock into manageable lengths for you to work with your other tools. A simple 10" miter saw may be limited in capacity to cut only a 1 × 8, but when you're dealing with off-the-rack lumber from the home center, 1 × 8 is likely the largest lumber with which you'll be dealing. Let's look at these tools in detail.

This is a barrel-grip jigsaw — chic and European and less common in North America. Too bad; some of us really like the lower center of gravity. If you can find a jigsaw like this one at your home center, we recommend it. If you can't — don't worry about it.

## JIGSAW

This tool seems so simple, yet it is a subtle thing, capable of immense finesse in skilled hands. There are lots of features on this tool that are rarely discussed from a furniture-making perspective, but that's exactly what we're going to do here.

First, there's the body style of the saw. There are two kinds of bodies: the common top-handle grip and the more European *barrel-grip* style. I absolutely hate to do this to you, but I encourage you to look for the barrel-grip saw. It bewilders me that the top-handle saw is the dominant style in this country. These tools are more tippy and harder to steer than the barrel-grip tools. This tippiness is not a big deal when you're just trying to notch some 2×4s on the job site, but it makes an appreciable difference in the shop. Keeping both your hands and the tool lower to the work improves your control. This maxim is not just for beginners; this applies to everyone.

The next most important thing is the blade-release mechanism. This is something you're going to be using quite a bit, so it should be simple. The best blade-release mechanisms are almost effortless: Pull a lever and the blade drops out or pops out. Lots of saws have sticky mechanisms — you don't want to have to grab the blade and wiggle it or tug it to remove it from the body. Eventually you will cut yourself.

Older saws need special screwdrivers or require you to twist a knob a good deal to remove the blade. Avoid these if you can

Here you can see what we're talking about. On the standard top-handle jigsaw, (behind the Festool) your hands will be much higher — 3" to 4" higher. That said, I wouldn't reject either of these jigsaws — both cost more than my monthly truck payment.

Shown is a properly set jigsaw with the orbital on 1. When you work in thicker material (or need to saw really fast), switch to 2 or 3.

because there are less frustrating ways to work. Speaking of blade-holding mechanisms, there are two dominant styles of blade-holding mechanisms on the market: a T-style and a Universal style or U-style. The T-style blade has a (surprise) T-shaped

Most people don't check the blade to ensure it's square to the baseplate, but it's a good idea. Even the best saws (such as this Bosch) will go out of alignment. If you don't check this occasionally, you'll be in for a rude shock when you try to do some precision work.

shank on top. The Universal-style blade has a hole bored in the blade. I've used both. I don't really have a preference. In fact, my preference is to buy a jigsaw that can hold either style blade. The jigsaw gurus tell me that this compromise results in a blade-holding mechanism that is weak. But I have never had a jigsaw blade come out of the tool while I was working.

Jigsaws have different *strokes,* which is the amount that the blade travels up and down in the tool. A 1" stroke is typical and fine. Shorter-stroke saws are generally at the very low end of the price spectrum and should be avoided anyway. You'll also see a lot of hype about the amperage of a tool. By and large, this is not important for furniture work. I'd give up a couple of amps of alleged power in exchange for a 12' power cord any day. And do check the length of the cord. A short cord will get hung up on your work where the plug meets the extension cord.

Another feature that gets played up is the orbital setting. The orbital setting is the amount that the blade will travel back and forth in the cut. Usually, most saws have four settings: zero, one, two and three. Zero means no forward movement,

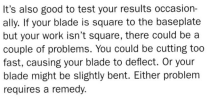

It's also good to test your results occasionally. If your blade is square to the baseplate but your work isn't square, there could be a couple of problems. You could be cutting too fast, causing your blade to deflect. Or your blade might be slightly bent. Either problem requires a remedy.

With a little practice you'll be able to cut very close to the line with your jigsaw. If you can leave just 1/32" of waste, then it's simple work to rasp (or sand) down to your line. If you cross the line while cutting, you'll have no line to rasp to. Make a relief cut into the corner before cutting the curve.

The jigsaw is a two-handed tool. A thumb on the baseplate will help steady the tool and will allow you great finesse as you round curves and track a line. We've removed the plastic guard on this saw for clearer pictures. With the guard in place, it's quite a feat to cut yourself.

which results in a slow cut but a clean one (generally). Three is when you need to cut plywood to cover your windows for an oncoming hurricane. It's fast and rough. Set your saw to one and you'll be fine until you move into the thick stuff.

How about a blower, do you need one? A blower puffs away dust from your cut line to make it easier to follow. I like a blower, otherwise I find myself doing all the puffing and turning blue. How about a worklight? It's not a must-have, but if your saw has one, you'll use it and like it. It can get dark down there by the blade.

Other features aren't so important. How you bevel the base of the saw is pretty irrelevant — some manufacturers play up the fact that the saw requires no tools. I rarely find the need to bevel the base. Once a year maybe. So no big deal. Do make sure that your blade is cutting straight down. You can check this first with your combination square, but keep the ruler away from the teeth of the blade. The teeth can be bent, or set, to either side of the blade on some blades. Register the ruler against the steel behind the teeth.

Then make a careful and straight cut off the end of a board. No curves (these tend to deflect the blade). Now check the finished cut with your combination square. If the cut is square, you're good. If it's not, then tweak the base of the tool until the resulting cut is square. Now cut a curve at a comfortable pace and check the work. The edge should be square to the face. If the blade deflects, then slow down your cutting pace.

You do need variable speed at the trigger — the more you press, the faster the blade goes. This is common on all but the cheapest tools.

## Jigsaw Use

Like any portable saw (hand or power) you want to have a pencil line that shows you where to cut. Always cut to one side of the line — the waste side. Cut as close as your skills allow. The less wood you leave, the less clean-up work will ensue, but the more disastrous the mistakes will become. I shoot for 1/32" of waste left or less.

The jigsaw is a two-handed tool. One-handed use is for hot dogs. One hand should grasp the tool's body and

trigger. Use the thumb on the other hand to press the base against the work. I use both hands to steer the tool. My trigger hand supplies the forward motion and does the heavy steering. My other hand provides the small adjustments that are critical to tracking my line. The thumb also keeps the saw from jumping up and down in the cut. If you keep the saw's plastic guards in place, this is quite safe.

You also need to know about relief cuts. These are the difference between success and disaster at times. Simply put, relief cuts are cuts you make into the waste that allow you to remove the waste one chunk at a time. They're sort of like waypoints for your tool. When your waste comes out in small chunks, it's less likely to droop and split and splinter, which can ruin your work. It also allows you to turn curves that are a bit tighter by freeing up space behind the blade, allowing it to turn.

I usually make a couple of relief cuts where my cutline is heading into a turn or coming out of a heavy turn. Also, I'll make a relief cut when I see that the waste is going to be 6" long or so. This really depends on how big your waste

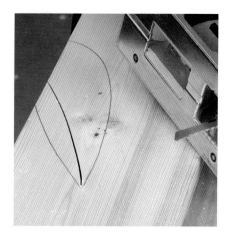

Learning where to make a relief cut takes some practice. If you have a sharp corner, such as this, that's always a good place to put a relief cut. You'll also want a few relief cuts in a long cut to prevent your waste from sagging and possibly breaking off.

piece is going to be and how droopy it will become during the cut.

We need to say a word about blades. Cheap blades will burn or leave a splintery mess in their wake. Buy nice blades and take care of them — wipe them clean with your WD-40 rag at the end of your shop time. After years of trying out different blades, we generally have two kinds of blades in our shop. I like the Bosch T234X Progressor blades, with 11 teeth per inch (*tpi* in shop lingo). Executive Editor Bob Lang likes the Progressor for straight cuts, but prefers the T101BR for curves where the Progessor is too bitey and rough.

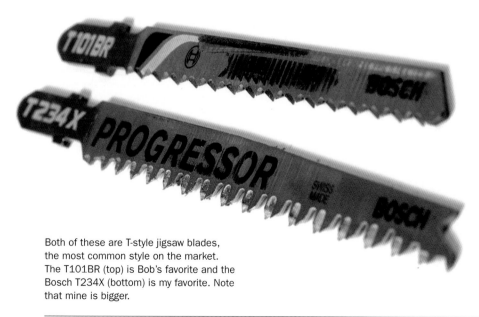

Both of these are T-style jigsaw blades, the most common style on the market. The T101BR (top) is Bob's favorite and the Bosch T234X (bottom) is my favorite. Note that mine is bigger.

## MITER SAWS

These saws were once the province of the high-end finish carpenter. Then the rough carpenters started using them (where they're called chop saws) as did the furniture makers. Each profession leans on a different feature of the tool to do their work. Finish carpenters like the combination of portability and accuracy. Carpenters like the speed and power. Furnituremakers like the accuracy and safety compared to a radial-arm saw (sometimes called the "radical-harm saw").

These tools are rarely perfect out of the box. They require tweaking for furniture work, plus they require a different way of working that we'll discuss later. But by and large they are incredible tools once you understand a few things.

### Styles of Saws

There are three major saws in the miter saw family:

**Straight Miter Saw:** This saw makes miters at any angle, usually between 47° left and 47° right at minimum. The cut this saw makes will always be 90° to the face of the work.

**Compound Miter Saw:** This saw does everything a straight miter saw does, plus the head can tip right (or both right and left) to make compound cuts. Compound cuts are angled in two directions, across the face of the board and across its thickness. This feature is used by trim carpenters for installing crown moulding.

**Sliding Compound Miter Saw:** This saw does everything the above saws do, but it also runs on a sliding carriage, which allows you to cut wide boards — most of these saws will cut a 12"-wide board; some go as far up as 16". These saws are as expensive as a good entry-level table saw and most of the features are little-used by a furniture maker.

So which saw do you need? Really? Probably just a straight miter saw. These are getting harder to find these days, so you might have to step up to a compound miter saw. And even these are getting cheap. Thanks to overseas manufacturing, I've seen good 10" compound miter saws for about $100 or a little more. What about the blade size? The 12" saws are notably more expensive, though it's nice for the occasional cut where you really need the extra width. However, we honestly think you can get by just fine with a 10" saw.

### Important Features

These saws can be loaded with extras, so let's cut through the clutter here. Two things are really important with this tool. First, it has to have a decent carbide-tooth blade that is capable of making clean finish cuts. Look for a blade with at least 40 teeth (and as many as 80). The more teeth you have, the smoother the cut, but having more teeth slows the cut and increases the chance you'll burn the work. And if you fall for a cheap saw that comes with a high-speed steel blade, you'll be upgrading it immediately and probably spending a good deal more money than you have to.

Second, you need a saw that is easy to adjust so the blade is 90° to the fence. Note that I'm not talking about the little handle up front that allows you to swing the head left and right. I'm talking about adjusting the tool so that when the head is locked at 90° it makes a perfect 90° cut. Sometimes you have to adjust the fence behind the blade, sometimes you adjust the points where the head locks down. We prefer this second method of adjusting the saw because it is faster and it doesn't ever result in you bending the fence. I've bent a couple, even while being careful. And when the fence is bent, you'll never get a square cut on both sides of the blade.

Your basic 10" miter saw is accurate enough and durable enough for a lifetime of woodworking. Beware of low-priced saws, even from national brands. One of the ways they lower the price is by equipping the saw with a poor-quality blade. You'll have to replace that blade immediately, and that almost always negates the price savings.

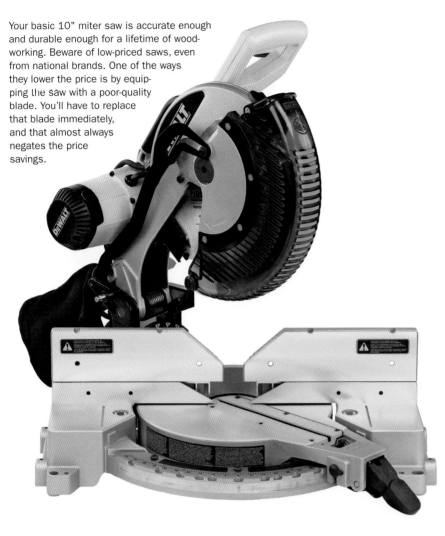

A carbide blade on top of a steel blade. Luckily, the steel blades are becoming more difficult to find, even on the cheaper saws. If you see a steel blade, don't buy it unless you need something to chew up your work in an unacceptable manner.

Follow the manufacturer's directions for squaring up the tool, and then make a sample cut and check it with your combination square. This brings us to another critical aspect of miter saws: How you make the cut. I've found that the number one cause of errors in this tool is not that the fence is off, it's that the work has shifted slightly during the cut, spoiling your accuracy.

The problem is these tools have fences and tables that are made of machined aluminum, which is slippery. So it's quite difficult to hold your work perfectly still during the cut. It's possible, of course, just difficult. Some manufacturers supply a hold-down clamp to secure the work against the table. These can be slow and can get in the way. The best solution I've found is to apply a layer of #120-grit peel-and-stick sandpaper to both sides of the fence. This works wonders.

The other way to spoil your accuracy is by taking too light of a cut and taking it too fast. For example, let's say you want to trim 1/32" off the end of a board. You line up the board as best you can and make your cut. It's not a lot of material so you make the cut quickly. Sometimes, not always, the blade can deflect out when you do this. This results in a cut that is not 90° to the face of the board. If you need to make a cut like this, take it a bit slower in order to keep the blade true.

The bottom line with this tool is that it's always best to check your work, especially if you don't have some sort of stop to constrain it from slipping around. So cut each joint and try each joint. You'll be fine.

Here's a common operation with a miter saw — trying to remove just a bit to sneak up on a cut line. If you make this cut too fast (especially in hardwoods or thick stock), the blade can deflect. Though it seems like you're making a light cut, slow down and check the cut across the thickness to ensure everything's OK.

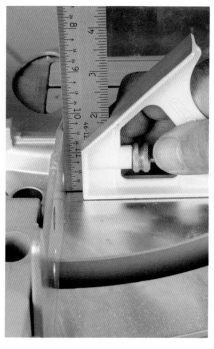

The fences on these saws can be bent during assembly. When you get your saw out of the box, check the fence with your square to ensure it's straight. If it's not, take the saw back and exchange it. A bent fence is almost impossible to fix and will cause a lifetime of headaches.

A less-common problem is that the fence isn't square to the table. Check this along several points on the fence. A twisted fence will wreak havoc with your accuracy.

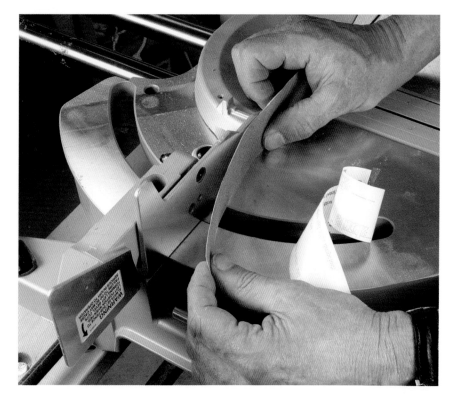

Personally, I don't understand why they make the table and fence so smooth and slippery. Their job is to support and grip the work. Even after using these tools for thirteen years, I still struggle with keeping the work immobilized as I cut it. If it shifts even a tiny bit during the cut, your cut won't be square. Adding a bit of self-stick sandpaper to the fence works wonders.

Other features of miter saws are less important. We haven't become fans of lasers on these saws yet. That may change, however, once they get them working just right. The raw amperage of these saws is mostly a non-issue. Almost all of them list their power as 15 amps, which is the maximum for a typical 120-volt household circuit and plug. All of the saws we've tested, even the cheapies, have enough power to cut standard material thicknesses with no complaint. The dust collection on all of them is quite poor — learn to live with it.

A few saws allow you to do stop cuts to make grooves or trenches across your work. You'll probably never use this feature. There are also high fences (best for crown moulding) and gizmos that allow you to micro-adjust your miter settings. These are not deal-breakers (or deal-makers).

## CIRCULAR SAW

When we decided on the list of power tools for our tool kit, we selected the jigsaw over the circular saw. But there are many instances where the circular saw would be the best choice; straight-line rips and cutting plywood are the most relevant. So we decided that the circular saw would have to be the first power tool added to that original list.

There is much to consider when selecting a circular saw, the first of which is the saw's size. The size of the saw is described in terms of blade diameter. You'll find saws that are from $4\frac{3}{8}$" to $10\frac{1}{4}$" with a number of entries between.

So, how do you choose? To begin, take a look at the depth of cut that can be made with the saw set at 90° and at 45°. As you begin building projects from this series you'll find that your materials will be mostly $\frac{3}{4}$" or $1\frac{1}{2}$" thick. So, the need to cut these materials should inform your purchase.

A $4\frac{3}{8}$" circular saw will cut only $1\frac{1}{4}$" in thickness set at 90°, and $\frac{3}{4}$" when angled at 45°. So, it's obvious this saw is not the one for your shop. You'll find that a $6\frac{1}{2}$" saw just clears a $1\frac{1}{2}$" cut at 90° but because the size is a bit odd, you may have trouble locating blades.

The most popular size of circular saw is the $7\frac{1}{4}$". Any store that carries circular saws will have a complete line of $7\frac{1}{4}$"

Large knobs can makes adjustments quick and easy when adjusting the depth or angle of cut.

saws from which to choose, as well as a number of different blades designs (we'll discuss those in moment). The depth of cut with the 7¼" saw at both 90° and 45° is more than required. This saw meets or exceeds the requirements of most woodworking so there is no need to look into bigger models that are heavier, higher in cost and unwieldy as well.

## Saw Designs

Circular saws are divided into two general categories — worm drives and in-line saws, also known as sidewinders. Worm drives are easily recognizable due to their design. The motor sits behind the blade, which is driven by a worm gear (the gear looks like a curled worm.) These saws provide a good line of sight while cutting

and will extend your reach across sheet goods, but they are more expensive than sidewinders. And, because wormdrive saws are much heavier saws — 14 to 16 pounds — they can be awkward to use because they tend to be front heavy.

Sidewinders, so named because the motor sits beside the blade, are the most common configuration. A sidewinder provides a better balance in your hand because the handle is directly above the motor. Bottom line: We recommend a 7¼" in-line saw.

## WHAT TO LOOK FOR IN A SAW

So where do you go from here? What about the power? Most saws boast of amps. The 7¼" saws generally have a 13- to 15-amp motor. Amps relate only the amount of electricity that the tools use, not the power sent to the blade. Is that good, or is horsepower better? Horsepower is generally measured when the saw is not in a real-world cutting situation. This too, is not an informative basis for comparison. The better way to select a saw is by price. A good sidewinder for woodworking will set you back around $100 to $150. Sure, there are saws that cost less, but they aren't going to last a lifetime nor be able to withstand the rigors of the woodworking shop. They would be great for the home-owner looking to use a saw occasionally.

Not only can you see the difference between the worm drive saw (left) and the sidewinder (right), it is obvious that the sidewinder will be a lighter, more easily controlled saw.

## COMPARISON SHOPPING

In side-by-side comparisons of saws, begin with an inspection of the saw's shoe — the bottom plate of the saw. You can find shoes that are aluminum or magnesium as well as plastic and other material. Our recommendation is to stay away from the plastic shoes and look for a metal base; cast metal would be best. A shoe with ribs will have added reinforcement in case (or when) you drop the saw on the floor — but that added strength adds weight to the tool.

The overall weight of the saw will affect comfort, and that is an issue in choosing your saw. Also, check the handle positioning and the balance of the saw. Making sure that the saw fits your hands and feels comfortable while in use is key in the selection process.

Next you need to look at the adjustments of the saw. The two adjustments are depth of cut and angle. You'll find knobs, levers and wing nuts used to allow these adjustments. Large knobs and smartly placed levers will make adjustments both quick, and accurate. Small, out-of-the-way levers and wing nuts are less handy.

The last issue to consider is how easy it is to change the blade. We've seen saws that require you to insert a nail through a hole in the blade to lock the blade. Or worse yet, to hold the blade as you try to release the arbor nut. These are not the best scenarios. A shaft-lock mechanism is the best option. This feature locks the shaft so it doesn't rotate, allowing easy use of a wrench to remove the arbor nut.

## A WORD ABOUT BLADES

A sharp blade is very important when using a circular saw. Dull blades are one of the causes of kickback, which is when the blade catches the wood but instead of cutting the piece, the saw is propelled back toward the operator. This is dangerous.

There are many choices when selecting a blade for your circular saw. First, you should always use a blade that is sized for your saw — if you have a 7¼" saw, use a 7¼" blade. Installing a smaller-diameter blade will not allow the saw to develop the rim speed needed for the machine to work at its full potential.

Second, base your blade decision on the type of work the blade will perform. If

Properly setting the depth of cut will help extend the life of the blade and lessen the possibility of kickback.

you're roughcutting lumber, a 24-tooth carbide blade would be right. But using that blade to cut veneer-faced plywood would result in a massive amount of tear-out.

There are blades that have 16, 18, 24, 40 or 60 teeth (and some in between, I'm sure). There are blades for plywood as well as masonry. You have to decide how the saw will be used in order to select the correct blade. Our tool kit would have a 24-tooth carbide blade (carbide tips on the teeth will stay sharp longer) for roughcutting stock and a 40-tooth carbide blade for the finish cuts.

Large knobs can makes adjustments quick and easy when changing the depth or angle of cut. The cut made with a circular saw should not be considered the last step in the milling process. A hand plane should be used to fine-tune most of the edges for better-quality results.

## USING THE CIRCULAR SAW

There are a few basic guidelines for using a circular saw. Adjust the depth of cut prior to cutting any material. Loosen the knob or lever and raise or lower the shoe until the blade is between ⅛" — ¼" beyond the lower edge of the material to be cut. Remember to tighten the depth knob before beginning the cut. Setting

the depth of cut too deep could lead to binding and kickback.

Because the circular saw cuts with the blade coming up through the material, it is best to cut with the face side, or best side, down. Any tear-out would then be on the back side of the material and away from sight.

Always start the saw with the front of the shoe resting on the workpiece; don't let the blade make contact with the wood until the blade has reached full speed. Move through the cut with the motor/ base resting on the good side of the workpiece, not the waste material side and do not remove the tool from the workpiece before the blade has come to a complete stop.

Another good rule of thumb is to have your workpiece properly supported. This does not mean laying the workpiece across two sawhorses while cutting the middle of the board. This tool is designed to cut through material causing one piece — the waste — to fall away.

To cut the end off of a board, make sure to have the waste material extended past any supporting surface. As the cut is finished the waste will fall away. In cutting sheet goods you may not want the waste to fall. In this case, support the work from below using several long

Aligning the blade with the cut line and using a speed square provides a temporary fence for a square or straight cut.

lengths of scrap so the work is fully supported. Some people cut sheet goods on top of 4' × 8' foam insulation board. Either way, set your cutting depth so you don't cut through the support below your work.

Clamping an auxiliary fence to the workpiece is an excellent way to achieve a straight cut, so long as the fence is also a straightedge. Note the gun shot notch.

## Making the Cuts Freehand

Many of the cuts made with the circular saw will be freehand cuts. This is where the saw is guided by hand and eye, not with guides or jigs. There are two methods for completing this type of cut while staying on your line and making straight cuts. The first is to use your eye to watch the relationship of the blade to the cut line.

With your safety glasses in place, tilt your head and watch the cut. The dynamics of the circular saw will enable you to make straight cuts more accurately than you can with a jigsaw. The circular saw, because the cutting area of the blade is wider than a jigsaw blade, will help to guide you on a straight path. It is possible, however, to veer from the cut line so keep your attention focused.

The second method of cutting by hand and having the resulting cut straight is to use the gun shot to help guide the tool. The gun shot is a notch in the saw's shoe that aligns with the edge of the blade. Maneuvering the saw while keeping the notch at the line will provide a straight cut — as long as you started the cut at the line to begin with.

## Cutting with Fences and Guides

Another much-used method of making straight cuts with the circular saw is to use a fence or other type of guide. As long as the fence is straight, the saw will follow that fence and the result will be a straight cut.

One type of guide is a speed square or an aluminum carpenter's square. To use this setup, position the saw so the blade touches your cut line, then move the speed square tight to the saw's shoe on the opposite side from the blade. At the same time, hold the square tight to the edge of the board to allow the shoe to ride against the square. This technique is best suited for cuts across the grain (called crosscuts) no wider than the square itself.

Making wide crosscuts requires a different fence or guide. The best fence is plywood; the factory edge works great. But, any scrap piece that has a straight-edge will serve. Use the fence just as you would a speed square, but clamp this guide to the workpiece.

This arrangement is one of the best ways to accurately make cuts with the grain (called rip cuts), too. Place the plywood in relation to the cut line as before and repeat the process of running the saw shoe along the cut, ripping a straight line. Be sure to have the work supported correctly.

## A Specialized Guide

If you plan to use your saw extensively, we suggest making a fitted guide that is designed to work with your saw for crosscuts or rip cuts.

Why make a fitted guide? Without a fitted guide, you have to do more measuring to position your auxiliary fence on your work. You're always having to add in the width of the saw's shoe when positioning your fence. A fitted guide allows you to position the fence perfectly on the cut line each time.

You'll need a piece of plywood and a straight piece of scrap stock (plywood will work here too) to build this fitted guide. The plywood needs to be about 5" wider than the shoe of the saw and the scrap should be about 4" in width, with a factory straight edge.

Attach the scrap to the left-hand side of the plywood keeping the straight edge

The jig has a wide fence to make clamping easy. Because this jig was created using the circular saw, whenever we clamp the jig exactly at the cut line, the result will be straight and on the layout line.

ited power of a corded drill. A handful of the corded drills have clutches and speed settings, and I don't know why there aren't more around. Probably because we love cordless drills — they must be the hottest-selling tool on the market.

There are a lot of factors to consider when buying a drill because they are used for so many different things. I'm going to tell you what's important for building furniture. First, you need a drill that is lightweight, balanced and will hold all the bits you need, from the tiniest wire bits up to $\frac{3}{8}$"- or sometimes $\frac{1}{2}$"-shanked bits. If you are buying a cordless drill, you probably should buy a 9.6-volt or 12-volt model. These drills generally satisfy all the requirements above — except they typically hold bits only up to $\frac{3}{8}$" in diameter, which is OK. Heavy drills (such as 18-volt drills) are hard to wield with any finesse. And you are so rarely far away from your charger while you're in the shop that the run-time issue is moot.

You need variable speed. This is found on all but the cheapest tools. Variable speed is where the more you pull the trigger, the more rpm you get. You want your drill to ramp up smoothly, though no drill is perfect in this department.

to the right. Clamp the assembly to a bench or worktable making sure that the single-thickness edge is hanging off of the bench.

Next, adjust the saw for the thickness of the plywood and cut through the plywood as the shoe rides tight against the scrap. This is just like making a rip cut with a fence, but this time the fence is attached. The freshly cut edge is now in line with the saw blade. Each time you make a cut, all you need to do is locate the jig exactly at the cut line and clamp it in place. Each time you run the saw against that scrap, while the saw is resting on the plywood, the cut will be correct to your layout. One thing to remember is that you need to set the depth of cut to the material you are cutting and the thickness of the plywood. This will shorten the thickness of cut of the saw but you get accurate results each and every time. If you need the additional depth, resort to the hand-held cut methods described earlier in "Making the Cuts Freehand." The jig has a wide fence to make clamping easy. Because this jig was created using the circular saw, whenever we clamp the

jig exactly at the cut line, the result will be straight and on the layout line.

## DRILLS

I'm going to guess that you already have some kind of drill. Maybe it's a corded drill; maybe it's a cordless drill. If I had to own only one drill it would probably be a cordless drill because these tend to have clutches and different speed ranges that make them ideal for driving screws in addition to drilling holes. However, nothing beats the raw and unlim-

I got by for years and years with a corded drill alone. Once I finally bought a cordless drill, I was glad I'd made the upgrade. Not only do you lose the cord, but you gain some features, such as control over your top speed and a clutch that prevents you from over-torquing your screws.

Maybe the big drill doesn't look so big to you here. Just wait until you have to heft this thing up above your head for the hundredth time. Then you'll want the wimpy 9.6-volt drill. If you work far away from your battery charger (like on an oil derrick) then get the big drill; otherwise, smaller is generally better (and cheaper!).

When you're in the store, close the chuck of the drill that you're considering and take a look at how closely the jaws close. The best chucks will close down to nothing. The lamest ones will allow you to get a toothpick in there. The tight jaws will let you grab the smaller bits that are occasionally important for woodworking.

A keyless chuck is a desirable feature. Though the keyless chuck might not hold as tightly as a keyed one, this is almost never an issue. The keyless chucks hold plenty tight enough and are so much faster and easier to use than their keyed cousins. While you're examining the chuck, take a look at the three jaws that grab the bit. Close the chuck on itself and take a look at where the three jaws meet. The best chucks will have a seamless fit. When the jaws come together they will look like one piece of solid metal. Lesser chucks will have a gap at the center. This gap will prevent the chuck from closing on small bits. Most of the time, this is not important, but when you need a tiny hole...

Let's talk a minute about clutch setting and speed ranges. These are important fine-tuning settings that you'll become more sensitive to the more you use your drill. Most drills (with a couple of notable exceptions) have two speed settings, low and high. In general, the low setting is for driving screws and the high setting is for boring holes. That's simple enough. Then you have the clutch of the drill to consider. The clutch has more settings than any reasonable person needs. Perhaps manufacturers see it as a way to get the upper hand on competitors. I just wish I didn't have to do so much fiddling and clicking to get the right clutch setting.

What does the clutch setting do? It's for driving screws. When you reach a certain amount of torque, the clutch disengages the motor from the chuck to stop the spinning action. This disengagement can prevent you from making some critical mistakes, such as snapping or stripping a screw's head. Or driving it too

deeply in softwoods — perhaps to the point where the screw won't hold.

How do you use the clutch? Here's how I do it: When I'm driving a bunch of screws into a cabinet back or the like, I'll set the clutch setting really low. When I drive the first screw I'm unlikely to fully seat it. So I click the clutch over a couple of notches and try again. When the screw seats where I want it, I'll drive all the screws for that project.

One last detail on the clutch: I don't much use it in the high-speed range. Most drills have a setting on the clutch designed specifically for drilling bits. So I recommend you set your speed range to high, set your clutch to the drilling setting then go for it.

The list of things you don't need on a drill is quite long. Wrist strap? No. Bubble level? Nope. Work light? Not likely. Laser? Please! Focus on the attributes that are important and you won't go wrong when picking a drill.

Setting the clutch as shown will disengage the clutch, allowing you to drill at full power and speed. This is in the drill's instruction booklet that you threw away.

## Another Type of Cordless Drill

Sometimes the easiest, fastest way to do a task is to use a hand tool instead of a power tool. Making small holes to get a screw started is an excellent example of this principle. One of the tools in your kit should be the simple, versatile awl.

You can use the pointed end of the awl for many things — marking lines that won't smudge or disappear, poking holes in the rim of a paint can so that the overflow from your brush doesn't spill over the side, marking holes to be drilled with a power drill, and making pilot holes for woodscrews.

You won't be faced with many choices when you go to buy an awl; there are basic ones at the local hardware store and fancy ones from mail-order woodworking suppliers. The steel should be straight and stiff, and it should be firmly attached to the handle. Start with an inexpensive awl. After using it for awhile, you'll find your personal likes and dislikes. You also may eventually find that you want two.

Machinists use awls for scratching lines, and awls intended for this purpose will have a handle like a screwdriver. For woodworking, you want a bulbous end so that you can push the point in to the wood with the palm of your hand.

The awls in the photo show a common variation in the handles of awls as

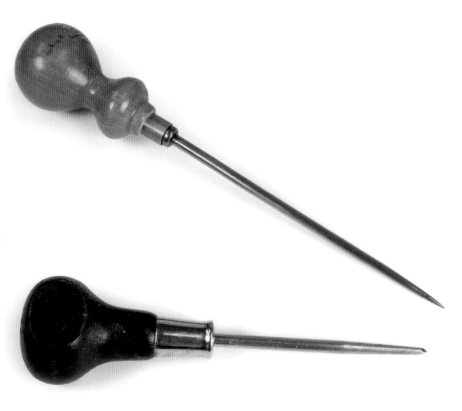

The shorter awl has flats on the handle that prevent it from rolling around when put down.

well as many other woodworking tools. The awl in the bottom of the photo has two flat sides, while the other one has a round handle. The round handle is more comfortable, but it can roll away when put down on a flat surface.

The other difference is in the way that the very tip of the awl is shaped and sharpened — and this is the reason you'll likely want two. One shape works best for marking, and the other works best for drilling small holes. The most commonly seen point tapers like a pencil point. This is an advantage if you are using it to scratch a line on your work.

The other point style is faceted. I took a small mill file, and in a few minutes filed four facets on a round-point awl. These straight edges will provide a cutting action when making a pilot hole for a screw.

To make a pilot hole with the round-tip awl, place it in the center of the opening and push down. You won't be able to go very deep because the wood fibers will crush and fill the hole. While using the faceted tip, twist the tip as you push down. The corners of the facets will cut the wood in the hole, letting you go deeper.

The faceted point on the left makes the awl an efficient tool for making a small hole.

Keeping your files clean is the key to keeping them working. A good file card (left) will have stiff brush bristles on one face to clean rasps. On the other side will be wire bristles, which are good for cleaning files.

## FINISHING TOOLS

After all your parts have been cut, you need to prepare the surfaces for finishing. And that's when you should turn to your files, rasps, sander and block plane.

### Rasp and File

Rasps and files are free form shaping tools. They can be used on their own to create shapes or they can clean up the work left by other tools, such as the jigsaw. The rasp is the coarser tool and you use it before you turn to the file.

There was a time in history when a discussion on rasps would be quite lengthy. There used to be hundreds of patterns and sizes available to the woodworker. Now you're going to be lucky if you find more than one kind to choose from at the store.

Files are a little different matter. They are actually a metalworking tool and

there are a lot of files available. For woodworking (and the metalworking involved in woodworking) I think you simply need one file; a bastard-cut file will do — either the 8" or 10" length. This file will smooth wood nicely.

Rasps are merely the coarser cousins of files. Finding a good rasp can be a challenge in some stores, but most home centers carry at least one. You'll typically find them labeled as bastard cut, second cut and smooth cut, which is an indicator of their coarseness. Bastard cut is the coarser one; smooth cut is the finer one. Because we're going to do most of the work with a jigsaw before turning to a rasp, I recommend you try to get a smooth cut rasp. Look for one that has one flat face and one face that curves out. Sometimes this is labeled as a half-round profile. This will allow you to shape inside curves.

Avoid the four-in-one rasps, sometimes labeled shoe rasps. These tools have two working ends, one coarse and one fine. They seem like a good idea, but the tools are actually too short for many woodworking applications. Longer rasps are better. You get more control from taking two long strokes rather than 10 short strokes.

In addition to your rasp and file, you'll need what's called a file card to clean them. As you use a rasp or file, the teeth will get clogged with wood fibers. The file card is a brush that cleans the tools so

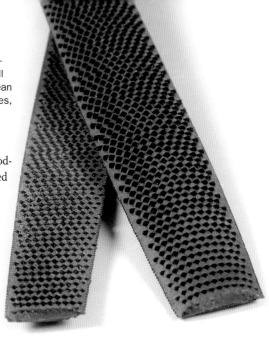

Get a rasp with a half-round profile like the ones shown here. The round profile allows you to sneak into inside curves that the flat face would butcher.

they continue to cut well. Most file cards are like a small hairbrush with two faces. One side has synthetic black bristles; the other has metal bristles. Use the black bristles to clean your rasp; use the metal bristles to clean your file.

One more accessory: a handle. Files and rasps have a pointed tang at one end. The tools are much more comfortable to use if you have a handle on one end. The handles, sold in the same section as the tools, simply screw off and on the tang.

The rules for using files and rasps are the same. Use the tools with two hands: One hand on the handle the other on the end. Like a saw, the tools cut only in one direction — on the push cut. If you drag the tool across the work on your return stroke you will dull the teeth faster and clog the tool.

After every few strokes, tap the tool against your sawhorse or workbench. This shakes loose the big particles. When

A good selection of rasps and files. The tool on the right that looks like a cheese grater is a Microplane, a high-tech rasp. They work great, but seem to dull faster in my experience. The rasp to its left is what you'll commonly find at the hardware store. The two files at the far left are both good for woodworking as fine finishing tools.

A typical file handle. Some people swear by them; others never use them. I'm somewhere in between.

The rasp and file are generally two-handed tools. You'll get better control and a more square cut if you adopt the two-handed approach.

the tool starts to cut slowly, clean it with your card file.

When working with a surface fresh from your jigsaw, begin by using the rasp. Always begin your work with light strokes, which will show you where you are cutting. After a couple of light strokes you'll know if you have the tool at the right angle and you can then add some downward pressure.

Once all the marks left by the jigsaw are replaced by marks made by your rasp, you can switch tools. Use the same techniques with your file as you did with your rasp and work the area until all the toolmarks left by the rasp are gone. The file

can leave a good surface, but I still usually finish things up with some sandpaper.

After a little practice, you'll find that these tools (even the cheap ones) are extraordinary shaping tools. You can round over an edge easily and quickly clean up tool marks that would take an impossible amount of sanding. They also allow you to easily incorporate sculptural elements in your work that make you look a lot more advanced than you are (and that's what this is all about, right?)

## Random-orbit Sander

Good sanding is the modern foundation of a good finish. And a good finish can

make an average project look fantastic. Though sanding is a chore, it's something you need to get good at to produce good work as you begin your craft.

We do a lot more sanding these days than our forebears, who used bench planes, scrapers and some hand-sanding to prepare their surfaces for finishing. And truth be told, I do very little sanding in my shop, but that's because I've spent years using hand planes, learning to sharpen and so on. But that takes time, and the real beauty of our modern sanders is that they can produce an extraordinary surface with a far smaller investment in skill.

Oh, there are still some skills involved in using a sander properly and most effectively, but they can be taught in an hour or so and the basic moves are easy to pick up without a lot of instruction. The downsides to sanding with a machine are that it's mind-numbing work and it generates a lot of unhealthy dust.

So if you want to start building today, you are going to need a sander. Don't buy a belt sander — that's for hogging material off. Don't buy a pad sander. These vibrating tools use sheets of sandpaper and aren't very aggressive. Buy a random-orbit sander. These high-tech tools are a marvel. Though they have a disk that spins rapidly, it's also wiggling eccentrically. The result is that the tools strike a nice balance between aggressively removing stock and leaving a fine finished surface.

There are three body styles available: the small palm-grip tools, the big right-angle tools (that look like an angle grinder) and an intermediate tool that's between the two. I have used them all and recommend you get a palm-grip tool for furniture work. It's inexpensive, the 5"-diameter sandpaper is available everywhere and the tool is lightweight enough to use one-handed and get you in tight spots. The bigger tools are better for sanding big tabletops and the like.

So what should you look for when buying a random-orbit sander? Here's the funny thing, I have yet to find one I really dislike. They all work pretty well.

Random-orbit sanders are excellent fine-finishing tools for the money and they don't require a lot of skill to learn.

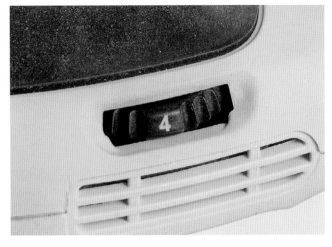

Generally, the variable-speed feature is unnecessary on a random-orbit sander. The only time I've slowed down the tool is when I was dealing with some really thin veneer. That's it.

After some experience with these sanders, you'll want to hook it up to a shop vacuum. The dust this tool makes is the worst. It's unhealthy and annoying. Adding a vacuum and hose to your sander will make your sanding faster (because the dust won't interfere) and (almost) pleasant.

Some vibrate a little more, some are a little slower, but they all pretty much do the job. These tools don't have a lot of bells and whistles available, so I think you can buy a basic tool and be just fine. Some of them are variable speed — I have yet to find a moment where I thought to myself: "Boy, I sure wish I could slow down the sanding process so I could really enjoy it." I'm sure there are some delicate jobs that benefit from this feature, but I think you'll be hard-pressed to say it's essential.

These tools don't have lasers, worklights or wrist-straps (yet), so that's not a consideration. But one thing you should pay close attention to is the dust collection. Dust collection on almost all of these machines is a spotty business, and sanding kicks up a lot of the dangerous dust — the sub-micron stuff that gets lodged in your lungs. If you own a shop vacuum, get the upgraded filters for the vacuum and buy the hoses that attach it to the sander. If you can't afford a shop vacuum, then you need a face mask that filters out this nasty dust. And not just a paper mask — I'm talking about a mask that's NIOSH approved. These are available at home centers and are the essential sanding equipment.

The other consideration is the sandpaper. Sandpaper can be expensive, but there's nothing more expensive than cheap sandpaper. The quality stuff (Norton 3X and Klingspor are both good brands) lasts a long time. I think you really need three grits to handle most project building. Get #100- or #120-grit paper for your

coarse grit. Buy the most discs of this grit because you will go through a lot of it. Do as much sanding with this grit as you can because it does the job fast. Then get a smaller quantity of #150-grit paper for your medium grit. This intermediate grit goes pretty quickly if you did a good job with the coarse grit. And then get a small quantity of #220-grit paper. Again, if you did a good job in the earlier grits, the #220 work will go quite fast.

People sometimes laugh when they hear there is a proper way to sand. After all, you simply put the tool on the work and move it around until everything is consistently sanded right? There actually is a little more to it than that, and proper use of the tool will ensure you get the job done in short order.

First thing to know: hand pressure. Try not to bear down too hard on the tool while you are working. It's tempting

to do this when you're sanding a rough patch, but it's not so good for the tool and there's a risk of you going too far when you get rowdy. Similarly, try to keep the tool flat on the work. It's tempting to sometimes tip the tool so one edge of the pad is contacting the work so you can work a small area of tear-out. This will work with a little skill and if the tear-out is shallow. If it's deep tear-out or you linger too long, you will create a valley in the work that may not be evident until you put a shiny finish on the work.

You'll need the biggest supply of #120-grit sandpaper (left) because it does the most work and needs to be replaced more regularly. You'll need less of the #150 (middle) and even less of the #220.

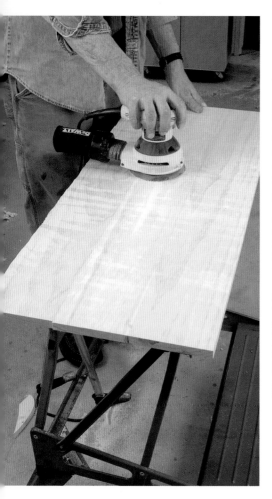

Move your sander in a regular pattern to ensure a consistent job. I'll start with overlapping strokes along the length of the board. Then I'll do overlapping strokes across the width. Then I repeat.

Always break the edges of your work before finishing. This makes your project nicer to the touch and makes your edges less susceptible to damage.

A raking light, such as the one shown here from a desk lamp, will point out the dings and scratches that your overhead lights will conceal. It helps to turn out your overhead lights as you sand critical areas (such as tabletops).

Second thing: Don't move too fast. Zipping around a board with a sander doesn't do the job. Manufacturers recommend moving the tool about a foot every ten seconds (at least, that's what a couple of engineers told me). I think that's too slow to be practical — try it and I think you'll agree. I go faster — maybe a foot every seven seconds.

Third: Work each surface in a consistent pattern. I like to work a panel left to right, slightly overlapping my passes. Then I come back and work the panel front to back in this way. This ensures I don't miss any spots.

Again, you'll do most of the work with the coarse grits. But how do you know when to switch to a higher grit? Once the workpiece looks consistently scratched to the naked eye, I'll take a desk lamp with a movable head or one of the yellow job-site lights and position it so there's a low, raking light across the work and give it a quick look. The raking light will point out any dings or divots or tear-out you missed as areas in shadow. If the board looks good under raking light, then switch grits.

The higher grits go faster. Much faster. Usually, I spend half the time (or less) with the #150-grit paper. And the #220 is used even less than that. After everything is sanded with the random-orbit sander, you might need to do a little hand-sanding with #220 paper in a few areas, sand the boards' edges and then break (slightly round over) the corners and sharp edges of all the touchable pieces. Sharp edges are fragile and don't feel good to the hand.

Breaking the edges is quick and greatly improves the tactile quality of your work. Use #150-grit paper in your hand and take down the corners slightly. A couple of strokes is usually enough.

You should be aware that you will have better results if you cut with the grain. Think of each board like a furry animal — the grain lines are the fur. If your tool is pressing down the fur as you cut, it's like petting an animal correctly. If you rub (or cut) the wrong way then the animal will get mad and the work will tear out.

## Block Plane

Buying and sharpening a block plane is probably the most involved task we're going to ask of you as you get started in the craft. The barrier here is sharpening the blade — lots of woodworkers get tied up in knots about this simple and very important skill. Here's the promise: Once you learn to sharpen a single woodworking tool, the same principles will allow you to sharpen a lot of other things: chisels, carving gouges, all manner of plane blades, turning tools, marking knives and so on.

Sharpening is one of those "minute to learn; lifetime to master" things. The principle is so simple: A sharp edge is the intersection of (sorry for the geometry) two planes. The smaller the point of the intersection, the sharper the edge is. The act of sharpening is simply the abrading of those two planes until they meet at the smallest point possible. That's it.

Like sanding, you start sharpening with a coarse grit and move up in grits. You can use almost any medium to sharpen. Sandpaper works well as you're learning. You'll also find diamond stones and oilstones at the home center. Pick a system that fits your budget. If there's an oilstone that has coarse grit on one side and fine grit on the other, that's what I'd get. Sometimes it's called an India stone. Buy a little 3-in-1 oil and you're in business.

## The Basic Strokes

There are lots of good books and web sites that can help you with sharpening. I'm going to tell you here how to get a good working edge that will get you started cutting pine and other work-a-day woods. My personal sharpening regimen is different, but everyone's is. The following requires the absolute fewest tools.

Disassemble the block plane and clean off the cutter. Notice that one end is wedge-shaped. This is called the bevel of the cutter. The flat part of the cutter that intersects the bevel is called the back of the blade. The back and the bevel are the two planes of your cutting edge and are what is to be abraded.

Begin with the back. There's a lot of metal here. Abrading all that metal flat would be a massive task. Remember that only the very end of the back is what does

Block planes are commonly available. Paying a little more will add some nice features — a blade adjuster, a mouth that you can close up for high-tolerance work and the blade pitched at a lower angle. That said, even the cheap ones work well on softwoods when sharpened.

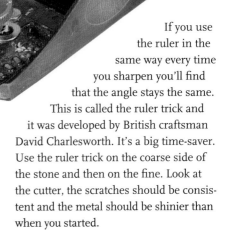

the cutting. That's all you need to worry about. So we're going to cheat so that we work only that area (and get to work much faster). Take a thin, cheap 6" ruler and stick it along one edge of your sharpening stone. Now rub the back of the cutter on the stone with the cutting edge on the stone and the back part of the cutter propped up on the ruler. The ruler holds the back end of the cutter in the air so you work only the area up by the edge.

If you use the ruler in the same way every time you sharpen you'll find that the angle stays the same. This is called the ruler trick and it was developed by British craftsman David Charlesworth. It's a big time-saver. Use the ruler trick on the coarse side of the stone and then on the fine. Look at the cutter, the scratches should be consistent and the metal should be shinier than when you started.

By propping up the back of the blade as you work the back, you'll greatly speed the polishing action of this critical surface. The ruler ensures that every time you do this it will be consistent.

Learning to hone the bevel takes a little practice. Take it slow and check your work frequently. A honing guide is a good $12 investment if you can find one at your home center.

A small block of wood can check the setting of your plane's iron. If the block of wood has the same amount of drag all across the mouth, then your blade is centered in the mouth and is projecting squarely — get to work!

Note the grain on the face of the board. See how it is heading up toward the edge being planed? Think of those grain lines as fur. If the tool is pushing them down as it works, the chances are your cut will be sweet.

Now turn your attention to the bevel. This is the part that trips people up because they have trouble balancing the tool on the stone on the narrow bevel. I like to use a little jig to hold the cutter for this part, but if you don't have a jig, it's still easy to pick up the skill. Start at the far end of the stone. Rest the tool's bevel flat on the stone (don't forget the oil). Now raise the tool just a tad so you're working only at the tip. Drag the tool toward you. Lift and repeat the stroke about four or five times.

Now feel the back of the blade with your thumb. There should be a little burr of metal curled over on the back. That's good; that means you really sharpened up at the tip of the tool. Work the bevel some more with your coarse stone and then your fine stone until your scratches look good. At the very end, you want to remove the burr. Put the ruler back on your fine stone and stroke the iron over the stone and ruler — this is called backing off. Wipe down the blade and reassemble the tool.

Setting a block plane is pretty easy. You want to project the iron equally all across the mouth. Turn the tool's adjuster to project the blade until it looks like it's just starting to emerge. You can feel this by passing your fingers lightly over the mouth or by sighting down the sole of the plane head-on. Then use a little scrap of wood to confirm your setting. Rub the block over the mouth. You should feel it drag as the iron removes a tiny shaving. And you should be able to hear it. Try it in several places along the mouth. If the drag feels the same and the sound is the same, then your iron is square in the mouth.

Using a block plane is a one- or two-handed operation — I prefer to use two hands as much as possible. Once you sharpen it up, you'll find endless uses for it. After you rip a board with your jigsaw, the block plane cleans up the sawblade marks, making the edge ready to finish (no sanding necessary). If two parts of a joint aren't in line with one another, the block plane can trim the proud surface flush.

## JOINERY TOOLS: BISCUIT JOINERS & POCKET HOLE JIGS

Joining flat panels to make a box is the ultimate and basic goal of a lot of woodworking. There are a lot of ways to get there, from nails to fancy locking sliding dovetails. All the methods work, and all are valid when used properly. The problem is that most of the techniques require a number of large machines with special bits or blades. We wanted to keep things simple and strong. So when it comes to case joinery, we think you should choose either a pocket-hole jig or a biscuit joiner.

The pocket-hole jig bores an angled hole (a pocket) in one half of your joint with a special bit included in the kit. The pocket is sized and shaped perfectly for a special screw designed for the jig. You put glue on your pieces, clamp them together and drive in the screw. Most people conceal the pockets by placing them on the underside or backside of their work and some people plug them with specially angled plugs.

The biscuit joiner simply cuts out a recess on the edge of the pieces you are joining. The recess is shaped and sized perfectly for a thin wafer of beech or birch, called a biscuit. Add glue to the recesses, add the biscuit and clamp up your work.

Both of these modern gizmos are accurate, fast and easy to master. They both cost about the same and both produce joints that are strong enough for most woodworking jobs.

### Biscuit Joiner

Choosing a biscuit joiner is going to be limited by what's available at your home center — most stores will have one or two brands at most. If you're ambitious, you can find a couple more to choose from at a local Sears.

They aren't significantly different at the low end of the price scale — but the ones that show up for less than $100 are usually things I'd avoid. These have plastic fences or oddball ergonomics or are a brand we have never heard of (all those factors are danger signs). Once the price of the tool hits about $150 or so, it's a contender.

Using a biscuit joiner is simple, but you really have to pay attention because

Biscuit joiners (left) cut a football-shaped recess in two parts to be joined. The biscuits fit into that recess and (with a little glue) hold the joint together. A pocket-hole jig (above) allows you to join two pieces of wood without clamping. The only real downside is the fact that you have to conceal the holes made by the stepped drill bit.

it's easy to make stupid mistakes without knowing it. Essentially, the tool is a small plunging circular saw. Press the tool against your work and it cuts one-half of a football-shaped recess. Press the tool against the mating part and it cuts the other half of the joint. Add glue and a biscuit and clamp things up.

It sounds easy, but I've seen a lot of beginners struggle with this tool. The biggest problem is that the tool is not aligned where it should be when you

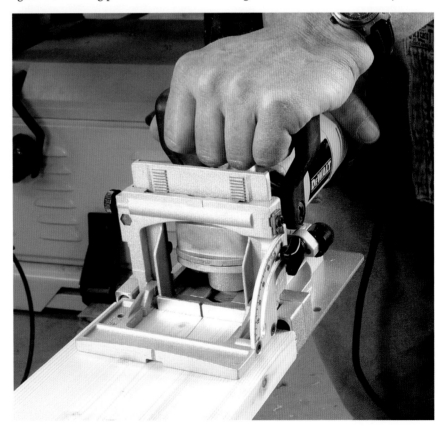

A textbook way of holding a biscuit joiner. Note that Bob's hip is braced against the rear of the tool. He'll shift his body forward during the plunge cut and use his arms to steady the tool.

make that plunge cut. It's not really a matter of being a little off on the left or right — the process is forgiving enough to allow you to miss your mark by a surprisingly large margin.

Where most people trip themselves up is in getting the up and down part right. If the fence isn't firmly on the work, or you tip the tool a bit, or it sags a bit under its own weight one of the slots is going to be off. You also can be thrown off by the tool's base. If it rests against anything — and you think you're referencing off the fence instead — you're in for trouble.

I think most problems come from overconfidence. The tool is so easy to learn and seems so effortless that the user starts moving too quickly. Plus, there's the problem of our sensitive fingers. Our fingers can feel a misalignment or ridge of just a couple of thousandths of an inch when pieces are not assembled in perfect alignment. I'm not saying you should be worried about a couple of thousandths — sandpaper can take care of that. But every error (even small ones) is magnified by the fact that it's an easy error for our fingers to detect.

There are a couple of ways to make sure your work is accurate. When you use the fence to position the tool, the trick is to slow down the pace of your work and ensure the fence is positioned flat on your work. Once you have the fence flat on the work, you need to make sure the tool stays positioned correctly as you plunge it into the work. A little misdirected hand pressure here or there can spoil the alignment. Senior Editor Bob Lang is a *connoisseur* of biscuit joiners and keeps one hand on the handle, one hand on the trigger and braces the tool against his body. When he plunges, he shifts his weight forward rather than relying on his arms to do the job.

The other option is to use your hand like a clamp, squeezing the fence and handle to plunge the tool. Personally, I've always put my fingers on the fence to keep it registered on the work. This operation opens up a remote chance for injury, but it does keep the fence in place.

The other way to get around the problem of the fence is to take the fence off and use the base of the tool as the reference surface. This involves working off your work surface, which might not always be convenient or possible. Once you remove the fence, you'll realize that when these tools are used this way they center a slot in 3⁄4"-thick material. Some engineer or tool designer was really thinking that day!

The other thing you'll find with biscuit joiners is that you have to take care of your biscuits. Keep them in their plastic tube or in a sealed plastic bag. Otherwise they tend to swell and become too thick to fit in their slots. And that really stinks when the glue is out and the assembly is halfway put together.

(By the way, whatever you do, do not listen to the joker who tells you that you can shrink the biscuits by microwaving them. That is — as far as I can tell — a sick joke. We zapped a bunch of them in our lunchroom microwave a few years ago and I officially became persona non grata when the biscuits scorched and filled the lunchroom with a nasty smell. Even when we tried nuking them for less time, nothing happened except the biscuits got warm and a little smelly. Anyway, you've been warned.)

With all these issues, why are we saying it's a good tool? Biscuit joiners have one big advantage over the pocket-hole jigs: they create an invisible joint. There is no hole or screw head visible. The overall work looks tidier inside and out. Usually you can hide your pocket holes inside your projects, but with biscuit joints you can put the joint almost anyplace.

If you never had to turn a corner, woodworking would be much easier. Glue alone will hold two pieces together if both surfaces are along the length of the grain. When one of the surfaces is the end of a piece, however, a glued butt joint will fail under very little force. To reinforce the glue joint, you can do one of two things; add a fastener such as a nail or screw, or cut parts of the wood away to make a joint. Most joints provide both long-grain gluing surfaces and hold the two pieces together mechanically. Dowels and biscuit joints fall somewhere in between. They aren't really joints, but they aren't fasteners either. The advantage to nails and screws is they not only strengthen the joint, they act as clamps to pull and hold the parts together as the glue dries.

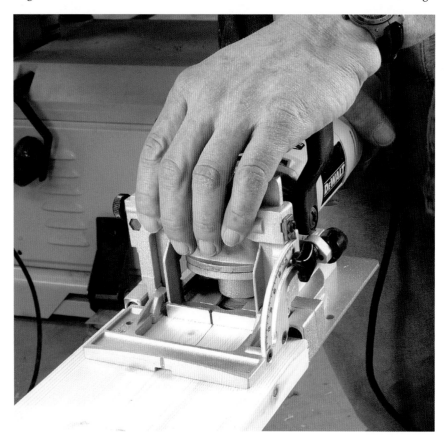
An alternate way to plunge: Squeeze the fence and tool handle together to make the cut.

Some woodworkers prefer to work without the fence when they can. Here we're using the Workmate instead of the fence, to control the tool. If you go this route, make sure your work surface is flat and debris-free.

The disadvantage to nails or screws is that most of the time you don't want to see any evidence of them in the finished product. If you can drive the fastener from a side that won't be seen in the finished product, you won't have to worry about concealing the evidence. Pocket-hole screws let you do just that by coming in at an angle from behind the finished surface. We're recommending it as the first joinery system to be adopted in the "I Can Do That" series. It is simple, strong and there are few things that can go disastrously wrong. In addition, it will enable you to put a lot of things together without needing to buy clamps.

Dowels and biscuits are an alternative, but we aren't suggesting either of those for the beginner. In the first place, you would need to invest in several clamps to hold the joints while the glue dries. Every time you move on to a larger project, you will need to get more clamps. The second reason is that pocket screws are simple to lay out and put together, and will keep your work moving along. You can screw a joint together and go on to the next one without having clamps in your way or a long wait for the glue to dry. The third reason is half practical and half philosophical. Dowels and biscuits were developed to make adequate joints in a production setting. Many woodworkers try one or both when starting out, only to leave their doweling jigs and biscuit-joining machines gathering dust as their skills develop.

Because they are a reliable, quick and hidden fastener, the pocket hole screw can often be found in advanced woodworking projects. When your skills have developed to the point where you can cut a nice mortise and tenon or dovetail joint, you will likely still find a use for pocket holes as a utility joint.

The difference between a pocket hole screw and a regular screw is the angle of the hole and screw. The 15° angle lets the head of the screw be accessed from the side of the piece rather than the end. This leaves a large elliptical-shaped hole, but if you plan ahead, you will make these holes where they won't be seen once the joint is assembled. The drill bit used is called a step drill. The large diameter is 3/8" to allow access for the screw head and driver, and the end of the bit creates a pilot hole for the screw threads. Because the angle is steep, you need a special jig to control the angle and the depth of the hole.

## Pocket Hole Jig

When you go shopping for a pocket-hole jig, your choices will be based mainly on price. What you need to come home with is the right drill bit and screws, a way to guide the bit while you drill the hole, a way to hold the guide to the wood while you drill, and a way to hold the two pieces together while you drive the screws. You will also need a #2 square-drive screwdriver. Most home centers will have a basic kit for around $50. You might also see a guide and drill bit combination for $20. The $20 kit doesn't include any clamps, and doesn't have a fence to align it to the end of the board you'll be drilling. The lack of an alignment fence makes this very frustrating to use, and when you add in the price of the clamps you'll need, you'll be close to the $50 mark.

The $50 kit is a step up, but isn't quite what you need. To use it you must clamp the work and the guide to your bench horizontally. This can be slow and tedious, and it puts your hands in an awkward position when drilling. What we recommend, if it's in your budget, is a system that holds the work piece vertically and that can be fastened to your bench with screws. You probably won't

This setup costs a bit more than the least expensive ones available, and less than the most expensive. It contains everything you need to get started in pocket-hole joinery.

find this at your local home center, but it's easy to find one online or through a catalog. We think the best choice for the beginner or the occasional user is the Kreg K3 standard pack. This includes all the bits and pieces mentioned above, and costs about $80.

Avoid any pocket-hole jigs that use a screw-type clamp to hold the work in place. The one we recommend uses the same locking pliers-style clamp to hold the work to the jig as you drill, and then to hold the two pieces together when you drive the screws. The more expensive kits have a lever-action clamp to hold the work in the jig, and a locking pliers-style clamp to hold the work together as you drive the screws. This is more convenient if you have a lot of parts to drill, or if you are working on panels more than 12" wide. With the Kreg K3, you can upgrade.

When you put the jig together, look for marks on the side of the part that holds the drill bushings that indicate the thickness of the stock you will be using. That should put the hole where you want it, exiting the end of the piece at or very close to the thickness of the stock. Next you need to adjust the clamp that holds the work on the jig. If you're using the locking-pliers clamp, fasten it to the jig, put a piece of wood in place and open the clamp. If it's too tight to clamp, loosen it up farther than you need to, close it and then tighten the screw until it makes contact with the wood. Open it back up, and tighten the screw another turn or two. The wood should be held firmly, but you should also be able to open and close the clamp without too much effort.

The last adjustment to make is to put the stop collar on the drill bit. When you drill the pocket hole, you need to control the depth so that the pointed end of the screw doesn't come out on the finished side of your work. With ¾"-thick material, a good place to start is with the end of the drill bit about ⅛" above the surface of the jig.

The screw will make its way through that last ⅛"; if you set the bit to go entirely through it can leave a little bump on the bottom that may keep the joint from coming together. Drop the bit in the jig, loosen the set screw on the collar, and slip the collar over the end of the bit.

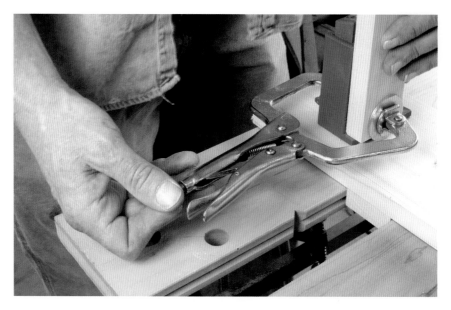

Adjust the clamp to hold the wood firmly in the jig without taking too much effort to set the clamp.

Lift the bit up about ⅛", letting the collar rest on the jig and tighten the set screw. Don't worry about being exact at this point. You will drill some test holes and make a practice joint to confirm your settings.

Place a piece of scrap wood in the jig and drill a hole, using the highest speed possible on your drill, checking to see that the stop collar doesn't slip on the drill bit and that the wood doesn't slip from under the clamp.

Remove the wood from the jig, place a screw in the hole, and drive it in. When the bottom of the screw head meets the bottom of the larger hole, you will feel it. Look at the end of the piece. The exit point of the screw should be close to the center of the board's thickness.

Next, you want to make sure that the end of the screw won't come out of the face of the piece you will be attaching. Hold the end of the piece of scrap with the screw in it against the face of the piece. There should be ⅛" or more between the point of the screw and the edge of the wood. If there isn't, you need

Setting the depth of the stop collar is simple. With one hand, you can push the collar down on the jig and hold the tip of the bit about ⅛" above the jig. Use your other hand to tighten the set screw on the collar.

Use the high speed setting on your drill to make the pocket hole.

The screw should exit the end of the wood near the center of the board's thickness. Don't worry about getting it precisely placed. The next step will let you know if your setup will work.

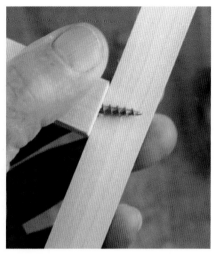

Hold a piece of scrap against the piece with the screw in it. Check to see that the end of the screw is about 1/8" away from surface.

to adjust the stop collar on the drill bit. You're almost ready to make a joint, but first you need to adjust the locking-pliers assembly clamp.

Open the clamp and then close it on a piece of scrap the same thickness as the material you will be using for your joints. Adjust the clamping pressure in the same way you adjusted the clamp on the jig; open it up farther than you need to, tighten the screw until it makes contact with the wood, then open it up and tighten the screw another turn or two. When you use the locking-pliers clamp to hold two pieces together, keep the larger of the two pads on the finished face. This distributes the pressure along the surfaces you want to have lined up when you're done, and won't mar the work.

The most typical use for pocket screws is in a face-frame joint and the clamp is used to keep the pieces lined up, not to pull them together. If one piece meets the other at the end, hold them in line with your hand as you set the clamp. If they come together at any other point, you need to mark the location with your square, and hold the piece to the line as you clamp. Obviously, the end needs to be smooth and square for the joint to pull together and hold properly.

You need to decide where to locate the holes in the width of the piece, and that will depend on how wide the piece actually is. You want to use at least two holes

if possible, as the parts could pivot on just one screw. If the material is 1½" to 2" thick, the middle of the board should be between the two closest-spaced holes on the jig. Once again, you don't need to be concerned about getting the board exactly centered; you only need to be close for the joint to work. If the work piece is wider than 4", use three or more screws. On wide pieces, the spacing between screw holes should be between 2" and 4". Don't waste your time measuring and marking exact locations, it's OK to do it by eye.

When you're ready to put the joint together, apply some glue to the end

Line up the two pieces and set the clamp to hold them together.

grain of the piece that the screws go in. As you practice, try varying the amount of glue that you use until you get just a small amount of squeeze out when you drive the screws. Using more glue than necessary will only create a mess to clean up, and can lead to some big problems when finishing. If you're driving the screws with a cordless drill, use the lowest speed available and the long driver bit that comes with the kit.

You're not limited to face-frame joints with pocket screws. You can also join pieces on edge, but when you do this, you lose the ability to clamp them together with the locking pliers. Because the screw is being driven at an angle, it tends to push the pieces out of alignment so it helps to clamp them together while you tighten the screw.

One last thing — you really do need to use the pan-head screws that come with the jig. If you try using a screw with a countersunk head, it won't stop when it hits the bottom of the large diameter hole. The clamping action of this joint depends on the pan head stopping so that the threads can bite into the second piece of wood and pull it tight to the first piece.

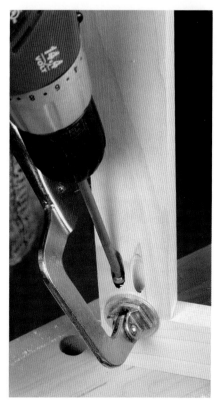

The long driver bit that comes in the kit keeps the drill chuck away from the wood.

## FASTENING TOOLS

Lots of furniture can be built using a hammer and screwdriver. Because these are two tools you'll never outgrow, you should select your first hammer and screwdriver with care.

### Hammer and Nail Set

You'd think that there isn't much to be said about buying a hammer. It's just a metal rock on a stick, right? Well yes, but buying the wrong hammer will trip you up. Buy a hammer for making furniture, not some hammer for chipping rocks. We recommend a claw hammer that has a head that weighs 16 oz. and a wooden handle.

The all-metal and composite hammers work, but I find them less forgiving on your elbows and arms. I get sore a lot faster. The wooden hammers are, by and large, cheaper, too. And here's another bonus: You can sand off the junky, gloppy finish on the handle and finish it to your liking. Sanding it nicely up to #220 grit and then adding a coat of wax or linseed oil will result in a hammer that is a joy to pick up. Seriously. Most new woodworkers are loathe to modify or improve the wooden handles of the tools. Hello? That's why they're made of wood — so you can make them suit you.

There are other things to look for, too. The business end of a hammer can be flat or slightly bellied. Go for the hammer with the bellied face — sometimes called a bell face. This results in fewer mis-strikes and allows you to drive the nail in much closer to flush than a flat-faced tool will.

Also, look at the claw. Does it stick straight out, almost straight out or does it curve down back toward the handle? If it doesn't curve much it's called a ripping hammer. These hammers are used for disassembling things — the claw is actually a crowbar. You want the claw to curve down — this gives you more leverage to remove a nail.

Using a hammer is straightforward, but keep these tips in mind. There are two basic grips. One is the power stroke. You grasp the end of the handle to get more bang when driving a nail. If you're after more control, choke up toward the middle of the handle and extend your thumb. This will reduce the force you transmit into the nail (which can be a

A good wooden-handled hammer and a few nailsets can serve you for a lifetime. Avoid the fiberglass and metal hammers. They are not as forgiving on your joints (as in your shoulder and elbow).

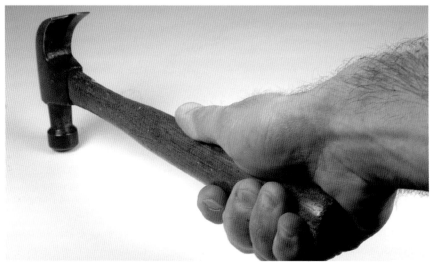

This is the power stroke with a hammer. When you build a deck, or really need to wallop something, grip the tool at the end of the handle. Sticking your thumb out will help steady the tool a bit.

By choking up on the handle you can gain some finesse and reduce the force (sometimes a good thing, really). Note again the position of my thumb.

A decent screwdriver that holds magnetic bits will replace a drawer full of cheap ones and you won't need to worry about wearing it out.

good thing) and it will help keep your strikes where you intended them to be.

Also, there's a lot of confusion about how to buy nails. Most places denote the length of a nail using the English pennyweight system. The origin of pennyweight is a mite murky, so let's stick to the facts. Pennyweight is denoted by $d$. So a two-penny nail is 2d. And a 2d nail is 1" long. For every penny you add, the nail gets ¼" longer. So a 3d nail is 1¼" long. A 4d nail is 1½" long. A 5d nail is 1¾" long. And so on.

You select your nail's length based on the thickness and density of the boards you are using. Here's how the old rule works:

1. Determine the thickness of your board in eighths of an inch. For example, a 1"-thick board would be 8/8. A ¾"-thick board would be 6/8. And so on.

2. For a wood of medium density (walnut or cherry, for example), pick a nail where the pennyweight matches that thickness — an 8d nail for 1" stock. A 6d nail for ¾".

3. For softwoods (white pine), select a nail that's one penny larger. For harder woods (maple), use one penny smaller. This seems complex at first, but it quickly becomes second nature.

Once you drive a nail into your work, you'll almost always want to *set* the nail so the head is slightly below the surface. Then, for nice pieces, you'll putty the hole. The tool to do this is a nail set,

which is essentially a pointy steel rod. The shaft is knurled so you can hold onto the tool easily. The tips come in a variety of shapes and sizes. Because nail sets are inexpensive, buy a variety of sizes, mostly ones with small tips, which are suited for woodworking (as opposed to deck building). Get at least one nail set that has a cone-shaped tip. Some finishing nails have a matching depression on their heads and the cone-like tip helps secure the nail set as you strike it.

There are only a couple of things to remember about using a nail set: When you hold it, it's best to keep the edge of your hand against your work — don't suspend your hand in space as you grip the set. Grasp the nail set between your thumb and forefinger. Pound away until the nail head is ¹⁄₁₆" to ⅛" below the surface of the wood.

## Screwdrivers

One of the easiest mistakes to make when buying tools is to snap up a bargain thinking you are getting all the tools you will ever need in one decisive move. This is especially true with screwdrivers. In the tool aisle there will always be a great deal on a complete set of screwdrivers. If you aren't sure what you need, and what the difference is between a good quality tool and a poor one, it's tempting to spend $20 for a set of screwdrivers, especially when a single screwdriver might cost $7 or $8.

You will need the ability to drive and remove several different sizes and types of screws, but you don't want to buy a cheap set and you don't want to spend a small fortune buying a bunch of individual tools. What makes the most sense is to invest in a good-quality handle that will hold different driver bits. Look for one that holds the same short bits that are used for driving screws with a cordless drill. The one in the picture has been in use for more than 10 years, and stores extra bits in the handle. It replaced a drawer full of miscellaneous screwdrivers.

The tip of any screwdriver is the part that takes all the abuse from the twisting forces exerted on it. The screwdrivers that come in sets won't last very long. If you buy an inexpensive set, you will soon find yourself the owner of several screwdrivers with damaged tips (the ones you need to use most often) and a few good ones you likely won't ever need. When you try to use the good ones you have left you will find they are a little smaller than they should be to fit the screw. This in turn will damage these drivers (or the screws) and eventually you will have fifteen or twenty tools that are only useful for prying open paint cans.

If you're using individual bits, damaging one bit or needing a new size or type has a quick, inexpensive solution. You should pick up a set of bits of differ-

This selection of bits will fill most of your woodworking needs; small, medium and large slotted, #1 and #2 square drive, and #1 and #2 Phillips.

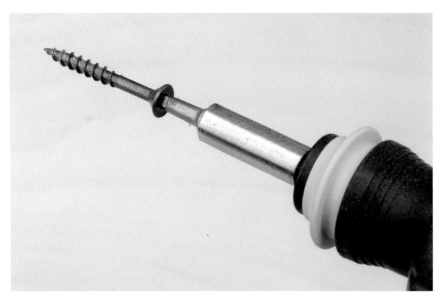

The square drive holds so well that the screw will hang on the end of the bit.

There is a large, #3 size of Phillips head, but it isn't likely you will need one unless you are working with large diameter screws. If you have a large screw, and your #2 bit has a sloppy fit in the screw head, you need to head to the store and get a #3 driver bit.

Square-drive screws won't slip out of the recess when the screw is tightened, and generally work better than Phillips. A square-drive screw will hang on to the tip of the driver by itself so it's easier to use if you have to reach in a tight spot. You can apply more force to the square drive without it slipping or damaging the screw head.

Pocket-hole screws use a #2 square drive, and the trim-head screws mentioned earlier use a #1 square drive. With either of these applications, don't use Phillips-head screws if you have a choice. Square-drive woodworking screws can be hard to find at your local home center, but they are readily available from online and catalog sources. Many woodworkers prefer the square drive for all applications, but you will still need to have other bits on hand.

Slotted screws used to be called common screws because the vast majority of screws were made with that type of head. The technology to manufacture other types was developed after the 1930s. The newer types are much easier to use, and less likely to damage either the screw or the screwdriver in use. There's an excellent chance that you will come across them, so having the appropriate bits on hand is a good idea.

If you have a cordless drill, you'll probably use it for driving screws as well as drilling holes. A magnetic bit holder will make your life much easier. It's a lot easier to handle and holds better in the drill chuck than the smaller individual bits. In addition, the magnet will hold the screw to the driver, making it much easier to place the screws where you want them. When you drive screws with your drill, adjust the clutch settings so that the clutch engages at the point where the screw is tight. This will keep you from driving screws in too far or stripping the threads. It will also extend the life of your drill.

ent sizes and types, but once again you should avoid the temptation of buying a cheap set that includes everything you'll ever need in favor of a quality set of the few you will really need.

The one size you will need most often is the #2 Phillips. The crossed recess of this bit is much easier to use than the common slotted screw because the driver will center itself in the screw head and won't slip sideways as you turn it. If you have a choice when buying screws for assembling woodwork, get Phillips, not slotted heads. Drywall screws are more brittle than woodscrews, but work fine in most cases and cost less.

The downside to the Phillips head is that the end of the bit will eventually wear out. When a Phillips-head screw is fully tight, the bit slips out of the recess in the screw head. This helps you keep from over tightening or stripping the screw, but it is hard on the driver. Get several extra bits of this size.

The #1 Phillips is smaller, and you won't use it as often as the #2. Usually it is only used for attaching hardware, not in building.

There is a wood screw called a trim head screw with a very small head that comes in either a #1 Phillips drive, or a #1 square drive. If you have the choice, go with the square drive. Like its big brother, the #1 Phillips is susceptible to damage and once the bit is torn up, it will start damaging the screws.

If you are attaching hardware and can't drive the screws without doing any damage you should make sure your pilot hole is the correct size. If it is and you still have trouble, try lubricating the threads of the screw with some wax.

Be especially careful with brass screws. They are softer than the tip of the screwdriver and are easily damaged. Try driving in a steel screw of the same size first to cut the threads, and lubricate the brass screws.

The magnetic bit holder chucks in your cordless drill and uses replaceable insert bits.

## WORKHOLDING

Your accuracy will be greatly increased if you can immobilize your wood as you work it. And that's why you need some kind of bench and clamps. Here is a bare-bones but workable setup.

### Workmate

You need a surface to work on, but it doesn't have to be fancy or even permanent. A couple of sawhorses and a solid door is a primo break-down work surface but I think the case can be made that you can build almost anything on a Workmate.

These wonders of engineering and marketing have dominated home garages since they were introduced in the early 1970s. (If you want to read a fascinating history of the Workmate, pick up a copy of Scott Landis' *The Workbench Book*.) The workmate is going to cost you anywhere from $50 to $100 (or hit the garage sales; they're everywhere). And for your money you're going to get a workstation that can be positioned at two heights: Kinda low, which is great for sawing and kinda high, which is good for everything else. Plus you get a big workholding kinda-sorta vise. It's not going to do the job of a big metal woodworking vise, but with the plastic dogs provided with the Workmate, you'll be able to clamp most things.

One nice thing about a Workmate is that it folds up reasonably flat so you can stow it away or throw it in your trunk. Plus, it's not something you'll ever outgrow. Even if you become a professional cabinetmaker and have $100,000 in tools you'll still find a good use for your Workmate.

There are some off-brands out there. We haven't used them. They might be fine; they might not. You're on your own there.

### Clamps

You need some clamps to hold your work while you cut it or drill it and to hold parts together while the glue sets or you drive a nail or screw. People spend a fortune on clamps, and someday you might also do the same. But to get started, we think you need only about six clamps.

F-style clamps are so named because they look kind of like an *F*. Usually they have a wooden or plastic handle. The typical and most useful of all F-style clamps has a bar that is about 12" long with a

You won't outgrow your Workmate — I've always had one in my shop. It's a bench, vise and (don't tell) a big stepstool. The new ones are good, but if you can find an older one, you'll have found a friend for life.

These two F-style clamps are absolutely your best friends when working wood. They hold things in place as you cut and shape them.

The threads on the clamp (bottom) are Acme threads. This is a durable, lifetime clamp. The cheesy threads on the clamp (top) above will strip out eventually.

throat (the distance from the bar to the tip of the clamping pad) of about 3".

How do you pick a good F-style clamp? Good question. I hate — let me repeat that, hate — cheap, cheesy clamps. They usually aren't much less expensive than the good stuff, but they are much less useful and durable. Even if you abandon woodworking, you'll probably keep your F-style clamps to hold stuff for household repairs.

So how do you separate the good clamps from the bad? The first place to look is at the metal screw between the handle and the pad. Look closely. Think

The teeth on the left are on the cheaper clamp. They're coarser and are only on a small portion of the bar. The teeth on the right are finer and there are more of them.

of the threads like mountains and valleys. Some screws will have threads with a pronounced flat or plateau at the top of each mountain. Some will have a sharp peak. Likewise, the mating valleys can be either flat or pointy.

The flat-topped threads are commonly called *Acme* threads and are far superior. They are more durable. They don't seem to get gummed up as much. They generally work faster. They are also more expensive, but they're worth it.

The other thing to look for on the clamps is the *teeth* or serrations that are cut into the bar. Cheap clamps will have teeth that are short and spaced far apart. Good clamps will have finely milled teeth that are generally bigger. I know all this stuff sounds minor, but it really makes a difference. Also, some clamps come with plastic pads on each head; some don't. Don't walk out of the store without pads for your clamps, otherwise you'll mar the work.

The F-style clamps will hold your work down as you cut, drill and shape it, though they also can be used for holding pieces together when you're gluing things.

For most assembly tasks, you're also going to want bar clamps. These are remarkably similar to F-style clamps in that they have the same issues with their

threads and their teeth. The other factor is the bar itself. Many woodworkers use pipe clamps for assembly chores. Pipe clamps are made from plumber's pipe. You screw the clamp parts onto the threads of the pipe — instant clamp of any length.

Other bar clamps come with a bar made of aluminum or some other metal. Now a lot of people are going to talk to you about how much these bars flex under clamping pressure. Truth is, they do all flex. But here's what's important: If the bars of any clamp are flexing so much that they're distorting your assembly, then there's something wrong with your assembly, not your clamps. A well-cut joint will close with just a little clamp pressure. If you're using your clamps to make up for a poor joint, you'll be sorry later — the wood always wins in the end.

So don't get too worked up about the bar material. Pick a bar clamp that fits your budget and has quality screw threads and teeth on the bar. You'll be fine.

Routers are available in many designs and at many different horsepower ratings. From left to right standing is a plunge router, a two-handle, fixed-base router, and a D-handle, fixed-base router. Lying at the center is a trim router, sometimes called a laminate trimmer.

## ROUTERS & ROUTER BITS

Selecting your first router can be a daunting task without guidance. With the many different designs, motors and options available, what do you look for?

Should you choose a fixed-base or plunge-base router? Is a D-handle design better than a trim router (sometimes called a laminate trimmer)? What about multi-base kits? And then the world of router bits opens for discussion. When does shank size matter? When do you choose a bearing-guided router bit over a non-guided bit?

Also, there's technique to be considered. In what direction do you move the router during normal routing operations? What is a climb-cut and when should you use it?

### Router Designs

There are two distinct router types: plunge base and fixed base. Plunge bases are spring-loaded units that, with the motor slid into the base, have the ability to adjust up or down as you work. Plunge cuts can be started and completed without moving the tool off the workpiece. While plunge-base routers do have a place in the shop, these routers, usually taller than fixed-base routers with handle placement set higher off the workpiece,

are a bit top heavy and awkward. Therefore, a plunge-base router is not recommended as your first router.

In fixed-base routers, removable motors are slid or threaded into bases that are then clamped around the motors to form a fixed unit with which to work.

Fixed-base routers include trim routers, as well as two-handle and D-handle designs.

Trim routers are small tools that are easily held with a single hand. Generally, there are no handles associated with these small routers; you simply wrap your hand around the tool and begin your cut. Trim routers would make a good introductory router except for the fact that they accept only ¼"-shank router bits. (You'll learn more about this shortly.) Also, small routers have small bases, and that makes it more likely you'll tip the tool as you work. Tipping the tool causes problems when routing. You can replace the stock base plate with a custom-made plate if you desire, but we think there is a better introductory router choice.

Fixed-base routers with two handles are most often thought of as a router for entry-level woodworkers. These routers sit flat in your workpiece with handles set close to the work. As you use the tools, the balance is right and there is no top-heaviness to speak of. But there is a problem as you begin or end your operation.

To reach the on/off switch, you must remove one hand from the tool. When you do that, the router is difficult to hold steady. This unsteadiness is reduced when the router has a "soft start" feature,

The base on a trim router is small and that presents problems with tipping the router as you cut. To improve the usefulness of this small router, add a shop-made, oversized base with an extra handle. Also, the tool is held with one hand.

D-handle routers are well balanced and can be held steady with a single hand. And the on/off trigger is right at your finger. It's hard to look anywhere else for a first router.

a gentle motor increase to full speed. (Without soft start, the tool has a small kick that can catch you off guard.) When ending a cut, if you take your hand from the router handle, the tool has a tendency to wobble — and because the router bit is still turning at a high rpm, that can be a dangerous scenario.

D-handle routers have the on/off switch set in the handle of the base; it's a trigger control. This, coupled with a well-balanced tool, allows the router to be easily operated without any tipping or wobble as you begin the cut, work through the cut and come to the end. This is the router we feel should be your choice as a first router.

What about multi-base router kits? Kits generally are two-base setups that include a two-handle base along with a plunge base. It's sometimes hard to pass on a deal such as this, but we've discussed the problems for someone just beginning to use a router. If you can find a multi-base setup that includes a D-handle base as part of the set, then I would look closely at the tool, as long as the desirable features discussed below are met.

## Horsepower & Variable Speeds

Horsepower ratings for routers can also be an indication of router size. Trim routers, which are the smallest in size, have the smaller horsepower (hp) ratings. Generally, these routers come in around 1 horsepower; some are slightly less.

The highest hp ratings belong to the largest routers. These routers are primarily used as table-mounted routers where the increased power can spin larger-diameter router bits to remove waste material quickly. Larger routers have horsepower ratings at 3 - 3½ hp. They are unwieldy to work easily as hand-held tools and we don't consider them to be a good first router. Routers in the middle category are normally rated with 1¾ or 2¼ hp. The difference in hp ratings is negligible, so choosing one over the other can be a toss-up. However, a D-handle base is more often found with the 1¾ hp routers, but you can find the 2¼ hp routers available with that base design. Then you should consider price and if you can work with a slightly heavier tool.

Variable speed is something to look for in your first router. Adjusting the speed is necessary when you're using router bits with a larger mass in the profile. As the bit's mass increases, you should slow the tool's rpm.

## Other Features

Other features one should consider when evaluating routers are the collets and how router bit changes are made — do you need two wrenches or is there a spindle lock?

A collet is part of the motor shaft assembly; it's the piece that holds the router bit safely in the router. On early routers, the collet was separate from the collet nut, but most routers today have a collet assembly where the two pieces are joined together. Collets are made to fit and work on the router model with which they came and should not be considered interchangeable between different models, although some companies produce a single collet design that can be used on many routers produced by that company. Also, collets sizes must match the shank on your router bits. Most routers, other than trim routers, include two collets: ¼" and ½". Other sizes, ⅜" and 8mm, are commonly found accessories. Collets should grip the bit shank tightly and not release once tightened.

Many routers come equipped with a spindle lock and a single collet wrench. To swap router bits, your thumb depresses a lock into the router shaft, then you operate the wrench with your second hand. This process is inefficient and can result in the setup slipping during changes, and sometimes the lock slips out of the spindle as you attempt to loosen or tighten the collet. The best arrangement is to use two wrenches: one wrench on the spindle and a second on the collet nut. Look for a router that comes with two wrenches. It's better if those wrenches are cast metal instead of stamped.

## A Look At Router Bits

What about router bits? There are a number of designs from which to choose; just as there are easy calls on what not to use. The vast majority of entry-level router work is to produce edge profiles. The best results are accomplished when using guided router bits — router bits that self-limit their travel into the wood.

Wrenches are as varied as routers. Cast is better than stamped, although we wouldn't walk by a router without cast wrenches. We would, however, pass on a router that insisted we change bits using a thumb-activated spindle lock.

The collet, the part of the router that grabs and secures the router bit, is the piece inside the collet nut. Today, these two important pieces are generally joined as a single unit. Different size collets accept different size router bit shanks.

If you're rummaging around a flea market or a garage sale, don't pick up pilotguided router bits — bits that have a portion of the shank extended below the cutting profile. That extension rides against the wood to guide the bit in the cut. Pilotguided router bits mar the edge of your workpiece and are likely to burn as they cut. Today, this design is all but vanished, but can at times be purchased.

A better choice is a bearing-guided bit. Bearings spin freely as the bit is moved along the wood. There is little chance of marring the edge, and if the cut burns as it shapes, chances are there is operator error involved (we cover that later) or your router bit is dull and should be replaced. Bits can be found with bearings placed above or below the router bit profile. Different bearing placement is for different routing operation. Generally, being new to routers, you'll be most interested in router bits with a bearing mounted below the profile.

Of course, there are times when a nonguided router bit is called for. In these operations, you are either making a cut free-hand — a procedure that's inefficient and difficult to master — or you'll guide the router in some other manner such as running the base plate along a straight-edge or using router guide bushings.

## Router Bit Profile Choice

The most often-asked question about router bits focuses on what profile or profiles should a woodworker purchase. The answer is whatever bit profiles you need. Of course, to someone not familiar with routers and router bits, that answer is meaningless. Our suggestion, if you're just beginning down this path, is to purchase a set of inexpensive bits in different profiles. As you become more experienced, watch to see what router bit profiles you use the most. At that point, purchase better-quality router bits with that profile. And don't be afraid to experiment with different profiles as you learn.

One important furniture profile is a roundover bit. Roundover router bits are available in a variety of sizes — ¼", ⅜" and ½" radii are the most common. These bits produce a smooth roundover detail, or if set for a deeper cut, the same bit forms a fillet (or step) in the design.

These router bits create a ⅜" roundover profile, but the router bit on the right is by far better. The bearing rolls along the edge of your workpiece as it guides the router bit. The piloted bit on the left is an older design. The shaft guiding the bit often produced a burnt edge below the cutting profile.

A few other router bits are commonly used in woodworking. A classic ogee profile — as is its cousin the classic Roman ogee — is used as a tabletop edge profile and sometimes found as a door edge design.

Rabbeting bits, used to produce stepped profiles along the edge of boards, are available in either a fixed setup that is good for a single rabbet profile, or the router bit includes additional bearings that can be switched to produce varying sized rabbets. There are dovetail bits used to create dovetail joints and sliding dovetail joints — more advanced router

Guide bushings, also known as template guides, are another method to guide your router bit. The bushing, available in different diameters, rides along a fence or pattern to guide your cut.

operations. Dovetail router bits can be bearing guided, but most often you'll find them without. And there are straight bits, including pattern bits.

Pattern bits have become more popular recently. These router bits are simply straight bits with a bearing mounted to guide the cut along a predetermined shape. That shape is only limited by what you can imagine — it can be a straight cut to house shelf standards for a bookcase, curved to form a round or oval tabletop, or an intricate design used on the side of a piece of case furniture.

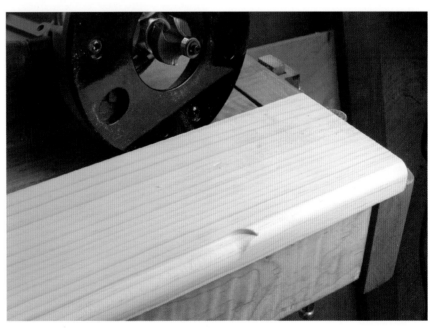

Roundover router bits produce two distinct profiles depending on the depth of cut. Set flush with the workpiece, the bit produces a roundover design. The same bit creates a thumbnail design which includes a small fillet if set deeper.

## Size Does Matter

When talking about router bit shank sizes, the mass of the cutter profile helps determine the shank size. Many profiles are available with either ¼" and ½" shanks. However, when the cutter profile becomes larger, the router bits are generally limited to ½" shanks. As a result, a trim router, due to its ¼" shank limitations, is not used for larger-diameter router bits.

So with many routers able to work with both router bit shank sizes, why choose one size over another? The answer most often given is for durability and longevity. A ½"-shank router bit experiences less vibration than the smaller diameter shank. That lack of vibration extends the useful life. But as discussed above, some routers use only ¼"-shank bits.

## Proper Router Techniques

Bit installation is important. A router bit should be fully engaged by the collet. A simple rule of thumb is to slide the bit completely into the collet, then pull the bit out anywhere from ¹⁄₁₆" to ⅛" before tightening. It's imperative to not leave the bit fully set into the collet; doing so could cause two problems. First and most important, the collet could tighten at the area where the shank blends into the cutter and not only on the shank. The connection could loosen as the collet slips down onto the shank and the router bit could fall free. Second, if the bit shank is against the motor shaft, as the tool is used and heat builds, any expansion could push the bit away from the shaft causing problems with your depth-of-cut settings.

The procedure for edge routing is to first securely clamp your workpiece so it will not move as you work. Next, move the router from the left to the right as you're routing an outside edge, or against the rotation of the router bit. On an inside edge, such as the interior edge of a frame, you have to move from right to left or again, work against the rotation of the router bit. That's why it's best to remember to move against the bit rotation.

Begin with the router bit away from the workpiece, but with the router base resting on your work. Wait for the tool to come to full speed (soft start), then move the router and bit into the work and move

slowly along the edge. As you reach the end of your cut, pull the spinning bit away from the workpiece and allow the router to come to a complete stop prior to removing the tool completely.

The speed at which you move is vital for a clean router cut. If you move too fast, the cut will be rough and jagged. But if you move too slow, you are apt to create burn marks on the routed edge. Finding the sweet spot is important. This is an area where being able to adjust the router speed (rpm) is nice. If you feel uncomfortable moving along the edge quickly enough to prevent burn while maintaining a clean cut, slow the spin of the router bit.

There are a couple tricks to eliminate burning. One trick is to increase your speed as you rout — find that sweet spot. If that fails, a trick we find useful is to rout the entire edge of your workpiece, then adjust the depth of your router bit just a fuzz deeper to run the edge a second time. This is a sure-fire method to a clean, burn-free edge profile. (Tip: Whenever you are routing a panel that has both long grain and end grain, you should work the end grain first. This helps to prevent tear-out as you profile the edges.)

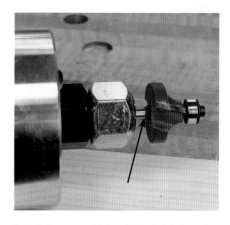

Install the router bit by sliding it fully into the collet then pull it out about ⅛". If the collet tightens around the transition point (shown by the arrow) it's probable the collet would slip and the bit could fall from the router.

## Pattern Routing

Pattern routing is gaining popularity in woodworking. Place your pattern on to your workpiece then draw a line along the pattern. It's better to remove most of the waste with a jigsaw or some other tool prior to routing. Next, clamp the pattern in position and rout the design just as you would an edge profile, allowing the bearing to ride along the pattern. Here,

If your first pass produces a charred profile, a technique used to remove the discoloration is to lower the bit a small amount then rerun the edge. Without having to remove a huge amount of material, the second pass is quick, the bit cuts cleaner and the charred edges disappear.

Pattern router bits are available in many lengths and bit diameters. Small diameters allow you to get crisp details in your work. Here an elaborate pattern, half the overall length of the workpiece, is used. (Flip the pattern to complete the piece).

Pattern routing can be as intricate as you need, or it can be simple and a great way to make matching pieces. And it's a real timesaver when woodworking.

whatever the pattern shape is, an identical shape is made in your workpiece.

To rout an inside area such as a handle, begin by transferring the pattern to the workpiece just as before, then drill a hole through the area large enough for your pattern bit to pass through — or your jigsaw blade if you have a lot of waste to remove. As before, the closer to your cut lines you can get, the easier the task will be. Clamp the pattern in place, then rout the waste from inside the pattern — remember that you're on the inside edges so you'll have to move the router from right to left.

## Climb-cutting

Until now, we've talked about moving the router against the rotation of the router bit. Working with the rotation is called climb-cutting. While this is an operation often used in woodworking, it has potential problems. When moving with the router bit rotation, the router bit has a tendency to grab the work and propel the router forward. If you're not prepared for this, the router can be pulled from your hands and your workpiece ruined. In this scenario, it's best to take very light cuts and not try to hog off heavy-duty waste. Even with that in mind, make sure to brace yourself as you cut. Stand in front of the cut and lock your elbow to absorb any kick.

With these potential problems, why would you climb-cut at all? When you're

routing hills and valleys, it's better to work down the hills. If you move only right to left, as you work up the hills, you're apt to tear out sections of your workpiece that are vital to the finished design as the spin of the bit cuts away from the workpiece. By climb-cutting from the apex of the hill down into the valley, the router bit, as it spins into the wood during a climbcut, cuts the waste material while pushing into the finished stock. This helps to keep the wood intact.

## Safety First

Remember to protect your eyes, ears and lungs when using a router. Eye protection is key whenever you're working in a woodshop, but it's of particular importance when using a router. The decibels reading for most routers is more than 100, which is over the danger threshold, so hearing protection should always be worn. And fine wood dust gathers in your lungs and accumulates over time, so it's best to wear a mask as you rout — especially when working with exotic woods.

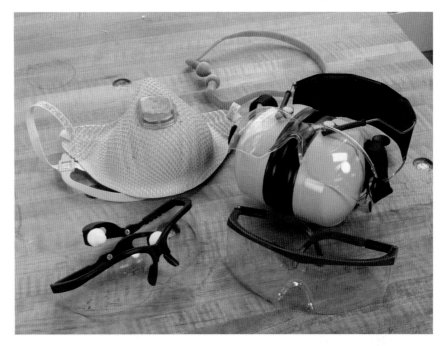

Safety gear — safety glasses, hearing protection and some type of dust mask — should always be used when routing.

# Techniques

## RIPPING

Ripping lumber is a lot of work. In fact, we try to plan projects to do the least amount of it possible. When you do rip — which is the act of sawing with the grain as opposed to across it – here's how to do it. Mark your cutting line all along your board — mark both faces of the board if you can. Use a combination square or play connect the dots. Cut outside of the line with your jigsaw — get as close as you can without crossing it. Secure the board with the sawn edge facing up. Use your block plane to smooth the edge down to your pencil lines. Check your edge with your combination square to make sure you are planing square.

**1** Mark your cutting line on both faces of your work — this will help you plane down to the line later.

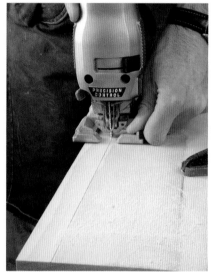

**2** Jigsaw as close to the line as possible without crossing it. Move the saw swiftly yet surely for a smooth cut.

**3** Use a block plane to remove the saw marks and create a square edge. Plane down to your cutting line (check both faces of your work).

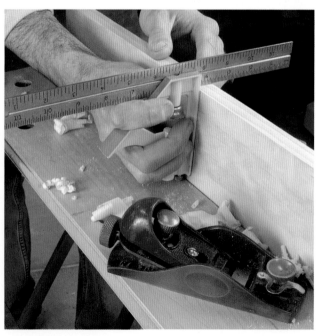

**4** Check your work in several places along the edge to ensure it's square. Work on the areas that aren't.

## LAYOUT — EGG CRATE SHELF JOINT

Long before the term "ergonomics" was invented, the combination square was designed to neatly fit the hand. In the egg crate shelf project, the square is used in several different ways, many of them with the left hand holding the square. Once you get used to using it and the way it works, you can use it as an all purpose layout and marking guide. Find a comfortable way to hold it firmly against the edge of your material.

### Layout

We want the joints to be in the same place on all the parts, even if our measurements are off a little. By clamping all the uprights together, we can measure and mark the locations of joints only once, and then use the square to transfer the marks to all the pieces by drawing a line across the edges of the boards. This saves time, and it also guarantees that the locations marked are in the same place on each piece.

Next we want to be sure that the slot we cut is the same size as the thickness of our wood. It isn't safe to assume that the ¾" material really is that size, so use a piece of scrap to get the size right, even if the material is too thick or too thin. Draw a line to represent one edge of the notch, and slide the blade of the square over to barely cover the line.

Holding the square firmly in place, the scrap is placed against it, and a pencil line is drawn against its edge as seen in the photo above right. After drawing the line, you can remove the square and look down on the scrap and the two lines. If you can see both lines against the edge of the scrap your layout is accurate.

If we're confident that the shelf will fit between the lines, then we can preserve the lines until the final fitting, cutting inside of them, and trimming down to them. The lines will let us know if our cuts are straight, and how much more material we have left to remove.

The ends of the notches need to be marked, and we'll use the end of the blade of the square as our guide after we adjust it to be centered in the width of the board. Measuring will get us close, but not exactly there. Make your best guess as

Measuring isn't always the best way to work accurately. Holding a block of scrap against the blade of the square guarantees that the line drawn will represent the thickness of the piece that will fit in the notch. It's much more important that the slot and the shelf be identical in size than it is to know the exact thickness of the shelf. Every time you measure and mark something you introduce the opportunity to make a mistake. I consider measuring to be a last resort, and avoid it when I can.

to the center measurement, and make a mark with your pencil.

Adjust the blade of the square to meet that mark, and draw a short line against the end of the blade. Now, flip the square over so that it's against the opposite edge of the board, and make a second mark. If these two lines coincide, you got lucky and hit the center on your first try. Chances are there's a gap between the two. Adjust the blade again, trying to place the end of it between the two marks. When

you have it set, make a mark from each edge as you did before. You should be able to get the lines to meet in a couple attempts.

We can also use the square to guide the jigsaw to make straighter cuts than we could make if we were trying to saw freehand, as seen in the photo at left. Clamp the board down, and with the square in one hand, and the jigsaw in the other, line up the saw so that the blade is just inside one of the lines.

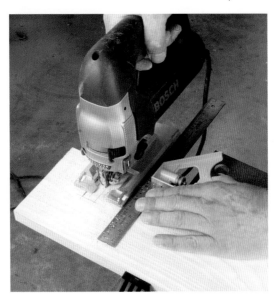

It takes some practice to coordinate sliding the saw and square to get in position to make the cut, and to hold the square steady as you push the base of the saw against it. Make some practice cuts in the wasted space between the two lines before trying to cut precisely to the line. When you're ready, hold the base of the saw down to keep from lifting it over the edge of the square. Release the trigger when you hit the cross line and wait for the blade to come to a stop before removing it from the cut.

After making both of the long cuts, make a curved cut in the waste toward one of the corners. This will give you room to maneuver the saw to cut the end of the notch.

## Cutting Joints

Back the saw away from the line while holding the square firmly against the edge of the board. Turn on the saw and push it in against the blade of the square to make the cut. Hold the base of the saw flat, and release the trigger when you get to the line at the end of the notch.

Making the square cut at the end of the notch seems impossible. There isn't a way to start the cut on the line, so you need to create some space for the blade. Run the saw blade down one of the previously cut lines, and aim for a corner. After the waste piece falls away, you have room to turn the saw as you head to the other corner. It may take a few times going back and forth, but eventually you can cut to the line. If you go too far, or end up with some ugliness, don't worry. This end of the joint will be covered up when you put the pieces together.

## Fitting Joints

We used a rasp to clean up the saw cuts, removing material back to the pencil lines. Holding it in both hands as shown helps to keep it square to the face of the board. When you get close, take a piece of scrap and see if you can fit it in the notch. If you can get it in with the pressure of your hand, you're ready to move on to the next joint.

If the scrap won't fit with hand pressure, take a close look at the joint and layout lines. Take a few more strokes with the rasp and try again. By checking the fit of each notch as you cut it, you will increase the chances of the entire project fitting together, and you will get instant feedback on your sawing technique.

When you assemble the entire piece, keep the joints lined up to each other as you push them in to place. Avoid the temptation to force them together. If you hit a point where the parts are stuck and won't go any further, examine the joints to make sure they are lined up, and look for any tight spots that are keeping them from going together.

When you're satisfied that you have a good fit, pull the joints apart about halfway, spread some glue carefully on the inside surfaces of the joints, then put the joint back together.

Using both hands helps to keep the rasp in a vertical position. Remove material evenly with long strokes of the rasp until you are down to the layout lines. Working to the lines will help you to keep the edges of the notches straight.

Test fit each joint as you go by fitting a piece of scrap wood. Take note of where the joints are too loose or too tight and correct your technique when you cut the next joint. Don't worry if the first joints have some gaps. The project will still come together if you're not perfect. The idea is to practice and get better with each attempt.

# Materials & Hardware

## MATERIAL SELECTION

Selecting the lumber for your project is almost as important as choosing the project. Trips to the home improvement store can be overwhelming when you are looking for material the first time. What lumber do you choose?

Resist the temptation to go directly to the vinyl-coated particleboard that some use for bookshelves. That is not what you need. Instead, look up and find the aisle marked "Lumber" — the material that you will need for your project is in that section of the store.

As you approach the lumber you'll notice that the aroma changes to a pungent, wood-like smell. This is where you'll start to notice the many choices available for your project.

And boy do you have choices! In the store that I visited I found that the first area I came to was the sheet-goods section. Sheet goods are plywood, both veneered and construction-grade selections, as well as Medium-density Fiberboard (MDF) and oriented strand board.

Let's look at dimensional lumber — material that is S4S (surfaced four sides). This lumber has had all four sides smoothed and is cut to a specific measurement.

## DIMENSIONAL LUMBER

Dimensional lumber is an enormous area that we need to continue to refine. All lumber has a grading designation. For our purposes, we're most interested in both #2 and prime grades, which is generally what you'll find at the home-center stores. The #2 grade denotes that these boards have knots that are large in size and possibly loose; the prime grade, on the other hand, is lumber relatively free of knots.

This clearly shows the difference between the #2 pine and the prime of the same species.

## How Dimensional Lumber Measures Up

| NOMINAL | ACTUAL | NOMINAL | ACTUAL |
|---------|--------|---------|--------|
| 1×2 | $3/4" \times 1^1/2"$ | 2×2 | $1^1/2" \times 1^1/2"$ |
| 1×3 | $3/4" \times 2^1/2"$ | 2×3 | $1^1/2" \times 2^1/2"$ |
| 1×4 | $3/4" \times 3^1/2"$ | 2×4 | $1^1/2" \times 3^1/2"$ |
| 1×6 | $3/4" \times 5^1/2"$ | 2×6 | $1^1/2" \times 5^1/2"$ |
| 1×8 | $3/4" \times 7^1/4"$ | 2×8 | $1^1/2" \times 7^1/4"$ |
| 1×10 | $3/4" \times 9^1/4"$ | 2×10 | $1^1/2" \times 9^1/4"$ |
| 1×12 | $3/4" \times 11^1/4"$ | 2×12 | $1^1/2" \times 11^1/4"$ |

Within dimensional lumber you'll find material such as 2×4, 2×6 and 2×8, etc. Lumber that is 2× is actually 1½" in thickness and the second measurement will be slightly less than the number shown, too. How much less? For numbers 6 and under, the actual size of the piece is a ½" less in width, so a 2×4 is actually 1½" × 3½". For the numbers above 6, such as 8, 10 and 12, the actual width will be ¾" less. It seems confusing but it is a standard within the industry.

Different species that fall into this category are treated lumber, SPF (spruce, pine or fir), hemlock and yellow pine. Depending on your area you might have one or all of these selections. Do you want to use this material for your projects? Sometimes you might.

Treated lumber is meant to be used outside. This is most often seen as deck material. If I were building a table for my deck I would consider using this material, however, I would have some reservations. Lumber intended for this use is treated with a type of chemical that helps preserve the wood when it is exposed to the elements. It is not for interior use. Take proper precautions when working with this stock.

The balance of the selections can be used in furniture, but there is something to consider. This lumber can have a higher level of moisture content (around 19 percent). Moisture is not a friend of

Looking down the edge of any board will help to uncover any defects in the lumber such as twisting, warping or crowning.

The use of the straightedge portion of the combination square will help to identify any cupping in the board. Return cupped boards to the stack and select others!

woodworking. Once a finished project is brought into the house moisture will dry or evaporate, which causes shrinkage across the width of the board (the length changes only minutely). That could result in your project having splits and cracks.

If you plan to use this wood in your project, OK. Just let it dry or acclimate to the surroundings before beginning. If you have a moisture meter to check the moisture content, it shouldn't be above 10-12 percent, depending on where you live. No moisture meter? You can wing it by choosing lightweight boards (water makes them heavy) or buying your wood and letting it acclimate in your house for a month.

## PRIME(ARY) LUMBER FOR FURNITURE

Lumber used most often for furniture is 1× material (1×4 or 1×6). Here is the good news, the variations between the stated measurement and the actual sizes is the same here as it is on 2× material, except that the 1× is actually ¾" in thickness. The width variances are identical to the 2× lumber.

Each home store might have different species of this type of lumber for sale. Mostly, you will find pine, poplar and red oak. In my area they also have aspen but in other locales across the United States, they have maple in place of the oak (check your store for species availability).

The biggest differences between this lumber and the thicker stock previously discussed are the moisture content and the grading. The moisture content in this type of lumber should be in the six- to eight-percent range.

Grading this lumber is the same as the thicker stock. In this discussion the lumber from the home stores should be considered prime, however, you will generally find #2 pine in these stores and the knots will be obvious (sometimes you can find #2 pine with clear areas; that allows you to make small cuttings without the problem of knots. And that will save you money).

Hardwoods will be better in quality. Poplar, red oak and other available species should be free of large or loose knots throughout the board. Avoid shrink-wrapped lumber.

The section of a tree from which a piece of lumber is cut can also help determine how the wood may "move" once you get it home. By looking at the end grain of a board, you can make an educated guess as to how stable the board will remain.

### Picking & Choosing

Now that we know the type of lumber for which we are searching, we have to determine how we should select from the individual boards.

To begin with, you are paying good money for this lumber, so if you have to pick through every piece in order to get the best board, so be it! Plan to look at a few pieces.

The first test is to look at the grain and overall appearance of the board. If the coloration is off as you view the piece, move on to the next one. If the grain doesn't look appealing, move on.

Next, I suggest that you carry your combination square into the store if possible. This will help you check the board for cupping (bending from side to side) by placing the straightedge against the face of the lumber. Areas where the straight edge of the square is not in contact with the board will allow you to see light between the edge of the square and the flat face of the lumber.

Or, at the ends of the board you can sight along the end grain of the piece to make this determination. If there is a cup in the board put it back and check the next piece. Continue until you get the boards that you want.

Finally, I look at the board from end to end, viewing the piece down the edge, this will expose any warping, twisting or crowning in the board.

Warping is a defect in lumber where the boards will move in one or more directions over the length of the piece, while twisting will cause the piece to not lay flat. A good way to check for this defect is to lay the piece onto the floor at the store. If one of the corners is off of the floor, press down on that corner. If the diagonal, opposing corner raises you have a board with twist. Put this piece back into the rack and move to the next. You can imagine how this type of problem will affect your woodworking.

To discover crowning you also need to look at the edge of the stock from the end. (Crowning is when the edge of the board is bowed, so it isn't straight.) A simple test for this is to place the piece on the floor while holding it on the edge. If the stock rocks from end to end (crown is down) or if it is touching only on both ends and there is space between the piece and the floor in the middle of the board (crown is up), you have a crowned or bowed piece. This affects your work by not allowing you to place the pieces side by side to achieve a larger surface, i.e. gluing a panel together. Choose another board.

Once all the selections are made and the tests are complete, you have chosen a quality piece of lumber for your project. This may sound like a good deal of trouble but I suggest that you make these steadfast rules for selecting lumber. If you bypass them you may find even more trouble while building your projects.

In addition to dimensional lumber, you may also find assembled or glued together panels at your home center. Should you choose these for your furniture? Maybe. The problem with most assembled panels is that they are usually comprised of a number of narrow pieces. This does not present the best look when staining a piece of furniture. But, if paint is your finish of choice for your project — take a look at them. Use the same decision making process and apply the same tests for these panels as you do in selecting dimensional lumber for the projects.

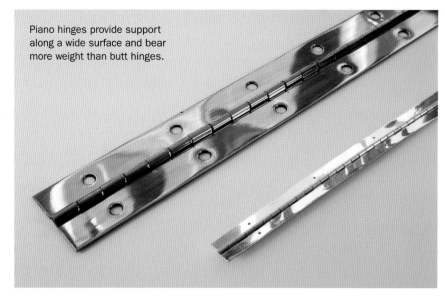
Piano hinges provide support along a wide surface and bear more weight than butt hinges.

## HARDWARE: PIANO HINGE

There are two important things to remember when setting hinges. The first is that you need to place the hinge exactly where you want it for it to function correctly. The second is you want the screws that keep it in place to stay there forever, or at least as long as possible. The piano hinge on the dimensional lumber bench is relatively easy to put in place, and the number of screws will give you plenty of practice, as well as some insurance if you don't get the first few in properly.

The simplest and one of the most accurate ways to locate the hinge is to arrange the top and the chest in a way that will let you put the hinge in place without trying to overcome the law of gravity.

Put the lid upside down on your Workmate, then place your assembled bench over it. You'll need to let the sides of the bench hang over the top of the Workmate. Once you have both parts in place, line them up where they will be after you've installed the hinge.

Piano hinges are usually sold in 1' increments. You can either use a 24" hinge and leave equal spaces on each end, or you can use a 36" hinge and cut it to fit. To cut the hinge, use a Sharpie marker to mark your cut line, and cut the hinge with a hacksaw or with a metal-cutting blade in your jigsaw. With either method, you need to clamp the work securely to your bench to make the cut. You don't need to fill the space exactly, you should cut it a bit smaller than the opening.

Put the hinge in place with the leaves of the hinge flat on the two pieces of wood. Hold the hinge in place with one hand, and use an awl to make a mark in the center of two or three holes. The hinge is held in place with small screws, so you don't need a big hole to get them started. You also don't have the space to get your power drill in position to make a vertical hole, centered in the opening of the hinge. If your holes for the screws are off-center, the beveled underside of the screwhead will move it as you tighten the screw.

When you attach the hinge, put two or three screws in one leaf, make sure the hinge is still in position, then put a few screws in the other leaf. This lets you

The edge of the lid is in from the edge of the bench. Set the combination square to the right distance, hold it against the back edge of the side, and push the back edge of the top in place.

When installing a piano hinge, first install just a few of the screws. Then test the hinge.

Check the action of the hinge before you finish your work. If you need to make adjustments, you won't risk damaging a painted surface.

check to see if the hinge will work the way you want it to before putting in all the screws. If you've made a mistake, you can remove the screws, adjust the position, then reattach the hinge with screws in different holes. You'll find it's difficult to move a hole.

Once you're happy with the way the hinge operates, make the rest of the pilot holes and drive the remaining screws. You'll face the same problem with driving the screws you had in making the holes — there isn't room to use your cordless drill without the chuck rubbing on the wood.

Even though there are a lot of screws to drive, if you have a good pilot hole, they will be easy to drive by hand, especially if you used softwood. If you used a hardwood, it will be more difficult. You might want to lubricate the screws with paraffin or another wax to make the screws easier to drive. Think of this as skill-building practice. Make a few holes, drive a few screws, and compare the results with the last round.

You'll notice that I put the hinge on before I painted the bench. Once I had the hinge working properly, I took it back off to paint the bench, then put it back on after the paint had dried. This may seem

like a waste of time, but there is a good reason to do it this way.

If I had to make any adjustments that involved removing some wood, or if the top rubbed against the side as the hinge opens and closes, I wouldn't be ruining

the paint job. Repainting to cover some damage would be a much greater waste of time, and there is enough risk of that happening to make it worthwhile to take extra time to reinstall the hinge.

# Skansen Bench

Jah, it's solid. Thanks to massive tenons and a thick seat, this bench will withstand both children and time.

BY CHRISTOPHER SCHWARZ

I've always liked things that are Swedish, impossibly overbuilt and yet somehow graceful. For example, my beloved Volvo 240DL, a certain foreign exchange student in high school and this bench from the Skansen living history museum in Stockholm.

This bench is from the Älvros Farmstead, a group of buildings from the 16th and 17th centuries that were moved to Skansen. I first spied this bench in the book "Making Swedish Country Furniture & Household Things" (Hartley & Marks). For this version I proportioned the parts so it could be built with dimensional pine — one 12'-long 2×12 and one 8'-long 2×8. Total cost: About $22.

At first glance, this might not look like an "I Can Do That" project, with its laminated top and wedged through-tenons in the seat. But I assure you, it can be built with basic tools.

### How the Joinery Works

The heart of the bench is the four through-tenons that connect the legs to the seat. The tenons are cut while you're shaping the legs. They don't have face shoulders, so they're cut easily with a jigsaw. The mortises are also easy. You just drill a hole for each mortise, then shape the mortise with a jigsaw.

Of course, it's the details that determine how easy all this will be, especially with the mortises. Let's begin there.

The seat is made of two 2×12s glued face to face. But it's best to cut the mortises before gluing up the seat plank — you'll get less deflection of your jigsaw's blade. Lay out the locations of the mortises on the two boards and drill a ¾"-diameter hole at each mortise location.

With your jigsaw, square up the mortises. After experimenting with several blades, I got the best results from a Bosch T744D blade, a 7"-long blade designed for cutting wood rapidly. It is a shade thicker than typical blades and has deep gullets. This helped prevent the blade from deflecting.

The only downside to this blade is that it will tear up the surface of your wood. Set the jigsaw's orbital action to "0" and

No mortiser required. With large through-tenons you can simply drill a starter hole for your jigsaw's blade then square things up. Don't rush the cut or the blade will deflect.

take your time. When the jigsawing is complete, straighten up the mortises with a coarse rasp.

Don't glue up the seat yet — we'll do that after everything is dry-fit.

### Get Those Legs in Shape

The legs are shaped with a jigsaw and a rasp. Lay out the pattern on one leg (you can download a SketchUp drawing of this bench from our web site). Then jigsaw

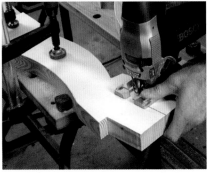

All in the jigsaw. The shape of and joinery on the legs is made entirely with a jigsaw. Follow close to the line and you won't have much cleanup work to do here.

## Parts List

| NO. | PART | STOCK | THICKNESS X WIDTH X LENGTH | |
|-----|------|-------|--------------------------|--------------------|
| | | | INCHES | MILLIMETERS |
| 2 | Top slabs | Pine | $1^1/_2 \times 11 \times 72$ | $38 \times 279 \times 1829$ |
| 4 | Legs | Pine | $1^1/_2 \times 7^1/_4 \times 20$ | $38 \times 184 \times 508$ |

Cheap clamps. With the seat planks glued together, drive 2" screws through the underside to clamp things up. Place a screw wherever you see a gap between the planks.

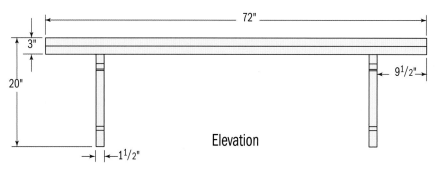

**Elevation**

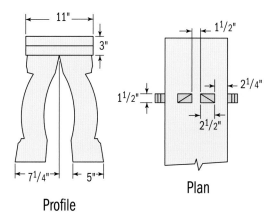

**Profile**

**Plan**

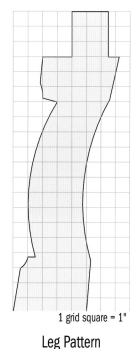

1 grid square = 1"

**Leg Pattern**

the shape and clean up your cuts with a rasp and sandpaper. Use that leg as a template for the other three.

After you have the four legs in shape, fit them to the mortises. Use a block plane to thin the faces of the tenons; use a rasp to thin the edges. Go for a tight fit, though the wedges will help fill little gaps. Fit the bottom seat plank over the tenons. Then fit the top seat plank on that.

Now you can glue up the seat plank using the tenons to keep the mortises aligned. Remove the top seat plank and coat the bottom seat plank with glue (avoid the tenons). Drive the top seat plank onto the tenons.

To clamp the two planks together, I recommend using 2"-long screws that you drive through the underside of the bench through clearance holes. Screws cinch

the planks together without clamps. After the two planks are screwed together, knock the legs out of their tenons. After the glue dries, you can remove the screws if you're a cheapskate.

### A Self-made Wedgie

Wedging the tenons is simple. You're going to wedge them diagonally, from corner to corner. This will expand each tenon in four directions. The first step is to cut a kerf in the tenons to receive the wedges. I used a handsaw. Any saw will

do. Saw from the top to the shoulder of the tenon.

For the wedges, you can use builder's shims or make your own. I made mine from leftover oak. I split out the wedges using a pocketknife and a hammer. The wedges are $^3/_{16}$" thick at the top, $2^3/_4$" wide, $2^1/_2$" long and taper to a point.

To assemble the bench, brush glue on the mortises and tenons and drive the legs home. Paint glue on the wedges and drive them into the kerfs in the tenons. Wait for the glue to dry, then trim the wedges.

To lighten the look of the top I chamfered all the edges with a block plane. The finish is a few coats of an oil/varnish blend. You could use paint — red is a traditional Swedish color.

When the bench was complete, I jumped up and down on it — it's solid. Heck, I think I could have parked my 240DL on it.

# Hall Bench

**BY ROBERT W. LANG**

Don't make the mistake of thinking you need a lot of tools and machinery to get started in woodworking. While it's certainly nice to have a jointer, planer, table saw and router, the only power tool I used to make this bench was a jigsaw.

We designed this project around available sizes of common lumber and put it together with a simple but strong method: nails and cleats. To add visual interest to this simple design, the ends are thicker than the front, back and top, and all of the joints are offset. This creates lines and shadows at the intersections. It also takes some of the pressure off your precision — if your measurements are slightly off no one will ever know.

Because I planned to paint this piece, I decided to use inexpensive material — #2 pine. I used 2 × 12 dimensional lumber for the ends, and 1 × 12 and 1 × 10 for the rest. If you want to use a clear finish to show the wood grain, you might want to upgrade to clear hardwood. Spend some time picking your material. You want the straightest pieces you can find with the fewest knots and other defects.

The shortest piece of 1 × 12 I could buy was 4' long. This length allowed me to cut between knots to get a clear piece for the top. I used the extra to make the $3/4$" × $3/4$" cleats that hold the front and back panels to the ends. I cut the top $1/8$" shorter than the front, back and bottom to provide clearance when it opens and closes.

The two end pieces and the front

and back panels were left at their full width; only the top and bottom need to be ripped to finished size. After cutting the ends to length, I marked out the feet at the bottom, made the cuts with the jigsaw, and cleaned up the saw marks with a rasp. I then used my combination square to mark the position of the front and back panels. I placed the panels against my marks as shown in the photo at right to determine the exact location of the cleats.

When I was sure that my layout marks for the top edges of the front and back panels were 1" below the top of the ends, I cut the cleats to length, allowing space for the bottom. I then put glue on the cleats and nailed them to the end panels. While the glue was drying, I glued and nailed the bottom to the lower edge of the front panel. I then put this assembly on one end panel, gluing and nailing it

I used the front and back panels as gauges to locate the cleats that hold them to the ends. This avoids measuring errors.

# Parts List

| NO. | PART | STOCK | THICKNESS X WIDTH X LENGTH | | COMMENTS |
| --- | --- | --- | --- | --- | --- |
| | | | INCHES | MILLIMETERS | |
| 2 | ends | pine | $1^{1}/_2 \times 11^{1}/_4 \times 16$ | $38 \times 286 \times 406$ | $2 \times 10$ |
| 2 | front & back | pine | $^{3}/_4 \times 9^{1}/_4 \times 27$ | $19 \times 235 \times 686$ | $1 \times 10$ |
| 1 | top | pine | $^{3}/_4 \times 10^{3}/_4 \times 26^{7}/_8$ | $19 \times 273 \times 683$ | cut from $1 \times 12$ |
| 1 | bottom | pine | $^{3}/_4 \times 7^{3}/_4 \times 27$ | $19 \times 197 \times 686$ | cut from $1 \times 10$ |
| 4 | cleats | pine | $^{3}/_4 \times ^{3}/_4 \times 8^{1}/_2$ | $19 \times 19 \times 216$ | |

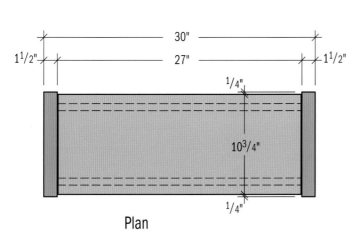

Plan

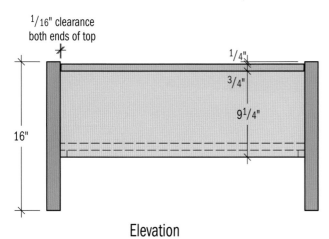

Elevation

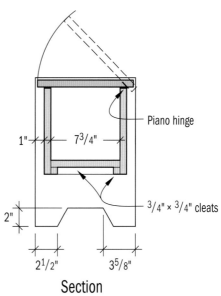

Piano hinge

$^{3}/_4" \times ^{3}/_4"$ cleats

Section

After marking the location of the front and back, and the height of the top, I glued and nailed the cleats in place on the sides.

Planning a logical sequence for assembling the parts is important. I attached the front and bottom together and glued and nailed them to the ends as a single unit.

to the cleat using 3d finish nails. Before putting the back panel on, I attached the other end.

I then placed the box face down on my bench and attached the back panel, using a couple of clamps to keep the assembly square and lined up with my pencil marks as shown in the photo (lower right). After setting the heads of the nails below the surface with a nail set, I was ready to attach the top to the back panel with a piano hinge.

With the top overhanging the back panel, I had room to surface mount the piano hinge. I used an awl to make pilot holes for the screws, and attached the hinge with just a few screws at first to be sure it opened and closed properly. Then I removed the screws and hinge and got the bench ready for paint.

I eased all the edges with my block plane and a rasp, then sanded with #100-grit paper to remove milling marks. If you use a random-orbit sander, stay away from the inside corners where the front and back panels meet the ends. If you get too close, the edge of the sanding disc can dig in. It's better if you stay an inch or two away with the sander, and work into the corners by hand.

I primed the bottom of the hinged

top and the bottom edge of the ends first. When this had dried, I put a screw into the end of each foot to hold the ends off the surface while I painted the rest of the bench.

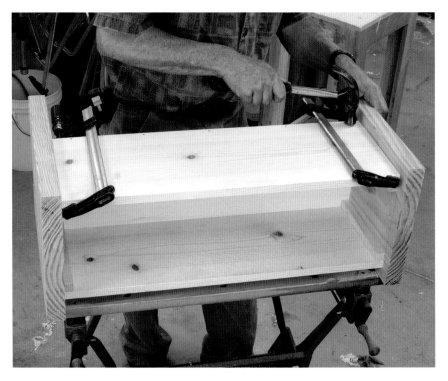

To get the back piece positioned exactly where I wanted it, I used a couple clamps to pull the parts into alignment.

# Piano Hinges

There are two important things to remember when setting hinges. The first is that you need to place the hinge exactly where you want it for it to function correctly. The second is that you want the screws that keep it in place to stay there forever, or at least as long as possible. The piano hinge on the hall bench is relatively easy to put in place, and the number of screws will give you plenty of practice, as well as some insurance if you don't get the first few in properly.

The simplest and one of the most accurate ways to locate the hinge is to arrange the top and the chest in a way that will let you put the hinge in place without trying to overcome the law of gravity.

Put the lid upside down

on your Workmate, then place your assembled bench over it. You'll need to let the sides of the bench hang over the top of the Workmate. Once you have both parts in place, line them up where they will be after you've installed the hinge, as shown above.

Piano hinges are usually

sold in 1' increments. You can either use a 24" hinge and leave equal spaces on each end, or you can use a 36" hinge and cut it to fit. To cut the hinge, use a Sharpie marker to mark a cut line, and cut the hinge with a hacksaw or with a metal-cutting blade in the jigsaw. With either method, you need to clamp the hinge securely to your bench to make the cut. You don't need to fill the space exactly, you should cut the hinge a bit smaller than the opening.

Put the hinge in place with the leaves of the hinge

flat on the two pieces of wood. Hold the hinge in place with one hand, and use an awl (as shown above) to make a mark in the center of two or three holes.

The hinge is held in place with small screws, so you don't need a big hole to get them started. You also don't have the space to get your power drill in position to make a vertical hole, centered in the opening of the hinge.

If the holes for the screws are off-center, the beveled underside of the screwhead will move the screw as you tighten it.

When you attach the hinge, put two or three screws in one leaf, make sure the hinge is still in position, then put a few screws in the other leaf. This lets you check to see if the hinge will work the way you want it to before putting in all of the screws. If you've made a mistake, you can remove the screws, adjust the position, then reattach the hinge with screws in different holes. You'll find it's difficult to move a hole.

Once you're happy with the way the hinge operates, make the rest of the pilot holes and drive the remaining screws. You'll face the same problem with driving the screws you had in making the holes — there isn't room to use your cordless drill without the chuck rubbing on the wood.

Even though there are

a lot of screws to drive, if you have a good pilot hole, they will be easy to drive by hand, especially if you used softwood. If you used a hardwood, it will be more difficult. You might want to lubricate the screws with paraffin or another wax to make the screws easier to drive. Think of this as skill-building practice. Make a few holes, drive a few screws, and compare the results with the last round.

You'll notice (above) that

I put the hinge on before I painted the bench. Once I had the hinge working properly, I took it back off to paint the bench, then put it back on after the paint had dried. This may seem like a waste of time, but there's a good reason to do it this way.

If I had to make any adjustments that involved removing some wood, or if the top rubbed against the sides as the hinge opened and closed, I wouldn't be ruining the paint job. Repainting to cover damage would be a much greater waste of time.

# Simple Side Chair

**BY GLEN HUEY**

After years of building furniture, mostly case pieces, I've come to understand that chair building is different. Where most casework involves working with panels and straight lumber, most chair building turns to bending stock or forming parts. When you find a chair that fits into the casework criteria, you should take every opportunity to build that piece.

This chair fits into that framework. I envision this chair sitting anywhere from around the dining room table, to welcoming guests to your home in the foyer, to being perched beside the dressing table in your bedroom. It is sturdy, comfortable and the construction is beginner friendly to say the least.

The focus of most chairs is the back and the seat. This chair has gathered the eye appeal with the shapely hour-glass back splat and the colorful seat that is woven with Shaker tape. One chair just might not be enough.

Set the miter saw to a five degree angle. Place the leg on the saw so that the cut begins about ½" down from the top of the leg. Use a stop block to hold the leg in place as you rotate the leg 90° to make the four cuts for each leg.

## For Starters — Get a Leg Up

Building chairs begins with the legs. Since you've already got the width and thickness of the pieces (1½" square) by buying stock material from the home center store, the next step is to cut them to length. You'll need two front legs that are 18" in length and two back legs that begin at 36" long.

To add interest to the chair, cut the top of each leg to a pyramid design. Set the miter saw to a 5° angle. Place the leg on the saw so that the cut begins about ½" down from the top of the leg. Four cuts are needed to create the pyramid — one at each face. Making the cuts is easy enough, but what might present a problem is aligning each cut to the previous cut.

This is best accomplished by setting a stop block to position each leg and each cut against. Place the leg against the block and make the first cut. Next, rotate the leg one turn and make the second cut. Repeat this pattern for each face and each leg. There is one set-up for the front legs and another for the back legs. The finished tops appear as small pyramids when viewed.

If you can't easily add a stop to your miter saw, you can also mark a line all the way around the top of each leg, ½" down from the top. This will be your cut line.

The rear leg (left) needs only a slight (5°) angle cut on the bottom to add about fifty percent more comfort to your chair.

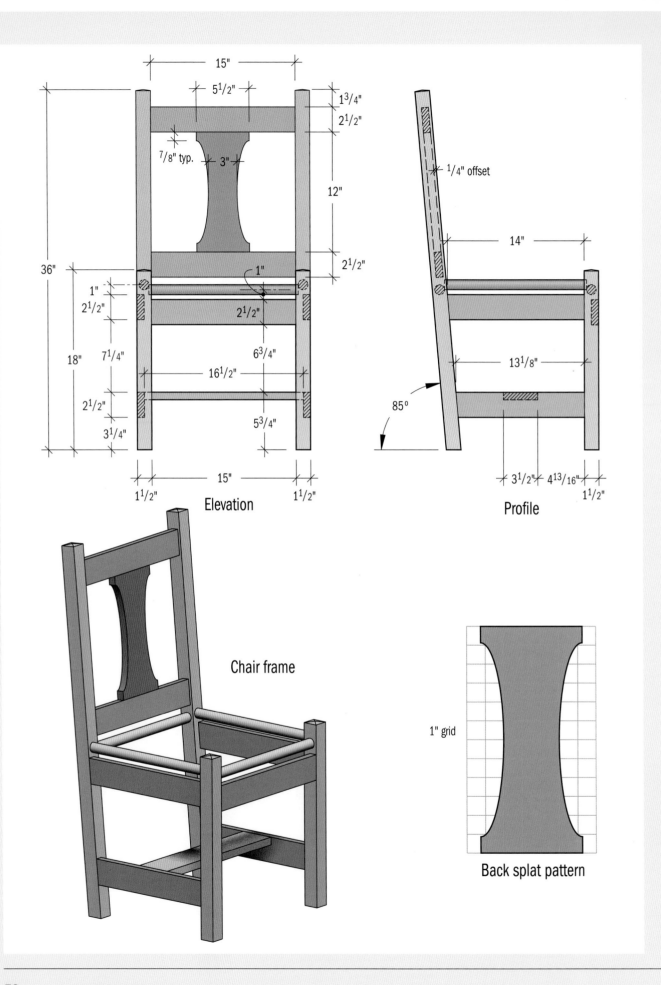

15"

5¹/²"

1³/₄"

2¹/²"

⁷/₈" typ.

3"

12"

¹/₄" offset

14"

36"

1"

1"

2¹/²"

2¹/²"

18"

7¹/₄"

6³/₄"

2¹/²"

16¹/₂"

13¹/₈"

2¹/²"

5³/₄"

3¹/₄"

15"

1¹/₂"

1¹/₂"

Elevation

85⁰

3¹/₂"   4¹³/₁₆"

1¹/₂"

Profile

Chair frame

1" grid

Back splat pattern

The dowel holes are offset from one another by 1/2". Make sure you've marked the front and left, or right face of each to avoid drilling the wrong hole in the wrong face. The depth of the hole isn't critical, but I tend to drill till the top of the cutting faces reaches the top of the hole. This is usually about 1/2" deep with most Forstner bits. To keep the hole perpendicular to the leg face, you can stand a try square next to your drill to give you a true 90° angle to follow.

Laying the pieces for the side assemblies on your bench and marking everything will make sure you cut the pockets in the right places. Pencil lines are much easier to sand off than holes in the wrong location.

A chair is not comfortable if the back is straight. I wouldn't want to spend much time sitting with that posture, it's unnatural. So, we need to add angle to the chair. Most times to add angle to the chair you need to bend the back legs. We aren't going to do that.

So how do you create a comfortable angle using straight stock? Easy, tilt the leg. At the miter saw, again with the angle set to 5°, cut the bottom of each back leg. Take as little material as possible in making this cut. You are not looking to shorten the legs, just add the angle.

## Hold That Seat, Please

In any chair the longevity of the chair depends on keeping the parts together. A lot of times you can find chairs where the seat is actually holding the parts in place. That is what this chair does.

The seat is wrapped around dowels that are positioned just above the stretchers and slightly offset from one another. Select the front face of the chair legs and mark the side and front edges. Locate the position of the holes and drill them into the front legs only.

To find the dowel positions, start from the pyramid cut and move down

1 1/2" for the center of the side dowel location. Slide down another 1/2" for the location of the front dowel hole.

Make these holes with a drill and 1" Forstner bit, squaring the bit to the stock from both directions. Cut the hole about 1/2" deep — it's not critical because you'll take an exact measurement after the chair is assembled.

Assembling the chair starts with the side profile. Lay the legs of one side of the chair on your bench. Orient the pieces so the angle cut on the back leg is parallel to the edge of the bench. Next, cut the rails for the sides. One end of each piece is cut square while the opposite end is cut at that five degree angle. Both cuts are made at the miter saw.

Fit the rails into position with the legs as shown (next page top left photo). Notice that the front leg (in the photo above) is positioned with the front dowel hole facing upward. The top side rails will fit 1/2" below the bottom edge of the side dowel hole or 1" from its center point.

Position the lower side rail starting 3 1/4" up from the bottom of the leg. Mark an X at each end of the rails to indicate the area for the pocket screws.

## Parts List

| NO. | PART | STOCK | THICKNESS X WIDTH X LENGTH | |
|-----|------|-------|----------|-------------|
| | | | INCHES | MILLIMETERS |
| 2 | back legs | oak | 1 1/2 × 1 1/2 × 36 | 38 × 38 × 914 |
| 2 | front legs | oak | 1 1/2 × 1 1/2 × 18 | 38 × 38 × 457 |
| 1 | front rail | oak | 3/4 × 2 1/2 × 15 | 19 × 64 × 381 |
| 2 | back splat rails | oak | 3/4 × 2 1/2 × 15 | 19 × 64 × 381 |
| 1 | back splat | oak | 3/4 × 5 1/2 × 12 | 19 × 140 × 305 |
| 2 | top side rails | oak | 3/4 × 2 1/2 × 14 | 19 × 64 × 356 |
| 2 | lower side rails | oak | 3/4 × 2 1/2 × 13 1/8 | 19 × 64 × 333 |
| 1 | bottom stretcher | oak | 3/4 × 3 1/2 × 16 1/2 | 19 × 89 × 419 |
| 4 | seat dowels | oak | 1 × 15 dia. | 25 × 381 dia. |

The "clamp-included" pocket hole jig (right) makes cutting twin holes on the ends of all the stretchers much easier. Once the holes are cut, lay the pieces on your bench, square things up and add the screws.

## Quick, Strong Connections

Use the pocket-screw jig to cut the holes in the side rails. Make sure that the ends of the rails fit tightly to the base of the jig; the angled cut will tip the rails to one side.

Place the holes, two per end, about ¾" in from the edges of the rails. Using a framing square will ensure that

the chair sides are square to the floor. Position the pieces to the legs as before and make sure that the bottom ends of the legs fit to the square and all faces are tight to the bench. Drive the screws to assemble the sides. Repeat the same steps for the second side, but this time the chair back or angle must face the opposite direction.

Because the angle is in the side assembly, installing the front rail is a snap. The ends are square-cut straight from the miter saw and the pocket-screw holes are drilled just as they were for the side rails.

Set the side assembly onto the front leg front face down to the bench. Position the front rail ½" below the bottom edge of the dowel hole. Hold the face of the rail flat to the bench and drive the screws to attach the front rail. Repeat the steps to attach the second side assembly to the front rail.

## Adding a Bit of Design

To add a few shadow lines to the chair back you'll need to set the rails by spacing them off of the front edge of the legs. To make it easy slide a scrap piece of ¼" plywood, or something else of a consistent thickness, under the rails before adding the screws.

You'll find that the chair is starting to gain in weight, so holding the pieces as you assemble the back is a bit of a task. To make it easier hang the seat portion off the edge of the bench and clamp the top portion of the back leg to your bench. Locate the rails according to the plan, add the spacers under the screw area to create the shadow and drive the screws to attach the back rails.

With the side assembly sitting on it's face on the bench, the front rail is screwed into position ½" below the dowel hole.

Once the chair is assembled you need to take an accurate measurement of the stretcher and fit it to the chair. It doesn't fit between two legs so the size will be different.

If you install the stretcher it will get in the way of other operations, but clamping it in place will add strength for the next step.

The side dowel is installed in a hole in the back leg that is drilled at an angle.

That hole is parallel to the side rail and is set ½" above that rail and centered in the leg.

Chuck the 1" Forstner bit into the drill and set the center point of the bit in position. Drill the hole to a depth of ½" while remaining parallel to the rail and square to the leg.

Measure the length of the dowels by placing rulers into the holes as shown in the photo (bottom right). This measure-

ment is exact for that particular dowel location and can vary depending on the depth you drilled the hole. So, each length needs to be measured. Cut the dowels at the miter saw to guarantee a square end.

There is no possible way to install the dowels in the assembled chair without releasing the hold of the screws. Work one dowel at a time and when the piece is placed in the holes reattach the screws

With the front faces of the rear legs clamped to the bench and the lower part of the chair hanging over the edge, it's time to add the back rails. To add some visual interest to the back, I used some scrap wood to hold the rails back from the front edge of the legs as I added the screws.

The dowel holes in the rear legs need to be drilled parallel to the side stretcher, not perpendicular to the rear leg, otherwise they just won't fit.

By using two steel rules in tandem I'm able to measure the actual required length of the dowels by measuring to the bottom of the dowel holes.

After marking the required length of the splat at the chair itself (above), use a home-made trammel to mark the curves to shape the splat (right).

before moving to the next dowel. Also remember to install the stretcher at this time.

## Another Shot at Design

The chair back splat is another area where you can influence the overall look of the chair. You can design something fantastic or simply leave it straight. I chose a simple arced cut.

To develop any design, first you need to find the length of the splat. This could be determined while installing the back splat rails or just find the measurement at this time.

Don't rely on rulers or measuring tapes for this. You want a snug fit. Lay the chair on its back then square cut one end of the splat stock. Raise the back off of the bench and slide the splat into position, keeping the square end tight to the lower rail. With a sharp pencil trace the intersection of the splat with the top rail. This is the exact measurement of the splat. Make the next cut at the miter saw.

To draw the arcs you'll need a compass that will expand to a radius of 10¾". That's not your average compass! So, you'll have to make your own. Use a piece of scrap or an older (read as not your every day ruler) ruler. Drill a small hole at one end of the piece just big enough for a small finish nail. In fact, I often use the exact nail for this step.

Next, move up the piece to the 10¾" line and drill a second hole for the pencil lead to go through. That's your compass a.k.a. a trammel.

Place a scrap of equal thickness perpendicular to the splat material as shown in the photo (above). Measure down 9½" from the intersection of the two pieces and place the nail. This is the pivot point of the compass. As you draw the line you will see that the arc starts about an inch from the end of the splat on all sides. Repeat the steps for the second side of the splat and you are ready to cut those with the jigsaw. Clean up any cut marks with a rasp and sandpaper.

Use the pocket screw as the connection of the splat to the rails. Position clamps over the two pieces, on the face of

With the splat held flush to the back face of the legs, the pocket screws are driven home, finishing the assembly of your stylin' chair.

Finish the chair before weaving the seat. See the illustration below for weaving details.

each piece to keep them aligned as you drive the screws.

Fill any screw holes with the available plugs. This includes all holes in the back and the holes in the side lower rails. Other holes will not be seen once the seat is finished.

Add glue to the hole and tap the plug into place. Allow the fill to dry before sanding smooth.

**Adding the Color**
The chair is finished with the same formula as the coffee table in this book. Rag on a coat of Olympic Special Walnut stain that is allowed to soak for five minutes before wiping away any excess.

That is followed by a coat of Watco Danish Oil in the walnut tint. This is also allowed to soak for a short time before wiping the chair clean. Once the oil had dried I elected to spray on a coat of shellac. Shellac can be purchased in a spray can and this will allow better control with all the pieces of the chair.

After applying a single coat of shellac which has dried, knock down any nubs with #400-grit sandpaper and add a coat of paste wax and its on to the seat.

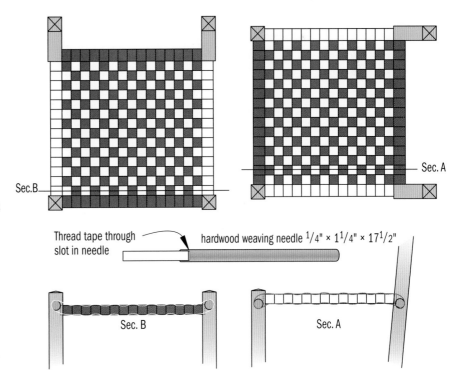

Staple the end of the warp strands to the underside of the front rail to start. Weave these strands front to back between the front and back dowels. Insert a 1"-thick piece of foam between the warp strands. Attach the weave strand to the hardwood needle. Thread the weave strand between the side dowels and between every other warp strand top and bottom. Staple the ends to the underside of the dowels.

# Patio Chair

**BY A.J. HAMLER**

I've always envied bakers, working around that fresh-baked aroma all day. This cedar patio chair — the best-smelling project you'll ever make — will have you feeling the same way.

Cedar is straight-grained, with minimal shrinkage and expansion, and doesn't cup or twist as much as other softwoods.

It works very easily, and it's the perfect wood for outdoor furniture as it naturally resists water, decay and insect damage.

Cedar comes in several species. Aromatic cedar, commonly used in hope chests and closet linings, smells great. But because the trees grow so slowly (a 20-year-old tree may be no more than 20' tall) it's on the expensive side for larger projects, plus it'll require a special order

from a lumber company. Spanish cedar is less expensive, but the dust can be an irritant for many. And it's still a special order.

But Western red cedar — I'll just call it cedar from this point forward — is the perfect compromise. It's inexpensive enough for furniture, most people don't find it an irritant and, best of all, you can find at home centers. And then there's

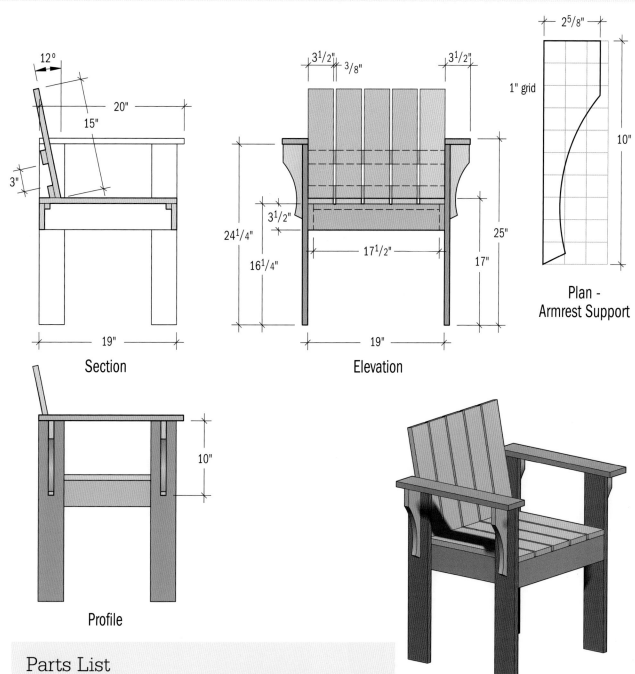

12°

20"

15"

3"

Section

19"

3 1/2"  3/8"

3 1/2"

24 1/4"

3 1/2"

16 1/4"

17 1/2"

25"

17"

19"

Elevation

2 5/8"

1" grid

10"

Plan -
Armrest Support

10"

Profile

## Parts List

| | | | THICKNESS X WIDTH X LENGTH | |
|---|---|---|---|---|
| NO. | PART | STOCK | INCHES | MILLIMETERS |
| 4 | legs | cedar | $3/4 \times 3^1/2 \times 24^1/4$ | 19 × 89 × 616 |
| 4 | armrest supports | cedar | $3/4 \times 2^5/8 \times 10$ | 19 × 67 × 254 |
| 2 | armrests | cedar | $3/4 \times 3^1/2 \times 20$ | 19 × 89 × 508 |
| 2 | seat box front/back | cedar | $3/4 \times 3^1/2 \times 19$ | 19 × 89 × 483 |
| 2 | seat box sides | cedar | $3/4 \times 3^1/2 \times 17^1/2$ | 19 × 89 × 445 |
| 5 | seat slats | cedar | $3/4 \times 3^1/2 \times 19$ | 19 × 89 × 483 |
| 2 | slat support cleats | cedar | $3/4 \times 3/4 \times 17^1/2$ | 19 × 19 × 445 |
| 5 | backrest slats | cedar | $3/4 \times 3^1/2 \times 15$ | 19 × 89 × 381 |
| 2 | backrest braces | cedar | $3/4 \times 2 \times 19$ | 19 × 51 × 483 |

that aroma. Believe me, you'll be thinking up excuses to make more cuts just to release another burst of that great smell into the shop.

Because this is an outdoor project, we'll use stainless steel screws wherever it may get wet. The stainless steel screws I bought are star drive. Star drive screws are fun to use, and the driver bit (included in the package with the screws) makes a very positive contact with the screw for sure driving; it'll even hold the screw without assistance. The pocket hole screws used for the seat box are protected underneath, as are the screws attaching the seat slats, so no need for stainless there. Speaking of waterproofing, if your finished chair will actually be out in the rain, consider using a waterproof glue such as Titebond III.

Almost all of the components for this chair measure ¾" × 3½", the actual dimensions of a nominal 1 × 4, so everything can be made from 1 × 4 cedar right out of the rack. That means most of the cuts are crosscuts and you won't need to do much ripping. Buy enough stock to be able to cut your components to avoid knots. (Alternatively, you can save money by purchasing 1 × 8 boards and ripping up your own 3½" stock. I've found that wider boards are generally more attractive and in better shape in the racks than narrower boards.)

Keep in mind that 1 × 4 dimensional stock can vary a bit — it may be slightly

The stainless steel screws used for this project are self-drilling, and feature a star-drive head.

more or less than exactly 3½" — so cut components accordingly. It's all right if the widths aren't quite the same, as long as you group like widths together. For example, if one board is slightly more than 3½" wide, cut all the legs from that.

Also, cedar sometimes varies in thickness; some I bought was as much as ⅞" thick. Again, this isn't a problem as long as you group like thicknesses together, and make minor alterations to project dimensions as needed. Another quirk of cedar boards is that one side is smooth while the other is almost always rough. No problem; just orient the boards with the rough side down or to the rear of the chair.

## Mission Meets Mountain

The design of this chair blends the classic look of Mission style with the construction details and outdoor hardiness of Adirondack furniture. I retained the overall shape and arm/leg details of a Morris chair, joined with the slat appearance of an Adirondack chair. Overall, I think the effect works nicely. Little attempt is made to hide the screws in Adirondack chairs, but most are hidden in this chair, making for a smooth, unblemished appearance.

The project consists of three main sections: sides, seat and backrest. It doesn't matter if you do the sides or the seat first, as long as you save the backrest for last

Since we're using standard 1 × 4 lumber, most of the cutting you'll do will be crosscutting, which can be quickly handled on the miter saw.

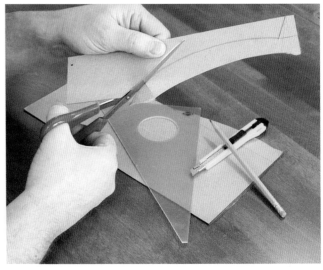

Transferring the pattern for the curved armrest supports to the workpieces is easier if you first cut a template out of stiff cardboard.

Cut out the armrest supports with a jigsaw. To keep the smooth sides facing forward on the finished chair, note how I've alternated the pattern to create *left* and *right* pieces.

Mark the tops of each leg as a guide to the exact center for attaching the armrest supports. Be sure to mark the legs *right* and *left* for proper orientation.

to take exact measurements from the assembled chair for a perfect fit.

Start by cutting the legs and armrests to length on your miter saw. Set these aside for now.

Trace the outline for the curved armrest supports onto a piece of cardboard, and use this to transfer the pattern onto a workpiece at least 41" long. Cut out the four supports with a jigsaw. Mark a center line on the top end of each leg and align the supports, then glue and clamp them in place. Don't forget to mark the sets for *left* and *right*. Drill a pair of

countersunk holes on the inside of each leg into the supports and attach securely with screws. I used a 2" screw at the top, and a 1¼" screw at the bottom. Locate the bottom screw so it will be hidden by the seat.

Attach the armrest by first gluing and clamping it to the leg pair for each side, making sure there is a 1" overhang at the front leg, then use a countersink bit to drill and then drive screws up through the back of the armrest supports and into the armrests from underneath.

## Take a Seat

The seat box is done as one unit, joined with pocket hole screws. Crosscut the seat box pieces to length and center the inside end of each of the side pieces in the pocket hole jig. Use the outer guides to drill a pair of holes using the ¾" setting. Note that I've attached my jig to a mounting board, which clamps securely to the workbench.

Assembling pocket hole joints in face frames using the jig's locking face clamp is simple, but joining boards end-to-end is more difficult, as the joints tend to move apart when driving screws in. I solved that by making a right-angle clamping fixture, into which I put both workpieces. Clamped securely at a 90-degree angle, the joint holds together perfectly when driving the screws. (By the way, I drilled a hole into the end of this assembly fixture and my pocket hole jig mounting board, so both can be hung on the shop wall when not in use.)

## Basic Assembly

With the leg sets lying flat, mount the finished seat box to the inside surface with three countersunk 1¼" screws after gluing and clamping it into place. I attached the seat box so the top edge is 8¾" below the top surface of the armrests, but you can adjust this a bit if you like. A couple of pieces of scrap support the leg set to keep it level while working.

8"

6"

### Pocket Screw Jig

3¹/₂" typ.          All stock ³/₄"

Hanging hole

24"

With the workpiece clamped securely in the jig, use the two outer guides to drill the holes for the washer-head pocket screws.

With the seat box and leg sets assembled, glue and screw a ¾" × ¾" cleat at the inside front and back, flush with the top of the seat box.

Crosscut the five seat slats to length and arrange them on the seat box — the two outside slats should be flush with the leg sets, but the interior slats should be spaced equally — and mark with a pencil. If your slats are a true 3½", the spacing will be just over ¼". Adjust accordingly for your stock.

Attach the two outside slats first. Glue and clamp them in place, then upend the chair and drive a pair of countersunk 1¼" screws through the cleats and into each end of the slat. Repeat with the three interior slats, being careful to maintain equal spacing.

Cut a pair of ¾" × 2" back braces, measuring the inside width of the assembled chair to get the exact length for a perfect, snug fit between the leg sets. With the backrest slats crosscut to length, hold the lower backrest brace in place and mount the slats with glue and 1¼" screws countersunk through the brace from the rear. As before, start with the outside slats then add the interior slats one at a time, matching the spacing on the seat slats. Fasten the upper brace in

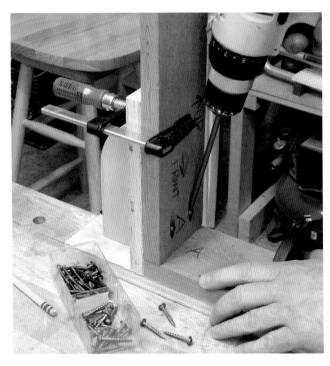

A shop-made right-angle clamping fixture keeps the drilled workpieces securely in place when driving the pocket screws

Attach the completed seat box to the leg sets with three countersunk 1¼" screws. Scrap wood under the leg set keeps everything level.

Countersink from the underside to drive screws to attach the seat slats. Since these screws are protected on the underside of the chair, I opted for regular screws here instead of stainless steel.

Although it isn't attached at this point, assembling the backrest inside the chair ensures a perfect, snug fit. Be sure the spacing of the backrest slats matches those in the seat.

With the jigsaw set at 12°, cut the bevel into the bottom edge of the backrest.

Drive a pair of 2" screws through each side of the leg sets to attach the backrest in place. The screws should anchor into the outside vertical slats, not the horizontal back braces.

the same way; the exact location of the upper brace isn't critical as long as it's below the rear of the armrest. Although not yet attached, the backrest should be a snug fit when finished.

Remove the assembled backrest from the chair to cut the bevel on the bottom. I opted for a 12° angle for the back, but you can adjust this a few degrees either way to your taste. Set your jigsaw to make the angled cut, and trim the bottom of the backrest through both the brace and slats, making doubly sure to cut the angle in

the right direction. Touch up the angled edge with a sanding block if necessary.

Put the backrest in place on the chair and set the angle so the bottom bevel is flush with the seat slats. Countersink and drive two 2"screws through the leg sets into the sides of the backrest. Locate the screws so they anchor into the outside back slats, not the ends of the back braces.

### Finishing Up

Sand all upper and outside surfaces, round over the front edges of the seat

slats, and your patio chair is done. Because cedar is so hardy in outdoor environments, no protective finish is needed. The cedar will weather nicely on its own, gradually acquiring a darker patina.

Should you ever desire to return your chair to a like-new appearance, a simple re-sanding will make the cedar look fresh-cut. (And give you an excuse to fill your shop with that delightful aroma once again.

# Mud Room Bench

**BY DAVE GRIESMANN**

When I was shopping at my local home center for the material for this project I had three words in mind. "No gluing up!" So with that I set out to find 11"-wide lumber for the seat and legs. As luck would have it, they carried lumber 12"-wide × 96", so I was set.

This simple Shaker-inspired bench is a great project because it requires only four pieces of wood, but still provides a terrific place to stop and remove muddy shoes before entering the house. The

top and two legs all come out of the 12" × 96" board, but I needed another board 3"-wide × 48"-long for the stretcher. I also needed a ³⁄₈" oak dowel to make some plugs to hide screws.

The first thing is to cut the 12" wide board into three pieces using the miter saw. Cut two pieces at 15¼" in length for the legs and the other at 54" for the seat. Then cut your 3"-wide board to a length of 44" for your stretcher.

Twelve inches was wider than I needed for the legs and seat (and more often than not the factory edge on a board from

the store can use a little help), so I ripped the three 12" pieces down to 11" in width. You can use a circular saw or jigsaw (see "Rules for using the tools").

Once you have the pieces cut to size you are able to lay out the location and sizes for the radii on the corners of the seat and on the bottom edge of the stretcher, as well as the cutout in the legs that give the bench a more elegant look (and make it easier for the bench to sit level on the floor). Last of all are the notches in the stretcher and legs to lock those pieces together. Start with the

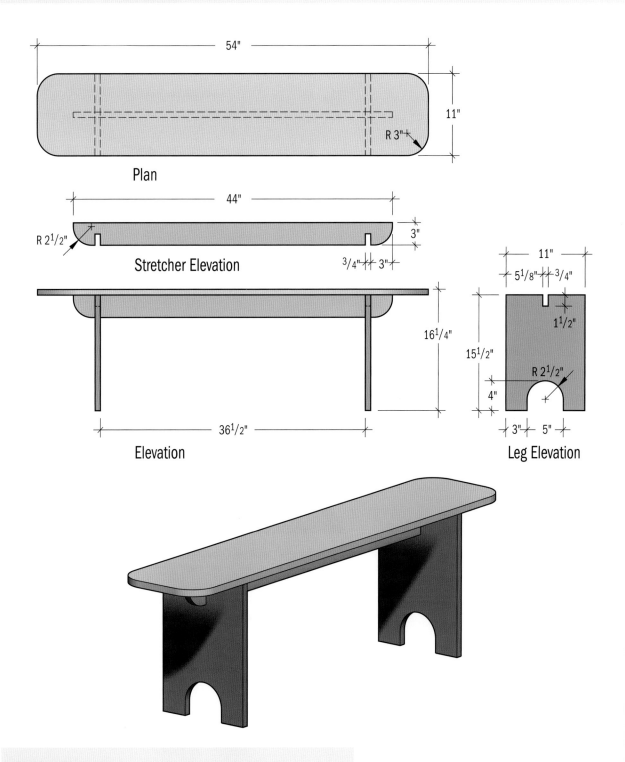

Plan

Stretcher Elevation

Elevation

Leg Elevation

## Parts List

| NO. | PART | STOCK | THICKNESS X WIDTH X LENGTH | |
| | | | INCHES | MILLIMETERS |
|---|---|---|---|---|
| 1 | seat | oak | $^3/_4 \times 11 \times 54$ | $19 \times 279 \times 1372$ |
| 2 | legs | oak | $^3/_4 \times 11 \times 15^1/_2$ | $19 \times 279 \times 394$ |
| 1 | stretcher | oak | $^3/_4 \times 3 \times 44$ | $19 \times 76 \times 1118$ |

round shapes. You can use a circle template or compass to lay out a 2½" radius on the bottom corners of the stretcher. Then lay out a 3" radius on all four corners of the seat. If these aren't tools that you have in your shop, you can use any convenient round shape in your shop to mark out an attractive shape.

Now turn your attention to the legs. Using a combination square, draw a line 4" up from the middle of the bottom of the board. This is to mark the highest part of your circle cutout. Using a drafting compass lay out a 2½" radius circle with the top of the circle at the end of the 4" line you just drew. To complete this layout, draw a line from each side of the circle down to the bottom of the board. Once you have this arch layout complete, repeat the process on the other leg.

Using your jig saw cut out the arches and radii, making sure to cut on the waste side, leaving your line. Once that is completed use your palm sander and finish the cuts by sanding to the line.

The next step is to lay out and cut the interlocking notches in the stretcher and legs. Layout a ¾" × 1½" notch centered in the top of each leg. Then measure and mark out a ¾" × 1½" notch 3" in from each side of the bottom of your stretcher.

Again using your jigsaw cut out the sides of each notch and cut a few straight relief cuts. A coping saw can help you finish cutting these notches and improve the fit. Use your palm sander and appro-

If you don't have a drafting compass or circle template, don't hesitate to substitute the bottom of a coffee can or a spool of fishing line. As long as it looks good to your eye, it works!

After marking the 5"-diameter circle and extending the marks down to the bottom of the legs, use your jigsaw to cut out the arches on both legs. Take your time in the curve. It's easy to cut outside your line.

Cleaning up the cuts on the radii is fairly easy with a random orbit sander. Make sure you keep the pad perpendicular to the face of the board or you'll round over the edges. The sander won't work on the inside of the arches. You'll have to resort to a rasp and file to clean up those cuts.

Depending on your comfort level with the jigsaw, cutting the mating notches for a tight fit can be tricky. You may want to cut the second notch by hand (I'm using a coping saw in the photo above). This allows you to sneak up on a tight fit.

Even though a long-grain to long-grain glue joint is stong, a handful of biscuits help reinforce the joint where the stretcher attaches to the seat (left). With the biscuit slots cut, add some glue and clamp the stretcher in place (above). If you've never tried wooden handscrews, you might be surprised at the amazing number of applications they have in your shop.

piate files to finish shaping the arch and the notches.

The next step is to attach the stretcher to the seat. I know I said no glue, but this is one place where it's a good idea. I also used biscuits to reinforce the glue joint. Line up the stretcher to the seat and mark several locations for biscuits. Make sure you stay away from the ends of the stretchers or the biscuit could show through at the radius. Once you have the biscuit slots cut, glue and clamp stretcher into position.

When the glue dries, position the legs in place in the stretcher notches and turn the bench upright.

Because the legs and seat came from the same board and the grain is oriented in the same direction, we can use screws to attach the legs to the seat without any worry of wood movement causing splitting.

Use a ⅜" countersink bit from the top of the bench to make the screw holes to attach the bench to the legs. Next cut four plugs from a ⅜" oak dowel to glue and cover each screw hole. Once the glue

dries, use a saw to cut the dowel plugs close to flush with the bench.

Using #150- and #180-grit sand paper on your palm sander; sand the entire bench. Take a rag soaked with water and wipe the bench down. This will raise the grain on the bench. When the bench is dry, sand it again using #180-grit sandpaper.

From here you're ready to finish however you wish. I finished my bench using an all-in-one mahogany stain from Minwax and then applied a few coats of wipe on poly.

I use a one-piece bit and countersink (lying on the bench) to make the clearance and countersink hole for both the screws and the plugs in one step. Just make sure you drill deep enough to allow the plug to seat ¼" below the surface.

The coping saw isn't my first choice for cutting the plugs flush to the top (it leaves more dowel than I'd prefer), but rather than go out and buy a flush-cut saw, I made do. Just a little more time spent on sanding and no one is the wiser.

# Folding Stool

**BY CHAD STANTON**

This simple project made from two pieces of dimensional pine can help solve seating shortages at your next gathering — and it folds neatly away until the next get-together.

All you need is a 4' 1x8, an 8' 1x4, some $^3/8$" x $1^1/4$" bolts and $^3/8$" nuts and washers, and a basic set of tools — all from the home center.

## Legs First

Begin by marking a centerline along the length of the 1x4, then rip it in half for the legs, seat cleats, handle and brace.

This cut is a quick and easy task for a table saw, however, the jigsaw can do the job, too. Set the jigsaw blade for no orbit (for the cleanest cut), then take your time and go slow to cut a straight line as you make the cut. (You can also clamp a straightedge parallel to the cutline, offset the width of the jigsaw's shoe, then keep the shoe tight to the straightedge as you make the cut. But don't be afraid to give it a go freehand.) Once the piece is ripped in half, use a block plane to smooth and clean up the saw marks. Each half will be approximately $1^3/4$" wide.

Using a miter saw, cut the four leg pieces to length. (Go ahead and cut the four cleats, handle and brace to length, too, and set them aside for now.)

The next step is the placement for the bolts for the stool to be able to pivot open and closed. Find the center (both length and width) of each leg and cleat and mark an "X." Also mark $^3/4$" in from one end of each piece and place another centered "X." Make these marks on both sides of the legs and cleats. Decide now which end is up.

These pieces need half-circle curves cut on the top ends, and quarter-circle curves on the other to allow smooth folding operation. Set a compass to $^3/4$" and with the point on the top "X," mark a half-circle radius. For the bottom of the legs and seat cleats, reset the compass to the width of the leg and mark a quarter-circle radius.

Use a jigsaw to cut the curves — but because they're likely too tight to stay perfectly on the line, cut a series of straight lines just proud of your arcs.

Then, shape the curves using a rasp or random-orbit sander.

The legs and cleats need bolt holes, and all those on what will be exterior faces after assembly must be countersunk, so the bolt heads and nuts won't interfere with the folding operation. Use a colored pen to mark the countersink locations.

Use a $^7/8$" Forstner bit to drill $^1/2$"-deep countersink holes. (A spade or paddle bit can be used, but a Forstner bit leaves a cleaner cut.) Verify that the hole is deep enough by placing a washer

## Parts List

| NO. | PART | STOCK | THICKNESS X WIDTH X LENGTH | |
| --- | --- | --- | --- | --- |
| | | | INCHES | MILLIMETERS |
| 4 | legs | pine | $^3/_4 \times 1^3/_4 \times 20$ | $19 \times 45 \times 508$ |
| 4 | seat cleats | pine | $^3/_4 \times 1^3/_4 \times 11^1/_2$ | $19 \times 45 \times 286$ |
| 2 | seat pieces | pine | $^3/_4 \times 7^1/_4 \times 16$ | $19 \times 184 \times 406$ |
| 2 | handle & brace | pine | $^3/_4 \times 1^3/_4 \times 7^1/_2$ | $19 \times 45 \times 191$ |
| 1 | long stretcher | pine | $^3/_4 \times 3^1/_2 \times 12$ | $19 \times 81 \times 305$ |
| 1 | short stretcher | pine | $^3/_4 \times 3^1/_2 \times 10^1/_2$ | $19 \times 81 \times 267$ |

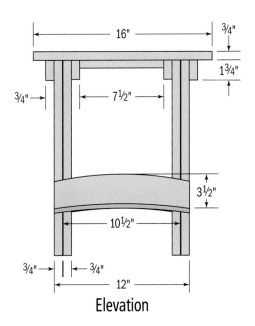

Elevation

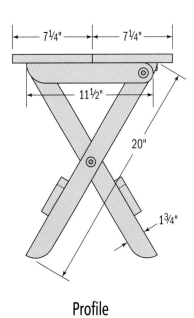

Profile

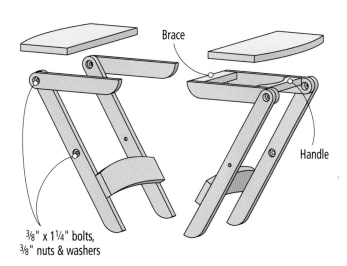

Brace

Handle

$^3/_8$" x $1^1/_4$" bolts,
$^3/_8$" nuts & washers

Exploded view

After cutting the leg stock down the middle with a jigsaw, use a block plane to clean up the cuts.

The legs and cleats need a half-circle curve at the top, and a quarter-circle curve at the bottom.

The holes that get countersinks (all exterior-facing bolt holes) are marked with a different colored ink.

and the head of a bolt or a nut in it; the fasteners should sit below the face of the board. Now drill centered $^3/8$" clearance holes to allow the bolts to go through.

## Leg Assembly

Assemble the legs and cleats together into pairs, with $^3/8$" fender washers behind each nut and bolt, and between the legs. Lock the nuts in place with Loctite or other thread-locking product, so they don't work themselves loose as you fold and unfold the stool.

The completed assemblies should mirror one another.

The leg assemblies are connected by the handle and brace. Both pieces are the same overall size, but use a jigsaw to cut a curve in the handle for comfortable grasping. Attach the handle and brace to the cleats with pocket screws as shown right.

## Sitting Pretty

Set the leg assemblies aside and turn to the seat. First, cut the two seat pieces to length from the 1x8 at the miter saw.

Now it's time to lay out the curved edges (if you leave the edges straight, the seat will bite into the back of the sitter's legs). Because this curve is too large for most compasses, make a simple trammel (also known as a beam compass) from a thin strip of wood and a pencil. Drill a hole in one end of the strip for the pencil to go through, then measure $26^5/8$" to the other end, and hammer a nail through the strip at that point.

Using the nail as a pivot point, mark the arc on the two seat pieces. Note in the photo right that I have an offcut supporting the trammel at the nail end, to keep it co-planar with the workpiece.

Mark the curve on both pieces, then cut them out with the jigsaw. Smooth the edges with a block plane and/or sandpaper.

## Put it All Together

With the leg assembly upside down, place it atop the halves of the seat. The centers of the leg cleats should line up with where the edges of the two seat pieces come together. (To make it easier, you can mark the centerline on the edge of the cleats as I've shown on page 77 — but you'll want to sand off those marks before you apply a finish.)

Drill two $^3/8$" countersink holes and two $^3/16$" clearance holes on the toe end of each seat cleat.

It's essential that there is no binding or pinching in order for your stool to fold smoothly. So use scrap pieces of wood (in the same thickness as the legs) as spacers, placing them between the cleat and legs as you locate the cleats on the underside of the seat pieces. Now use 2"-

A few drops of a thread-locking product will keep the bolts in place as you fold and unfold the seat.

Use pocket screws to attach the brace and handle to the cleats.

A thin strip of wood, a nail and a pencil is all it takes to make a simple trammel for marking large curves.

A scrap of wood helps to locate the cleat position to the seat as you screw them together.

long #8 wood screws to attach the cleats to the seat.

The final pieces are the stretchers — without them, the stool could collapse under load.

Rip the remaining piece of your 1x8 (you should have a 16"-long piece left) in half, then smooth the edges with a block plane. You'll end up with two pieces that are each approximately $3^5/_8$" wide. After cleaning up the cuts with a block plane, you'll be close to the $3^1/_2$" width noted in the cutlist (the precise width is not critical).

Now cut them to length, and use your trammel to lay out curves that match those on the seat. Cut the curves with a jigsaw, and sand the edges smooth.

With the seat folded and lying flat on the bench, align the stretchers to the legs, mark your nail locations, then drill $1/_{16}$" pilot holes. Nail the stretchers in place using $1^1/_4$" nails.

## Stain & Finish

The smooth folding action of the legs has a tight tolerance; paint or a thick coat of polyurethane might interfere with that. So, I recommend using a stain (if you don't like the looks of raw pine) and wipe-on poly. And don't leave your stool out in the harsh weather — it does, after all, fold up for easy transport and storage.

In the opening photo, you might have noticed the matching table. That's simply a scaled-up version of the stool. You'll find a SketchUp model for it — along with the model for the stool — at popularwoodworking.com/ articleindex/i-can-do-that-folding-stool.

The final step in assembly is to nail the stretchers in place (after drilling pilot holes for the nails, of course).

# Round Taboret

**BY DAVE GRIESMANN**

Recently my wife put in a request for a small simple round-top table for our entry way. I did some checking around the internet and eventually saw an Arts & Crafts table that fit the general description, but our house has more contemporary furniture than that. So I thought about it for a while, changed a few features as well as the material (no oak in this one) and came up with a simple design that required minimal lumber and a chance to use my new trim router.

I knew with this piece I wanted to paint the base and have a natural finish top. Where I got lucky was finding one of the home centers that carried some maple boards. I picked up a ¾" × 6" × 96" maple board and then headed over to the racks with the pine. All that was needed here was a ¾" × 6" × 96" board, a ¾" × 4" × 24" board and a ¾" × 3" × 108" board.

In my shop, I cut my 6" maple and pine boards into 22" lengths and edge glued them together to make two 22" × 22" blanks for my top and sub-top. The butt joint is one of the simplest of all woodworking joints, but when working with material that is already at its finished thickness, it can be a challenge to hold the edges of the pieces level with each other.

A simple way to solve this problem is to add biscuits to the edge joints. Though the biscuits aren't necessary for strength, they make it easy to align the pieces during glue-up. Use three biscuits at each joint, do a little sanding after the glue dries and you're done.

With the top and sub-top set aside to dry, I turned my attention to building the legs and stretchers of the table.

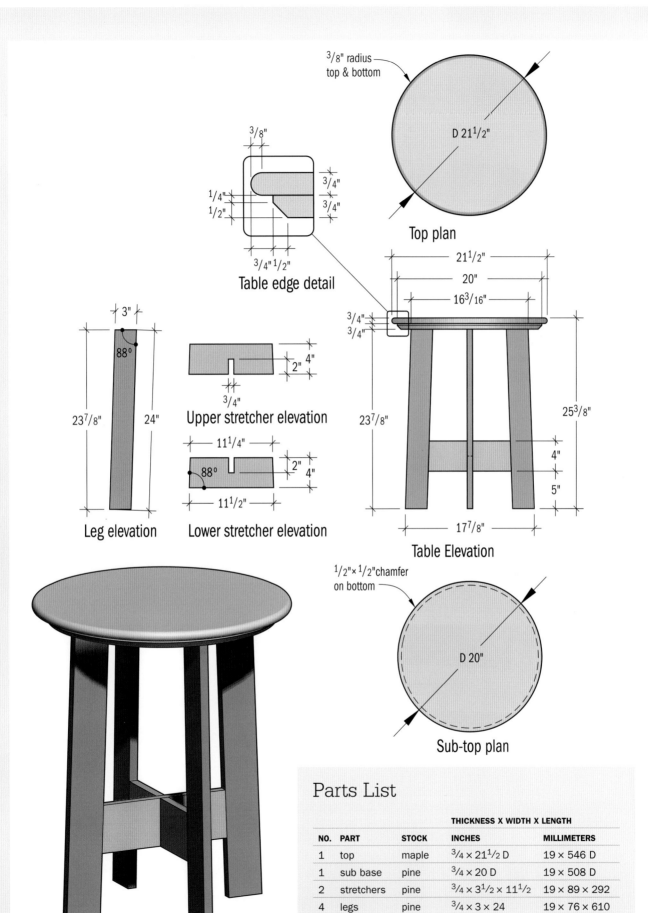

3/8" radius
top & bottom

D 21$\frac{1}{2}$"

Top plan

3/8"

3/4"

3/4"

1/4"
1/2"

3/4" 1/2"

Table edge detail

3"

88°

23$\frac{7}{8}$"    24"

Leg elevation

2"  4"

3/4"

Upper stretcher elevation

11$\frac{1}{4}$"

88°

2"  4"

11$\frac{1}{2}$"

Lower stretcher elevation

21$\frac{1}{2}$"

20"

16$\frac{3}{16}$"

3/4"
3/4"

23$\frac{7}{8}$"

25$\frac{3}{8}$"

4"

5"

17$\frac{7}{8}$"

Table Elevation

$\frac{1}{2}$" × $\frac{1}{2}$" chamfer
on bottom

D 20"

Sub-top plan

## Parts List

| | | | THICKNESS X WIDTH X LENGTH | |
|---|---|---|---|---|
| NO. | PART | STOCK | INCHES | MILLIMETERS |
| 1 | top | maple | $\frac{3}{4}$ × 21$\frac{1}{2}$ D | 19 × 546 D |
| 1 | sub base | pine | $\frac{3}{4}$ × 20 D | 19 × 508 D |
| 2 | stretchers | pine | $\frac{3}{4}$ × 3$\frac{1}{2}$ × 11$\frac{1}{2}$ | 19 × 89 × 292 |
| 4 | legs | pine | $\frac{3}{4}$ × 3 × 24 | 19 × 76 × 610 |

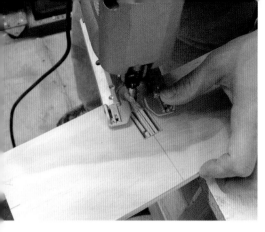

When cutting the half-lap notches, cut to the inside of the pencil lines, then nibble away the waste with successive cuts. A rasp and file will smooth the rough edges.

Biscuits attach the legs to the stretchers (or stretchers to the legs, depending on your point of view). While the slot in the stretcher is centered on the end, the slot in the leg is centered 7" up from the bottom.

If you look at the illustration on the previous page you can see that the legs of the table slant in from the floor to the top. To accomplish this I set my miter saw to cut at an 88° angle and cut the ends of my 3" wide boards. From here I slid the boards down 24" and make another cut at the same angle. These two cuts give me my four finished leg lengths and the legs slant perfectly.

Next are the two stretchers. Keeping my saw set at 88°, I take my 4" wide pine board and cut one end. I then flip my board over (end-for-end, keeping the same edge against the miter saw fence) and measure 11½" at the widest part of the board (don't measure from what will be the top of the stretcher, or it will end up too short) and make another cut at 88°. This gives me a stretcher that has two miters kicked in toward the top of the board. With that piece complete, I repeat the process on the second stretcher.

The two stretchers are going to have a half-lap joint at the center so the two stretchers will interlock. To create this joint, I lay out and mark a ¾" × 2" notch at the center of both stretchers — but with one notch at the top edge of one stretcher and the other at the bottom edge of the other stretcher.

From here I clamp one of the stretchers to my bench and using my jig saw I cut out the sides of the notch (leaving the pencil marks) and start cross cutting to

remove the waste in between. From here I use my files and rasp to fine tune the joint so it is a tight fit.

The legs attach to the ends of the stretchers using biscuits. Mark and cut the biscuit slots on both ends of the two stretchers. Make the matching slots on the legs centered 7" up from the inside bottom of each leg.

While dry fitting the leg/stretcher assembly I noticed that I couldn't get good clamp pressure across the legs because of the slant of the legs. With that in mind I went back to my scrap and cut out four blocks that were 90° on one side and 88° on the other. I applied glue in each of the biscuit joint slots and on all four biscuits. When it came to putting the clamp on I used my scrap pieces to counter the slant of the legs and acted as if I were clamping all straight boards.

While the leg assembly was drying I went back to my sub-top and top and removed the clamps, removed any glue marks with my sander and was ready to begin to make my square tops round.

Starting with my sub-top, I used a tape measure and drew an X from corner to corner on the underside of my piece. This located my center point.

I then used a long piece of scrap and drilled a hole at one end to accept the tip of a pencil and measured in 10" on center and drilled another hole for a nail. I hammered the nail into the center point

Clamping on a angle can cause the clamps to slip, messing up the procedure. A couple of scrap blocks cut at a complementary angle bring the clamping surface back to 90°.

Using a ½" high, 45 degree chamfer bit in my trim router, I carefully cut the bevel profile on the underside of my sub-top. This isn't a requirement for any building reason, but refines the underside of the table.

To finish the edge of the top I used a ³⁄₁₆" roundover bit on both the top and bottom edges. A little hand sanding will blend the radius to the top and edge, removing the slight "edge" left by the router.

of my sub-top just enough for the nail to stay in place but still be easily removed. From here I simply used this home made compass to draw the circle.

I clamped the sub-top to my bench and then, using my jigsaw, I carefully cut out the circle leaving the line inside my cut. (You will have to adjust your clamp several times so you can get the full circle cut). Switching between my files, rasps and sander I smoothed up the edge of the top, then added a chamfer to the bottom edge (top left photo).

While I was making circles, I went to work on making my top in the same manner as I made my sub-top except I

adjusted my home made compass to be 10¾" (for a 21½" diameter top), then added a roundover profile to the edge.

Next I unclamped the legs and cleaned them up using my sander (sanding to #120-grit), then I assembled the two halves. I centered the legs on my sub-top and marked the leg locations. I then marked an X at each leg location by drawing lines from corner to corner of my traced leg marks and drilled a small hole through the sub-top at each leg location.

Flipping everything over, I placed the sub-top back in place on top of the legs and then drilled ⅜" holes through the sub-top into the center of each leg about

½" deep. Then, after cutting a ⅜" dowel cut into four pieces, I applied glue to the holes and the dowels and tapped them into each leg. After the glue dried I cut the dowels flush and sanded the sub-top.

After final sanding the top to #120-grit I drilled through the sub-top and attached it to the top using four 1¼" × No.8 screws.

I applied several coats of wipe-on polyurethane to the maple top. Using flat black latex paint, I painted the sub-top and legs. I applied the paint using a foam brush and a small trim roller. Top it all off with a coat of paste wax on the top.

The legs are attached to the sub base using dowels whose locations are determined from below (left). Then holes are drilled and the dowels are put in place from above.

# Victorian Side Table

**BY MEGAN FITZPATRICK**

While vacuuming a few weeks back, I was thinking about what to build for this issue's "I Can Do That" project when it hit me ... actually, when I hit it with my vacuum. I've had a small Victorian table/bookshelf in my guest room for years, tucked away in a corner where I rarely see it. It's suffered from a broken foot for as long as I've had it. I decided the time had come to fix the problem so that I could put the table where it belongs — next to my favorite reading chair.

I brought the table into our shop, took a look underneath and realized that, because we've introduced a router to the toolkit, it was ideal for "I Can Do That." So I headed to the big box store for select pine (4' lengths of 1×2, 1×12 and 1×8, as well as a ½"-thick piece of pine 4" wide and 4' long — once you get out of the realm of dimensional lumber, the nominal size and actual sizes are the same). I also grabbed a 2' × 2' piece of ½" plywood and a can of mahogany gel stain.

### First, Make a Perfect Pattern

There are a great many curves in this piece — while you could use a jigsaw to cut out the sides and feet, then laboriously smooth and sand them with rasps, files and sandpaper, it's far easier to take the time to make one perfect pattern out of ¼" or ½" MDF, hardboard or plywood. We prefer to use ½" materials for patterns if we have it handy, because it gives the router bit bearing a wide surface on which to ride.

Take the time to make a good pattern and save it, so you can quickly make a bunch of these tables should you find yourself in need of a few handmade

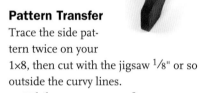

A reader's table. This Victorian side table is ideal for placement alongside a comfy chair — it has a V-shaped shelf underneath to hold a handful of your favorite books.

presents for the holiday season.

I drew the entire side pattern on a piece of ½" plywood (with the pattern's straight top edge at the factory edge of the plywood), then cut with a jigsaw about ¹⁄₁₆" outside my lines. No matter how good the blade, the plywood will tear out a bit, so I wrapped sandpaper around a big dowel and used that to clean up the cuts down to the line.

Getting the pattern to look perfect may take some time — but it's worth it. Do it right (and use a sharp router bit), and you'll have almost finish-ready edges on your workpieces.

Trace amounts. Trace your pattern two times on your 1x8; try to keep the grain figure centered and continuous for a good look.

### Pattern Transfer

Trace the side pattern twice on your 1×8, then cut with the jigsaw ¹⁄₈" or so outside the curvy lines.

While you can set up for pattern routing at this point, I found it easier to first cut the two sides apart (and simultaneously make the straight cut for the top of both pieces) by using the miter saw (or you clamp a straightedge to guide the shoe of your jigsaw for a straight cut, or simply let the router make the final cut).

Now clamp the pattern in place on one side piece, and install in your router a ½" straight bit with a top-mounted bearing. Adjust the depth of cut so that the blade will completely engage your workpiece, and the bearing will ride on your pattern.

For most of the work, make the cuts by moving the router from left to right, or with the direction the router bit is spinning, But as you start to move out of the grain toward the outer edge of the piece, climb-cut — that is, cut against the grain — to avoid breaking off the delicate points. Try to keep moving at a steady pace; if you leave the bit in one location for too long, you'll burn the edge of your workpiece (not a big deal — it can easily be sanded out). Also, you'll get a cleaner edge if you make one pass to remove the bulk of the waste, then ride the bearing along the pattern as you make a final light pass to cut the final shape. Do the same on the second side.

## Strong Feet

You'll notice in the illustration that the feet are separate from the sides. It's important that the grain runs across the feet so that the $1\frac{1}{2}$" ends don't snap off (which is exactly what happened to my antique inspiration piece). You can make a pattern and use a router to cut the feet from the end of your 1×12, but because they are simple curves, I just drew them directly on the pine, cut them with a jigsaw then sanded them.

Attach the feet to the sides with three countersunk screws — a 2" one in the middle of each foot, and 3" screws located $1\frac{1}{2}$" or so to each side of center (I eyeballed it; there's no need to measure).

## Shelves & Top

The shelf cleats are simply a $\frac{3}{4}$"-thick, $3\frac{3}{4}$"-square piece, cut in half diagonally. They're secured by three $1\frac{1}{4}$" countersunk screws in each. The two 20" shelf pieces are cut from the $\frac{1}{2}$" stock and are simply butted together at a 45° angle then

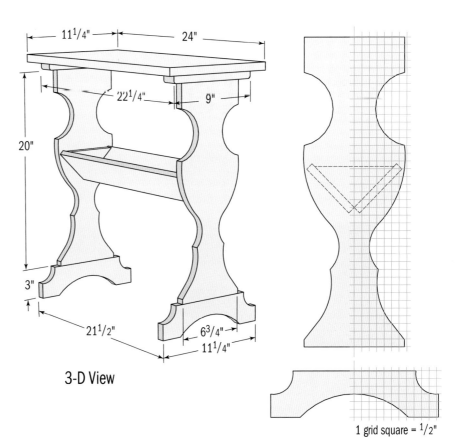

3-D View

Side & Foot Patterns

1 grid square = $\frac{1}{2}$"

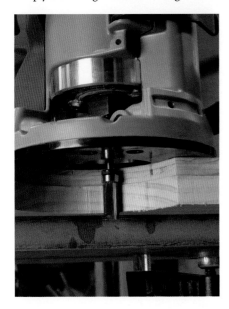

Ready to rout. Grab your router and before you plug it in, install a $\frac{1}{2}$" straight bit, then adjust the depth of cut so that the blade hits your workpiece and the bearing rides on your pattern.

## Parts List

| NO. | PART | THICKNESS X WIDTH X LENGTH | |
|---|---|---|---|
| | | INCHES | MILLIMETERS |
| 2 | Sides | $\frac{3}{4} \times 6\frac{3}{4} \times 20$ | 19 × 171 × 508 |
| 2 | Feet | $\frac{3}{4} \times 3 \times 11\frac{1}{4}$ | 19 × 76 × 285 |
| 1 | Shelf cleat | $\frac{3}{4} \times 3\frac{3}{4} \times 3\frac{3}{4}$ | 19 × 95 × 95 |
| 2 | Shelves | $\frac{1}{2} \times 4 \times 20$ | 13 × 102 × 508 |
| 2 | Top cleats | $\frac{3}{4} \times 1\frac{1}{2} \times 9$ | 19 × 38 × 229 |
| 1 | Top | $\frac{3}{4} \times 11\frac{1}{4} \times 24$ | 19 × 285 × 610 |

secured to the cleats with three nails per end. (Don't forget to drill pilot holes.)

Cut the top cleats from the 1×2 and before screwing them down to the top of each side, round the ends with a rasp and sandpaper.

Cut the top to size, and if you like, add a decorative profile on the top edge using a $\frac{1}{4}$" roundover bit (or any profile you like.)

I stained this piece with two coats of gel stain before attaching the top, and added a top coat of wipe-on poly for protection. (Gel stain sits on top of the wood more than traditional, penetrating stain,

so it cuts down a bit on the blotching inherent to pine.)

With the finish done, flip the top over, position the cleats, drill countersinks and drive $1\frac{1}{4}$" screws through the cleats into the underside of the top to secure it.

Now, choose a selection of your favorite books and stock the shelf. You're ready to read.

# Coffee Table

**BY GLEN HUEY**

A coffee table is generally the focus of the living room. Sure the couch is the big comfortable sitting place, but the coffee table is the heart of the area. Where else do you prop up your feet? Where are the important magazines stored, to be pulled out when needed? The answer is your coffee table.

This particular table caught my eye because of the overall design. It is not too Country or Arts & Crafts and it will fit into either design quite well. It will also look proper within a contemporary setting.

The construction of this piece is uncomplicated. The top and shelf units are made of four individual pieces of lumber, which will help limit the total amount of wood movement versus using one solid

glued panel. The legs are comprised of two pieces each and are attached to the top and shelf with screws. Add in the pieces that put the finishing touches on the sides and ends and this coffee table is ready for a finish.

And the finish could not be any easier to complete if it were painted, which would also be a nice look if you chose not to use the red oak as shown, but first things first.

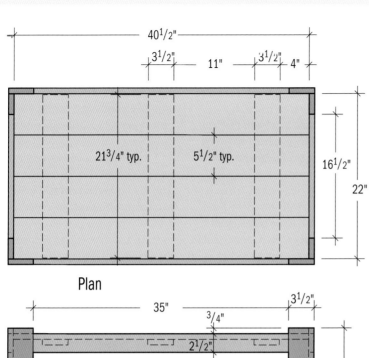

Plan

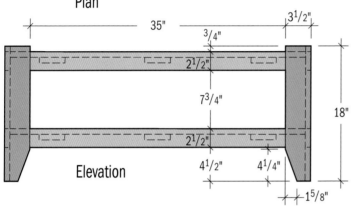

Elevation

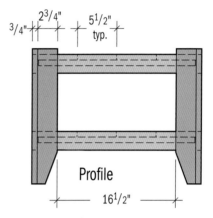

Profile

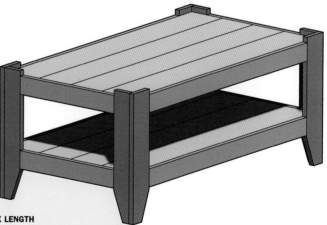

## Parts List

| REF. | NO. | PART | STOCK | THICKNESS X WIDTH X LENGTH | |
|------|-----|------|-------|---------------------------|--|
| | | | | INCHES | MILLIMETERS |
| A | 8 | top & shelf slats | oak | $3/4 \times 5^1/2 \times 40^1/2$ | $19 \times 140 \times 1029$ |
| B | 6 | battens | oak | $3/4 \times 2^1/2 \times 21^3/4$ | $19 \times 64 \times 552$ |
| C | 8 | leg sides | oak | $3/4 \times 3^1/2 \times 18^3/4$ | $19 \times 89 \times 476$ |
| D | 4 | end rails | oak | $3/4 \times 2^1/2 \times 16^1/2$ | $19 \times 64 \times 419$ |
| D | 4 | side rails | oak | $3/4 \times 2^1/2 \times 35$ | $19 \times 64 \times 889$ |
| Screws | | 40 No. $8 \times 1^1/4$" | | | |
| | | 16 No. $6 \times 1^1/4$" pocket screws | | | |
| Nails | | 24 3d finish nails | | | |

## Making the Top and Shelf

Construction begins with the top and shelf pieces. Each of the two identical assemblies is made of four pieces of stock cut to the required length. Take the time to knock the sharp edges off of the pieces. This can be done with #100-grit sandpaper, or if you would like a more pronounced rounding of the corners, use a hand plane to make the cuts on all the edges of each piece.

Position four of the top/shelf pieces on a flat surface, such as your bench top, with the best face down toward the bench and align the ends. Add clamps to help pull the pieces tightly together as well as to keep things from shifting as you attach the battens.

The battens are pieces of 1 × 4 that are cut a ¼" less in length than the overall width of the assembled panel. Position three battens so they are about 2" from both ends and one is centered. To attach the battens use one screw (1¼" × No.8) directly in the center of each of the 1 × 6 pieces. Use a tapered drill with a countersink before installing each screw.

Having the screw located in the center of each piece will help to keep the wood stable with seasonal adjustments. The pieces will be allowed to move but the total movement is, in essence, cut in half because the pieces will only move from the center outward. If the pieces were screwed at both edges, the screws would restrict the movement and a crack or split might occur. Repeat these steps for the second assembly and set them aside for the time being.

## A Leg Up

Cut the leg material to size and set four of the pieces to the side. The remaining four pieces need to have ¾" taken from one edge. Mark the cut line and use a jigsaw to make the cut as close to the line as possible without crossing. Use a hand plane to straighten and square the cut edge to the line.

I made the angled foot cuts at the miter saw, though they also could be made with the jigsaw and cleaned up with a hand plane. In using the miter saw we can't set any angle past 45° (+ -). We need to make a steeper cut, so we need to base the cut off of the 90-degree setting. Position the saw to cut a 15-degree angle, place a temporary stop in place (bottom right photo) and set the cut to leave 2⅛" of stock at the bottom edge of the leg. Make

Knocking the corners off of all the edges will provide a shadow line as the pieces are place side by side. Don't try to find the joint — celebrate it!

Lay four pieces together as shown, aligning the ends, and add clamps to hold them in place. Attach the battens and the top and shelf are complete.

Patience is required when cutting the leg stock. Get close to the line and finish the edge with a plane.

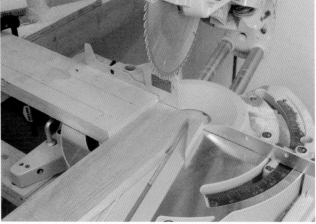

A set-up as shown will allow you to create the beveled feet whether you have a sliding compound miter saw or simply use a miter jig with a hand saw.

A strong glue joint and the correct orientation of the legs is important.

Stack the pieces of the table in any way you can to ready them for clamps. I found a neat way to use soda cans.

the cut on the four full-width pieces, then set the stop so the cut is made at 1⅝" on the pieces that were ripped with the jigsaw.

After the legs are assembled, the idea is to have identical views while looking at either face. You'll notice that the difference in the layout of the two cuts is exactly ¾" which is the amount ripped off with the saw.

Add glue to the ¾" edge of the narrow blanks and clamp the leg assembly together. Make sure as you tighten the clamps that the pieces don't slip. A little trick I've learned over the years is to add a little playground sand to the glue before adding clamps. The sand keeps the pieces from sliding, but indents into the wood, so the joint will still pull tight. Repeat the steps for each pair of leg blanks and set the legs aside to dry.

## Time to Assemble

Position the top with the face down and raise the unit off of the bench with a couple of ¾" scraps. Next you need to find a way to position the shelf so your hands can be free to position the legs and add clamps. You can get a friend to help or think outside the box and find a special support system. The shelf should hit the legs 3½" above the terminating point of the angled cut. I found that two stacked soda cans worked great.

Set the cans at each corner and position the shelf, face down, on top of the can supports. Next, position the legs at each corner and add a clamp to each side. Once the clamps are in place, mark the location

Mark the top or bottom edge of your shelf. You will need to get those cans out and precisely locate the shelf back in position.

Everything may be in position, but if your table is not square to the flat surface, you will find it extremely difficult to add the finishing pieces to the table.

of the top edge of the shelf as it hits the legs. This is so you can correctly position the shelf after removing the cans.

Loosen the clamps slightly and slide the shelf upward. Remove the cans and tighten the clamps while repositioning the top at the marked lines. Do the same for the opposite end and you are ready to attach the legs to the top and shelf.

Before joining the two, make sure that the entire table, as it is to this point, is square to the bench. Tapping the unit with a rubber mallet or a hammer and a block of wood can make slight adjustments. Again, use the tapered pilot-drill and drive a 1¼" × No.8 screw through each leg and into both the top and the shelf. Each leg will have a total of eight screws installed.

Before the clamps are removed, cut and fit the remaining pieces that complete the sides and ends. A snug fit is required. Use a pocket hole jig to drill a hole at the lower edge of each of the rails. Follow the manufacturer's instructions to create the pockets. After the pieces are fit and readied for the screws, attach the pieces to the leg assemblies with the recommended screws.

Drive nails into the side rails, three per side, and through the end rails into each piece that makes up the top and shelf. Two nails per piece — one ½" from each edge. Use a drill bit or begin the hole with the nail itself in the drill. The nails will allow for seasonal movement and help keep the wood flat because as the lumber moves, the nails will bend to and fro. Screws hold things fast and wouldn't allow for this natural happening.

Joining the legs to the top and shelf is easy with screws. Please don't use drywall screws, they will break, leaving you with much bigger problems.

The remaining pieces need a tight fit. Butt one end to the legs and mark the cut end to achieve that fit.

A pocket screw connection will hold the rails in place while you add the nails to complete the construction.

With a piece of the scrap wood and a plug cutter, you can make plugs that exactly match your project.

Knock down all sharp edge and corners before starting the staining process.

With these four finishing products you will complete your finish in a short time.

The construction is complete once you have filled the screw holes. The countersink part of the pre-drill leaves room for a ⅜" plug. These plugs can be purchased from the supply store, or cut from scrap material with a matching ⅜" plug cutter. Add glue in the hole and on the plugs and tap them in place with a hammer. Trim any additional material with a small saw or a plane and allow them to dry before finish sanding.

## Preparing for a Finish

Before we look into that easy finish I mentioned, we need to get the table ready for finish. This involves sanding the flat surfaces with #120- and #150-grit sandpaper as well as rounding the ends of all the tops of the legs and the sharp corners. Use a file or rasp to ease the edges of the leg tops and carefully sand the areas smooth.

Once everything is sanded and ready, the staining is next. The staining process begins with a coat of Olympic Special Walnut wood stain. Use a clean rag to apply the stain. Rub on a heavy coating, allowing the stain to sit and penetrate the wood pores for about 15 minutes. Then wipe away any excess stain. This has to sit for at least 24 hours before moving on.

Once the stain is dry we move to the second coat of finish. This is a coat of Watco Danish Oil — Dark Walnut. Apply this in the same way as the stain. Put on a generous coat, allow the oil to seep for 15

Wipe on, let sit, and wipe away. Repeat that twice, once with the stain and once with the oil and you are ready to add your top coat of shellac.

minutes and wipe away any excess. Please take caution with these oily rags as they can become fire hazards if not properly treated. (Hand the rags on the edge of a garbage can and let them dry. Then they can be safely tossed into the garbage can.)

After the oil has dried for more than 24 hours we can apply the next coating — shellac. Rag a coat of shellac over the entire table. Try to not lap your application. Putting additional shellac over an area that already has a coat may produce lap marks, which will show in the final product. Keep a wet edge as you apply the top coat.

When the shellac is completely dry, a few hours later, lightly sand with a piece of No.0000 steel wool or a piece of #400-grit sandpaper. This will knock down any nibs left from the shellac. The final coat before using your table is a layer of paste wax. Rub it on, allow it to set and dry, then polish the surface to a warm sheen.

If you are like me, you will find a number of uses for a finish this easy. Move the table into your living room and add books — or maybe just your feet.

# Factory Cart Coffee Table

**BY DREW DEPENNING**

At the turn-of-the-century, no factory existed without several industrial carts (also known as trucks) at its disposal. From hauling lumber to carrying crankshafts to serving city ice, these workhorses served many functions.

Today, many of these antique carts have been restored for another purpose — furniture.

But if you don't have several hundred dollars (or more) to spend on a restored antique cart, you can build one that will serve for years in your living room.

Century-old chic. Inspired by re-purposed factory carts, this coffee table is a modern design solution for supporting your favorite books — and the occasional pair of feet.

## Reclaimed Timber

To give my table the look of 100 years of use, I built the top with the most distressed wood I could find — boards from shipping pallets that were in our storeroom.

Let me warn you: Bringing these boards back from the brink of the dumpster is more time-consuming than you might think. For that reason, the measurements found in this article are based on a "clean" top built with 1x6 dimensional lumber.

The goal is to have a top 27" deep and 44" wide. Two 1×6 × 10' boards of No. 2 pine will be enough lumber for the top (and it's easy to find at the home center).

But if you prefer a more rustic look, ask at your local grocery store if you can grab a few pallets (or check outside by your office loading dock) and pry off more boards than you think you'll need.

Sand down a spot on each board to help you select wood of consistent color. Don't forget to wear a dust mask — your lungs and sinuses will thank you.

Now, using your jigsaw (the cut will result in pleasing irregularity), trim or cut the top boards to 27" in length. (If you want a perfect 27" and square cut on all the boards, set up a stop on your miter saw).

## Build the Box

The base frame of the table is built from 2×6 dimensional lumber. Two 2×6 × 8' boards should suffice for this project.

Because I want the tabletop to over-hang the base by 1" on all sides, I'll cut the length of the side pieces to 42".

If you're using random-width pallet wood for the top, arrange the boards how you like, then adjust the length of your side pieces as necessary to accommodate a longer or shorter overall cart length.

After your sides are measured and cut with your miter saw, cut two 22"-long end pieces from your second 2×6.

To determine the length of the center brace, arrange the sides and ends in a rectangle on the floor, then measure up the middle. That's the length to cut for the center brace.

After setting your pocket screw jig to work with 1½" stock, drill three pocket holes at each end of both end pieces on the inside faces of these boards. Do the same for the center brace.

On your bench, slide the side piece against a square block of scrap and use this setup to hold your end pieces at 90° while you drive home the 2½" pocket screws.

Scraps for a shelf. Use two 10¼" scraps to keep your brace centered and level.

Once the outside frame is completed, cut two pieces of scrap to 10¼". Use these scraps to act as a shelf while you screw the center brace in place.

## Distressed to Impress

If you're using pallet wood for the top, here's where you'll spend the extra time: bringing these boards back to life.

Using #100-grit abrasive in your random-orbit sander, begin to remove the layer of grime. To expedite the process, you might want to use something more aggressive, such as a belt sander.

Again, don't forget your dust mask. If you don't use one, don't be surprised when your facial tissues look like cleanup rags from an oil spill.

Clean up the boards, but be sure to leave some of the nicks and saw marks — this is the character you want to keep.

If you're using new dimensional lumber, smacking it with a set of old keys is a great way to apply dings to the top to give it distressed character.

Take your top boards to some rough concrete (a sidewalk works great) and bang up the corners and sides. This will

Dust protection. The dust from pallet lumber is nasty stuff. Wear a dust mask to spare your sinuses and lungs.

make the top look as if it's seen plenty of industrial action.

Finally, use a #120-grit disc on your random-orbit sander to knock down all the corners and smooth down the dents.

## Finish with Charm

Original carts often had the name of a company or city printed on the side. You can add that touch by using stencils and black spray paint. Use plenty of blue tape to avoid over-spray.

Use a hair dryer to set the paint, then rough up the label with your sander.

Finish the frame and top boards with a few coats of amber shellac before nailing the top boards in place.

With the frame on the floor, place one top board at the end of the frame. Use a combination square to square up the 1" overhang then nail the board in place.

Here, you can use finish nails or even regular framing nails for an industrial look. (If you use cut nails, don't forget to first drill pilot holes.)

With this piece as your reference, square and nail the remaining boards.

Before you attach the casters, nail two blocks of 2×6 scraps at each of the inside corners of the frame. This will give the casters support on all four corners.

I purchased the steel casters for my project online from one of many industrial supply companies. At your home center, you'll probably find 6" casters with rubber wheels. They may not look old-fashioned, but they won't mark your floors, either.

To attach the casters, first drill pilot holes, then slip washers on your lag screws and use a wrench to drive the screws.

Finally, prop up your feet and enjoy your piece of custom furniture. And don't forget to use a coaster!

## Parts List

| NO. | PART | STOCK | THICKNESS X WIDTH X LENGTH | |
|-----|------|-------|--------|--------|
| | | | INCHES | MILLIMETERS |
| 2 | Sides | SPF* | 1½ × 5½ × 42 | 38 × 142 × 1067 |
| 2 | Ends | SPF | 1½ × 5½ × 22 | 38 × 142 × 559 |
| 1 | Center brace | SPF | 1½ × 5½ × 39 | 38 × 142 × 991 |
| 8 | Top boards | No. 2 Pine | ¾ × 5½ × 27 | 19 × 142 × 686 |
| 8 | Corner braces | No. 2 Pine | 1½ × 5½ × 4 | 38 × 142 × 102 |
| * Spruce, pine or fir | | | | |

| HARDWARE | |
|----------|--|
| 4 | Casters, 6" wheel diameter |
| 16 | Lag screws, ¼" x 1" |
| 16 | Washers, ¼" |
| 18 | Coarse pocket screws, 2½" |

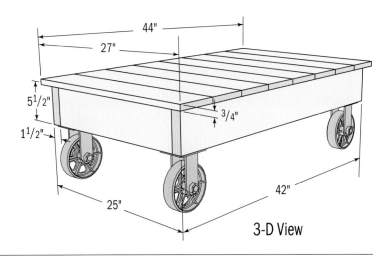

3-D View

# Tapered-leg Table

**BY GLEN D. HUEY**

Small tables are useful just about anywhere in the home. They can be easy to build, but a good design is important. To make the design more interesting, tapered legs (often part of Shaker, country and Federal furniture) are part of this design.

The taper begins below the aprons and continues on a slope until it reaches the floor. Tapering lightens the look and keeps the legs thick enough at the top to provide adequate joinery strength.

Additionally, this table's base is slightly wider than it is deep, and the top overhangs the ends more than at the front or back — the increased work surface adds to the overall design.

## Where to Begin

At the home center, pick up a piece of 1x8 red oak that's 8' long (for the top), a piece of 1×6 poplar that's 6' long and the stock for four legs — at my store I found 36"-long pieces of 2×2 poplar. Select the straightest, flattest boards you can find. And select the red oak with the best-looking grain.

At the miter saw, position a stop block to accurately cut the four legs to length. Next, cut the aprons from the 1×6 making sure to cut two each of the two different lengths. Adjust the stop block to cut the top material to length — three pieces make up the top and those three pieces need to be edge-glued.

The top has a clear finish, so it's important to examine the pieces to find the best grain match. Flip and turn the boards for the best look, one that keeps the grain flowing across the panel. Draw lines across the joints so you can easily orient the pieces into position again.

Don't limit yourself. If you understand how the parts of a table come together, there's no limit to size. Simply change the apron length, in pairs, and you can build whatever size table you like.

On the back face of the middle board, add three pocket-screw holes along each edge — one hole 4" off each end and center the third hole. Add a thin layer of glue to the meeting edges, orient the boards as before and install the screws while keeping the ends aligned. When done, set the panel aside while the glue dries. After 20 minutes, scrape the excess glue from the panel.

## Let's Taper the Legs

The taper on tapered legs is on either two faces of the legs (as with this table), or on all four faces, which is more often seen on furniture of Federal design.

To keep things simple, work one face at a time. Move down from the top end of your legs to the width of the aprons. You could begin your taper here, but to be safe — so your taper doesn't extend up into where the apron attaches — move

down another inch, then square a line across the face of the leg.

Rotate the leg 90° in either direction, slide down to the floor end of the leg and make a mark that's ½" from the previously marked face. With the second face up, connect the end of the line with the mark set at ½" as shown.

Securely clamp the leg to the edge of a worktable with the waste area overhanging the edge. With a sharp blade in your jigsaw, and the blade set 90° to the saw's base, carefully cut on the waste side of the line. Make the cut from the foot toward the top of the leg.

Keep the base of the saw flat to the face of the leg. The farther into the cut, as the jigsaw base fully settles on the leg, the easier it is to keep the jigsaw square to the leg. Also, if you have a variable-speed jigsaw, turn down the speed a notch or two as you cut. This allows better control throughout the cut.

After the cut is complete, smooth the face to your layout line with a block plane. Work to maintain a 90° corner and

Connect the dots. With the start of the taper drawn on one face, rotate the leg, mark the amount of the taper at the foot of the leg then connect the lines to show the total taper.

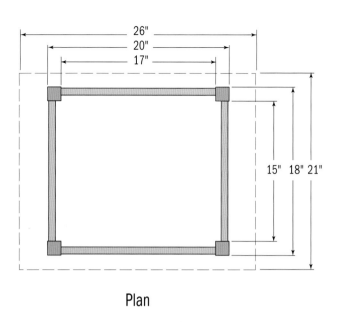

Plan

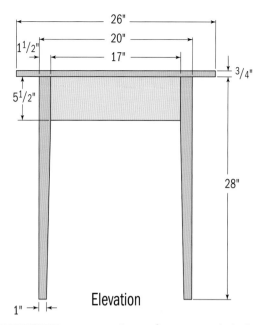

Elevation

## Parts List

| NO. | PART | STOCK | THICKNESS X WIDTH X LENGTH | |
|-----|------|-------|-------|-------|
| | | | INCHES | MILLIMETERS |
| 4 | Legs | Poplar | $1^1/_2 \times 1^1/_2 \times 28$ | 38 × 38 × 711 |
| 2 | Short aprons | Poplar | $^3/_4 \times 5^1/_2 \times 15$ | 19 × 140 × 381 |
| 2 | Long aprons | Poplar | $^3/_4 \times 5^1/_2 \times 17$ | 19 × 140 × 432 |
| 1 | Top | Red oak | $^3/_4 \times 21 \times 26$ | 19 × 533 × 660 |

don't worry if you plane a little bit beyond the line.

The second taper layout is made on that smoothed face. At the floor end of the leg, mark a point that's ½" from one edge. Connect from the ½" layout mark to the line where the taper begins on the edge nearest your ½" mark. That line is the second cut line. Use the jigsaw to cut just off the line on the waste side, then plane the face to the line. Repeat

Cut with a jigsaw. If you begin the taper cut at the foot, the task gets easier as you move up the leg. Just make sure to clamp the waste area off the side of your workbench.

the steps on all four legs and you have completed a set of tapered legs.

### On to the Aprons

Use your pocket-screw jig to install two screw holes at both ends of each apron piece. On the long apron pieces, add two pocket-screw holes along one long-grain edge, spaced about 2" from the ends; on the short apron pieces install a single pocket-screw hole that's centered. These holes are used to secure the top, so over-size the pocket-screw holes along the top edge of the aprons with a slightly larger diameter bit to allow for seasonal wood movement.

Gather the legs in a square with the tapers facing inward. To check the arrangement, each pair should form an inverted V-shape. If your gathering does not, rotate whichever leg is out of sorts until the V-shape is found.

On the top of the legs — the area that remains square — label each leg where the apron pieces attach. This helps keep the orientation correct throughout the

construction. Before you attach the legs and aprons, sand the aprons to #120-grit.

If you attach the aprons back from the face of the legs, you'll add a nice shadow line to the design. For this, slide a scrap of ⅛" hardboard under the apron before driving any screws. Clamp a leg to your worktable with the labeled face toward the apron, slide the elevated apron into position then add the screws. Next, position the second leg to the apron, clamp the leg then drive the screws. Complete two matching assemblies, then add the remaining aprons to the base.

### The Top and Finish

The top's length is correct, but you'll need to trim it to width. Level the joints with a plane, sand the panel through #150-grit, including the edges, then knock off the sharp corners with sandpaper. At the same time, smooth any sharp corners on the base.

Add two coats of your favorite paint to the base and a few coats of amber shellac to the top (sanding between coats). Attach the top when it's dry. As the final touch, I added a trompe l'oeil "inlay" with the same paint as I used on the base.

# Game Table

**BY GLEN HUEY**

Back in the day, gentlemen would sit for hours at the local barbershops and while away the time discussing the day's events and playing checkers. Hours might be spent sliding pieces from square to square.

Jumping the opponent's checkers was the way to clear his pieces from the board and to reach his back line where one would utter those fateful words, "king me". The king, two stacked checkers, possessed new powers that would allow it to move in new directions. With those added powers came a better chance at clearing the board.

Removing all of the opponents checkers would make one the winner. It would allow him to obtain the local title or possibly begin a heated argument that went on for days by itself.

What could be better than to bring those long passed days back into your home with the building of this game table? The time spent with family members playing at this table will bridge many gaps and start many a conversation about life.

## It All Starts at the Top

The table top is the most important part of this table. That's where we begin. Select the material for the frame and make a 45° cut on both ends of the pieces leaving 23" of length at the long side of each piece. Cut all four pieces the same length.

The 23" figure comes about due to the size of the game board. The board is 18" square and using the stock for the frame at 2½". To wrap the board with this stock you need to have pieces for the frame at 23". If you choose to change the board size remember to adjust the frame size as well.

## Parts List

| NO. | PART | STOCK | THICKNESS X WIDTH X LENGTH | |
|---|---|---|---|---|
| | | | **INCHES** | **MILLIMETERS** |
| 4 | board frame | oak | $^3/_4 \times 2^1/_2 \times 23$ | $19 \times 64 \times 584$ |
| 4 | board supports | poplar | $^3/_4 \times 1^1/_2 \times 19^1/_2$ | $19 \times 38 \times 495$ |
| 1 | board | plywood | $^3/_4 \times 18 \times 18$ | $19 \times 457 \times 457$ |
| 2 | inside fit aprons | poplar | $^3/_4 \times 3^1/_2 \times 19^1/_2$ | $19 \times 89 \times 495$ |
| 2 | outside fit aprons | poplar | $^3/_4 \times 3^1/_2 \times 21$ | $19 \times 89 \times 533$ |
| 4 | legs (pre-miter) | poplar | $^3/_4 \times 3^1/_2 \times 27$ | $19 \times 89 \times 686$ |
| 2 | leg connectors | poplar | $^3/_4 \times 2^1/_2 \times 6$ | $19 \times 64 \times 152$ |
| 2 | stretchers | poplar | $^3/_4 \times 3^1/_2 \times 19^1/_2$ | $19 \times 89 \times 495$ |

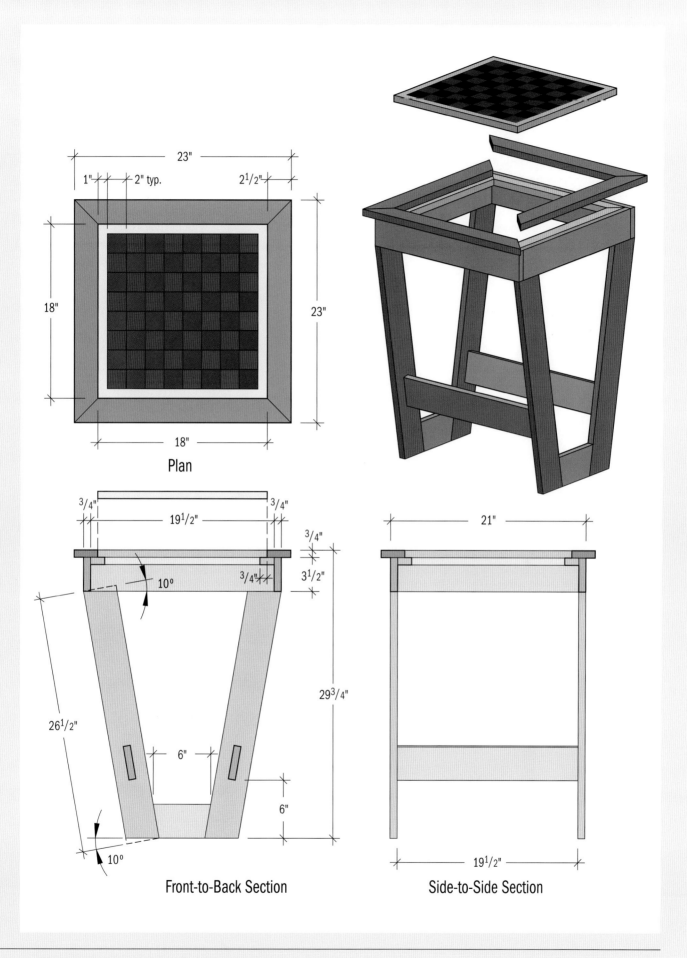

23"

1"  2" typ.  2½"

18"  23"

18"

Plan

¾"  19½"  ¾"

¾"  ¾"  3½"

10°  ¾"

26½"  6"  29¾"

6"

10°

Front-to-Back Section

21"

19½"

Side-to-Side Section

With the frame pieces cut to length you'll need to use the pocket-screw jig to locate and drill two holes per end on two of the pieces (see photo below).

Putting the frame together is as simple as driving the pocket screws. Place a clamp on the piece that is accepting the screws so it won't move. Position the pocketed piece against the clamped frame member and drive the screws to make the connection. Repeat this step for each corner and the frame will come together.

For extra reinforcement I added screws to the corners (lower left) then cut plugs from matching stock to fill the

countersink area. Any time during the project add a small amount of glue to the holes and tap in the plugs.

Next, prepare the stock for the board supports. Each piece has a mitered 45° cut at each end made at the miter saw. These pieces are attached to the inside edge of the frame with ¾" lying on the frame and ¾" sticking into the center area to catch the game board when it is positioned. Attach the support pieces with #8 × 1¼" wood screws. Be sure to use the tapered countersink for these holes too.

## A Strong Leg to Stand On

The apron for the table is built to snugly fit around the support pieces. The best method to gather accurate sizes is to use the support frame to align the apron. Two pieces are the inside fit aprons. These pieces are cut to the same length as the support pieces. The two outside fit aprons will extend past the support pieces and cover the ends of the inside fit aprons. Return to the pocket-screw jig to cut two holes per end on the inside fit apron pieces.

With the holes cut connect the apron pieces with the pocket screws. The assembled apron should just slip over the

Set the angled cut flat to the jig and drill the holes perpendicular to the cut end. The remaining pieces will accept the screws and no holes are required.

When driving the pocket screws, it's best to clamp whatever you can to the bench. This helps to ensure a tight, flush fit when the screw is tight.

Drill a hole with a tapered countersink at each corner, four in total, then add a screw to help to hold the corners of the frame tight.

Attach the board supports using screws.

Fit the apron parts to the board supports.

Use pocket-hole screws to assemble the apron parts.

Using a miter saw, cut a 10° miter on both ends of each leg. These cuts should be parallel.

After cutting the leg connectors to length, attach them to the legs. Make two of these leg assemblies.

support pieces and allow the top to fit into the apron. Don't make the connection of the top to the apron just yet. You'll want to separate the two assemblies before you are finished with construction.

The legs are started at the miter saw. Set the saw for an 80° cut or 10° off of a square cut of 90°. Position the material for two legs at the saw and cut the angle at what is to be the top of each leg. Leave the saw set at that angle for the next set of cuts on the legs.

Set the top apron assembly on one side and position the angled cut on a leg against the bottom edge of the aprons. Pull a measuring tape from the bottom edge of the apron and mark at 25½"

down the leg. This is where the second cut of the leg is placed.

Making that second cut is a snap. Position the leg material so that both legs are flush at the top end and cradled into the saw tight to the fence. Slide the two pieces, making sure that they stay aligned, into position to make another angled cut at the mark (lower left photo). It is important to have the cuts angled the correct way. When this cut is complete you'll have a parallelogram shape to the legs or both cuts angle in the same direction. Repeat the steps for the second set of legs.

Next, add pocket-screw holes to the top end of each leg and align them with

the bottom edge of the apron making sure that the edge of the leg lines up with the side of the apron. It doesn't really matter which opposing aprons you select to attach the legs to since the apron is square, but I attached the legs so the end grain of the outside aprons sat on the leg top — there may be additional support with this choice.

Add the legs to one side of the table, then cut the leg connector to fit in position. This connector also cuts at the same angle as the legs. Make the cut on one end then flip the piece, measure the distance between the legs at a mark that is 2½" above the floor and make the second cut at that point. In this sce-

Attach each leg assembly to the bottom of the apron assembly using pocket screws.

Lay out the location for the stretchers and attach them to the legs.

nario you'll have the cuts set at opposing angles. Place two pocket-screw holes at each end and attach the connector to the legs. Repeat the process for the second leg assembly and you're ready for the stretchers.

The stretchers have square cut ends and pocket holes, two at each end, that allow you to attach them to the legs. Position the stretchers to the legs with the screw holes facing inside the table. I like these stretchers to be centered in the leg. To accomplish this easily I cut a scrap at the miter saw to the appropriate width, 1⅜" for this example, placed it at the front edge of the leg, pulled the stretchers tight to the back of the scrap and set the screws to make the connection. The base is complete.

## Making the Game Board

Cut and fit the piece of plywood that is the game board to the opening in the table. This piece should be a loose fit so it can be removed if necessary. You see, you can also have a different game on the bottom of the board.

To mill this board use your jigsaw to cut close to the layout lines and then hand plane to bring everything into shape. Remember that if you're cutting across the grain of the plywood it is best to score a line with a sharp utility knife before cutting. That way as you cut to the line the top veneer of the plywood will not splinter.

Once the game board is fit you are ready to complete the table. Add the

plugs to the top frame if you haven't already, install pocket-hole fillers into any hole that is easily visible and sand everything to #150-grit. Use #100-grit sandpaper to knock off any sharp edges and move to the finishing stage.

The game board is a checker board and to make your own board you need a few additional tools. Gather a utility knife, framing square (or square of some kind) and a roll of painter's tape that is 2" wide. Of course you'll need two or three different colors of acrylic latex paint.

To begin the board you'll need to layout the lines that define the checker squares. Find the center of the board and draw a line across the entire piece. Next, move each way in 2" increments each time, drawing a line as before. You should end up with eight squares and 1" of space on either edge which will be the outside border of the board.

Rotate the board 90° and repeat these steps for the opposing lines. Make sure that you continue the lines clear to the edge of the plywood piece. These will become important after the first layer of paint. You now have the sixty-four spaces for the checkerboard.

## Paint Makes the Square

Add painter's tape to the outside edges of the squares which protects the borders from the first paint color. Traditionally, black and red are the colors of the checkerboard, but there is no reason you couldn't choose different colors. I selected black for the first layer. Whatever color

you decide upon, make the first layer the darker of the two.

Apply the paint in a light coat moving from side to side on the board. When that coat is dry (you can speed it along with a hair dryer), add a second coat of the same color, brushing in the perpendicular direction. This coat completes the first layer of paint.

Remove the tape from the borders. See those lines for the layout? Stretch the tape from end to end aligning it with the lines. Apply tape to every other section as shown. Rotate the board and add tape in the second direction as well.

Now you need to remove the tape from any areas where the tape is double layered. Align the rule or straightedge to the tape and use a utility knife to cut the tape on all four sides of each square that needs to be removed. Carefully peel away the tape to expose the black painted surface below. Each square will be two thicknesses of tape.

Once the necessary areas are removed it is time to add paint. For this layer you need the second color and two coats will be needed to cover the exposed areas. Begin by brushing on one coat of paint moving from top to bottom. The second coat will be applied moving from side to side. This process provides better coverage. After the second layer is dry you can peel all remaining tape to expose the painted checkerboard.

To complete the painting you will need to apply tape around the outer edge of the checkerboard. The tape will

Measure and mark the game board itself, using the table frame as your guide.

To lay out the checker grid itself, start from the center and measure out. It's much easier.

After taping off the 1" border, a base coat of black paint is applied to the whole board.

Tape is first stuck down in one direction, skipping every other space. This pattern is repeated in the other direction, then the tape is trimmed and removed where doubled.

Two coats of red paint are then applied over all the exposed squares. Again alternate directions between coats to hide brush strokes.

With the paint dry, the tape is removed, and the checkerboard pattern is revealed. I retaped the board to add a third contrasting color to the bare wood border.

be the barrier that will prohibit paint from touching the completed squares. I elected to paint a third color — one that will show favorably against the oak of the frame. You can also decide to allow the border to match the second color added to the checkerboard.

The completed board fits into the frame of the top. All that's left to complete the project is to apply paint to the base (I used black and added a layer of an oil/varnish finish for protection) and to apply two coats of Watco's Special Walnut finish to the oak.

Set this game table in your home and rekindle the past with a rousing game of checkers. Will you be kinged and become the local champion or have to succumb to another master of the house?

To complete the table I applied a couple of coats of black paint to the base, then added a top coat to protect the paint from scuffing. Finally, I added a coat of Watco oil to the top/frame of the table.

# Tiered End Table

**BY DAVE GRIESMANN**

When I was drawing the sketches for this project I was reminiscing about the styles of furniture we had in the family as I was growing up. Back then the modern furniture had sharp corners, with straight or really drastic angles. But what I remember most was that all the kitchen appliances were burnt orange, harvest gold or avocado in color. With that in mind, you now know the reason behind my color choice in finishing this table.

Beyond the nostalgic coloring, I love the fact that this end table also doubles as a great location for storing books and for showing off pictures or other memorabilia, without taking up all of the top surface of the table.

Since I knew this piece was going to be painted I decided to build it using poplar. If avocado isn't your thing and you'd rather not paint, another option would be to use birch plywood, also available at your home center store. Iron-on veneer tape can be used to hide the plywood core and offer a more finished look to your project. But I was smitten by the avocado bug, so poplar and paint were my choices.

While I was at the home center choosing my lumber, I made sure to get lumber as close as possible to the finished sizes I needed. Meaning small stock for the bottom riser and wide stock for the rest.

Even thought I purchased the widest stock I could find, I still had to cut and glue up boards for the tops, side and risers. Whenever I needed to glue up a panel, I used biscuits to help align the two pieces during gluing. This also cut down dramatically on the sanding.

While my glued-up pieces were in the clamps drying I turned my atten-

## Parts List

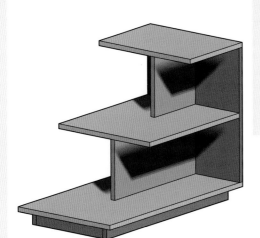

| NO. | PART | STOCK | INCHES (THICKNESS X WIDTH X LENGTH) | MILLIMETERS (THICKNESS X WIDTH X LENGTH) |
|-----|------|-------|-------------------------------------|------------------------------------------|
| 1 | top tier | poplar | $^3/_4 \times 18 \times 12^3/_4$ | $19 \times 457 \times 324$ |
| 1 | middle tier | poplar | $^3/_4 \times 18 \times 22$ | $19 \times 457 \times 559$ |
| 1 | bottom tier | poplar | $^3/_4 \times 18 \times 32^3/_4$ | $19 \times 457 \times 832$ |
| 1 | top divider | poplar | $^3/_4 \times 10 \times 10$ | $19 \times 254 \times 254$ |
| 1 | bottom divider | poplar | $^3/_4 \times 10 \times 20$ | $19 \times 254 \times 508$ |
| 1 | back | poplar | $^3/_4 \times 18 \times 20^3/_4$ | $19 \times 457 \times 527$ |
| 2 | riser sides | poplar | $^3/_4 \times 2 \times 30$ | $19 \times 51 \times 762$ |
| 2 | riser ends | pine | $^3/_4 \times 2 \times 13$ | $19 \times 51 \times 330$ |
| 1 | middle riser stretcher | poplar | $^3/_4 \times 2 \times 28^1/_2$ | $19 \times 51 \times 724$ |

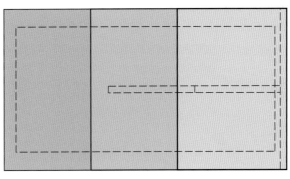

Plan

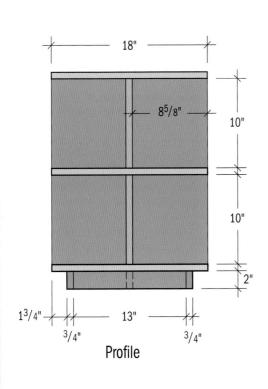

Profile

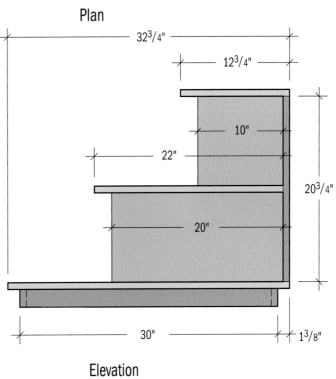

Elevation

tion to building the bottom riser. I had purchased four pieces ¾" × 2" × 36" I ganged three of them using a clamp and my left hand to hold the three tight and squared up one end of all three.

Once I had the three pieces squared I ganged two of them together and cut them to 30" in length and the third piece to be 28½". These will act as the two sides and middle stretcher of my riser. For the two ends of my riser I squared up one end of my fourth piece and cut it into two 13"-long pieces.

To assemble the riser frame, I used my pocket hole jig and screws. I drilled two holes on both ends of the two end pieces and on both ends of the center stretcher. Once I had everything aligned, I used 1¼"-long pocket-hole screws to assemble the riser.

Now I turned my attention back to my clamped up pieces. Once I had the clamps off I used a scraper and my random orbiter sander with #80- and then #100-grit sandpaper to clean up any glue squeeze out and to flatten the pieces.

Once I had my boards flattened I cut my three tops, two dividers and my back to size using my jigsaw. I cut close to the lines and used my block place to clean up the edges.

With all the pieces cut to size I was ready to assemble the project. I gathered up my cordless drill, a box of square drive No.8 × 1¼" self-tapping deck screws, a couple of No.20 biscuits, my biscuit cutter, a square and a piece of ¾" × ¾" × 20" scrap. That's all that is needed to assemble this piece. (Well, that and bit of patience, since the process is a bit repetitive.)

Starting with the 18" × 30" bottom tier, I used my scrap piece to mark where the ¾"-thick back sits on top of the bottom. I also marked where the ¾"-wide × 20"-long bottom divider is centered on the bottom. With these two locations marked I pre-drilled the holes to attach the back and the bottom divider. I first attached the back to the bottom, then flipped the assembly onto its back and attached the bottom divider.

With the assembly still laying on its back, I marked on the back where the middle tier will attach, pre-drilling into the back. I also marked on the middle tier where the bottom divider will attach. Once I had this laid out I went ahead and pre-drilled and attached the middle tier to the bottom divider. I then flipped the assembly onto the bottom tier and attached

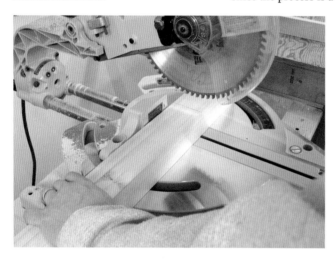

When using the miter saw to trim pieces to length, it's a good idea to gang identical lengths. By holding the identical-length pieces flush at one end (a clamp can help with this, all of the pieces will be the same length, avoiding problems during assembly.

Square cuts on the ends of the boards will ensure a square frame, but it's still a good idea to check for square as you screw the riser together.

You could use a square and ruler to lay out the locations of the back and bottom divider, but I find using a scrap of the actual pieces themselves gives me a more accurate representation of the pieces.

After marking the locations for the back and divider, I drill pilot holes for the screws through the top surface. Working from this side will guarantee the any blow-out from the drilling will end up on the bottom surface.

To keep the screws flush to the bottom surface, I first used a countersink bit at each hole location, then screwed the bottom tier tightly to the divider.

When cutting the biscuit slots in the middle tier piece, it's very important to keep the base of the biscuit jointer accurately located on your layout line. If the biscuit is not parallel to the line, the biscuit will not fit into both slots.

The last tier is screwed in place into the top edge of the back and the top edge of the divider. Pre-drilling is still important at this step, as is making sure your screw is driving straight (not at an angle) into the piece below.

I didn't use glue to attach the riser to the bottom for two reasons: Glue can cause problems with seasonal movement, and I wanted to finish the piece with the base detached.

the middle tier to the back, again countersinking the screw heads.

Once the middle tier is attached, you won't be able screw up through the middle tier to attach the top divider. Instead, I used biscuits to attach it. I marked the ¾" × 10" location of the top divider on the middle tier and its location in the middle of the back. I again predrilled the back, then marked two biscuit locations on the divider and middle tier pieces. I then set my biscuit jointer to cut No.20 biscuit slots and cut two slots in both pieces.

From here I used an acid brush and spread glue on the biscuits, and on the bottom of the top divider and tapped the divider into place on the middle tier. Lastly, I attached the back to the divider with screws.

We're almost to the end. To attach the top divider and top tier, I followed the same process to lay out the location of the divider on both the back and the top tier piece. The divider is again biscuited to the tier below and attached to the back by screws.

Because I'm painting my table, I went ahead and attached the top tier to the assembly using screws through the top. If you're staining you would be better off using biscuits to attach the top tier piece.

Even though I'm painting, I don't want my screws to show. So while the glue was drying, I filled the countersunk holes with paintable wood putty. After the putty dried I sanded it flush to the top surface.

The last assembly step is to attach my riser to the assembled unit. With the riser still loose from the table, I used my

pocket-hole jig to drill three holes on the inside of both the side and the middle dividers. I then turned the piece on its side and marked an X from corner to corner to center the riser and then attached the riser to the bottom of the piece.

With just a little finish sanding, I was ready to apply my finish. I chose to stain the riser a dark walnut to give the table a feel of floating off the floor. I removed the riser and stained it separately. I applied three coats of avocado paint to the table. Then I reattached the riser to the table.

The concept used to build this table also set my mind to thinking about building a tiered shelving unit to match. With the practice gained on this table, the shelf should be an easy project — someday.

# Contemporary Coffee Table

**BY ROBERT W. LANG**

This small coffee table is a great introduction to building furniture. It doesn't require much material and it's an opportunity to develop your skills. This project is sturdy, attractive and easy to build. All of the parts come from standard widths of lumber. I used poplar from my local home center, and I made the table from one 6'-long piece of 1x8, one 8' length of 1x6 and two 8' lengths of 1x4.

Start by gluing the top from two pieces of 1x8 and one piece of 1x6. If you

are cutting the parts from 6'- or 8'-long boards, leave them a couple of inches long, then trim them to the final length after the glue has dried.

The goal during glue-up is to keep the faces of the boards aligned. Use a couple straight strips of wood below for a level work surface and, if you need to, clamp straight pieces across the top and bottom to hold the edges in alignment while the glue dries.

Let the glue dry overnight, then trim the top to length. Clamp a straightedge across the top to guide your jigsaw or

circular saw to make the cut. When the top is at its finished size, set the blade of your combination square at 2" and draw lines in from each corner on the underside of the top.

## Start From the Bottom

Use the angled side of the combination square to draw a line at a 45° angle from the corner of the top to the intersection of your layout lines. Cut the legs to length. Then mark the center of one edge of each leg.

Stand the legs in the corners and line up the center marks with the angled lines

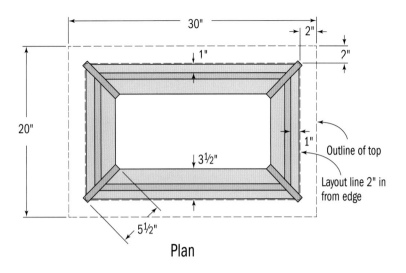

Plan

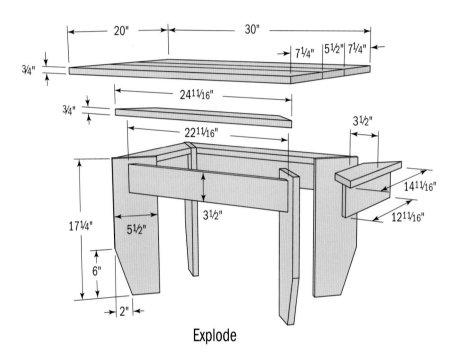

Explode

## Parts List

| NO. | PART | STOCK | THICKNESS X WIDTH X LENGTH | |
|-----|------|-------|------|------|
| | | | **INCHES** | **MILLIMETERS** |
| 1 | top | poplar | $^3/4 \times 20 \times 30$ | $19 \times 508 \times 762$ |
| 4 | legs | poplar | $^3/4 \times 5^1/2 \times 17^1/4$ | $19 \times 140 \times 438$ |
| 2 | long rails | poplar | $^3/4 \times 3^1/2 \times 24^{11}/16$ | $19 \times 89 \times 627$ |
| 2 | short rails | poplar | $^3/4 \times 3^1/2 \times 14^{11}/16$ | $19 \times 89 \times 373$ |
| 2 | long aprons | poplar | $^3/4 \times 3^1/2 \times 22^{11}/16$ | $19 \times 89 \times 576$ |
| 2 | short aprons | poplar | $^3/4 \times 3^1/2 \times 12^{11}/16$ | $19 \times 89 \times 322$ |

*Glue up top from two 1x8 and one 1x6 pieces

Lay out all the pieces on the underside of the top. You won't have to measure, and all the pieces will be the exact size you need.

After cutting, put the parts in place and mark the locations for the screws.

on the top. Use your combination square to set each leg at a 45° angle to the edge, then trace around the ends of the legs.

When the leg locations are marked, use the lines to determine the exact lengths of the rails. Cut the rails a few inches longer than the dimensions in the cutlist, with a 45° angle on one end of each piece. Place the angled end against the line, with the back of the rail even with the back of the leg.

Draw a line up the edge of the rail from the layout marks drawn at the other end, then draw an angled line across the face. Cut the second end of each rail to the line.

After cutting the rails to length, draw a line 1" in from the outer edges of the rails. This is the location for the outer

face of the aprons, and you can put them in position to mark the lengths exactly without measuring. Cut the aprons to size at the miter saw with a 45° cut on each end, then mark and cut the angle at the bottom of each leg.

## Check, Layout, Drill

Place the rails and the legs in position on the tabletop. The rails and legs join with two types of screw connections: countersunk screws through the legs into the long rails, and pocket screws through the short rails into the legs.

Mark the rough positions of the screws with the countersunk screws near the edges, and the pocket holes toward the center of the rails. Be sure to locate the screws so they won't run into each other during assembly.

Drill through each leg into the ends of the long rails. A bit with an integral countersink makes this a one-step process. Use a pocket-hole jig to drill through the ends of the short rails. Sand all the parts before assembly.

Connect the legs to the long rails first. Apply some glue to the end grain of the rails and wait a few minutes (a.k.a. "sizing"). Apply a fresh bead of glue and screw the legs to the rails with #8 x 1 3/4" screws.

When all four legs are attached to the long rails, connect the two subassemblies with the short rails. For stronger joints, size the end grain with glue. To keep the

boards from shifting, clamp the subassembly down to your worksurface before driving the pocket screws.

Size the mitered ends of the aprons with glue before assembly and run a narrow bead of glue on the long edge of each apron to hold it to the rail. Drill pilot holes in the apron ends then fasten them to the legs with 4d finish nails. Set the nails below the surface and fill the holes.

## Top it Off & Finish

The top is screwed to the base through the rails. The pan head screws used for the pocket holes work well. The solid-wood top will expand and contract as seasons change, so take that into account when drilling the screw holes.

At the center of the short rail, drill a clearance hole slightly larger than the diameter of the screw's shank.

In the long rails, the holes should be larger to allow the top to move. Drill a 1/4" hole and use a washer under the screw head, or drill two smaller holes and tilt the drill back and forth to connect the holes and make a slot.

Place the assembled base on the upside-down top and drill pilot holes for the screws. Use a bit the size of the unthreaded part of the screws, and be careful not to drill through the top.

When the top and base are assembled, give the entire table a finish sanding with #180- or #220-grit sandpaper. Round or bevel the sharp edges at the corners of the boards with coarser sandpaper, then go over it again with the finer grit.

I used a water-based stain, and after letting the stain dry overnight, I brushed on two coats of a water-based polyurethane finish. This is a durable coating, but it can show brush marks after the finish dries. I rubbed the dry surface with a non-woven abrasive pad to remove the brush marks and leave the surface with a satin sheen.

# Contemporary Side Table

**BY MEGAN FITZPATRICK**

The first step in building this contemporary side table is to go shopping for the basket that serves as a drawer — then adjust the plans as necessary to fit your choice.

The one shown here is an 11"-deep, 7"-tall, 17"-long sea grass basket from Organized Living – but a basket, tray or cloth tote of many sizes and shapes would work (and you can easily change the style of the project with your "drawer" and finish choice).

The key thing is that your basket/tray/tote not be deeper than $11^1/4$", which is the actual width of 1x12 — the widest dimensional lumber available at the home center.

So, with my basket selected, I headed to the home center for No. 1 white pine.

This project is dirt-simple and, including the $24 basket, costs less than $100. It took just a couple of hours to shop, build and apply the finish — yet I've seen similar projects in various catalogs and stores priced anywhere from $200 to $600.

I know it's easy to fall into the trap of "I could just build that," then never get around to it — but with this side table, there's simply no excuse.

## Stock Layout

The shelves, sides and top are all the full $11^1/4$" width of the 1x12 stock, so all you need to do is cut the pieces to length.

I started with the shelves, so I marked then cut one 18"-long piece at the miter saw, and used it to mark the length of the other so they'd match. Then I did the same with the $27^1/4$"-long sides. After making your cuts, confirm the parts match their partners; if they're off even a little, stack them flush at one end, then trim them simul-

taneously at the miter saw. They need to match.

Note that if you don't have a miter saw, or if yours won't make an $11^1/4$"-wide cut, you can easily use a circular saw, running it along a straightedge to keep the cut square.

Hold off on cutting the top to length until you've assembled the base.

Now lay out the shelf locations. I decided on a 7" opening at the top for books and the like. My basket is also 7" — but I

wanted a little room at the top to be able to easily reach in to pull it out, so that took an 8" opening.

After I marked the shelf locations, I showed the basket to the side to make sure it would fit. Trust, but verify.

Before moving on, sand the sides and shelves to #150-grit or more to remove mill marks. (You can probably get away with stopping at #120-grit if you're going to paint your side table.)

Measure, mark, then cut the first shelf and use it to lay out the length of the second shelf. Do the same for the two sides.

## Grab Your Drill

The joinery is simply two pocket screws on the underside of each end of both shelves. But because this was all moving along far too quickly, I decided to add a dash of fuss (two minutes' worth) by measuring and marking locations for the pocket screws before drilling. I hope the cats and bugs are impressed by the perfect symmetry that no person will ever see.

The only (slightly) tricky thing about using pocket screws for assembly is making sure your parts stay perfectly aligned as you drive the screws. But clamp a thick, straight piece of wood along the layout line (and to the bottom of the Workmate to keep the side from shifting), and the challenge is overcome. You'll also see in the picture top right that I've another clamp pulling the shelf to the block — that's because the shelf boards developed a slight but noticeable warp after I cut them to length; the clamp pulled the warp out to make the shelves nice and level.

After you drive the pocket screws on one side, flip the piece on top of the second side and again clamp the block to your layout lines to keep things in place as you finish assembling the base.

But before you tighten the clamps, grab a 12" combination square and confirm that the setup is indeed square.

Once the base is all together, set it on the ground and confirm the length

A block clamped in place to the layout lines makes it simple to hold the shelves perfectly in place as you drive the pocket screws. (Note: Because I'm using pine, a softwood, I used coarse-thread screws.)

A nail set helps you avoid inadvertently marring ("Frenching") the tabletop as you drive the nails slightly below the surface.

## Parts List

| NO. | PART | STOCK | INCHES | MILLIMETERS |
|-----|------|-------|--------|-------------|
| | | | THICKNESS X WIDTH X LENGTH | |
| 2 | sides | pine | $^3/_4 \times 11^1/_4 \times 27^1/_4$ | 19 × 286 × 692 |
| 2 | shelves | pine | $^3/_4 \times 11^1/_4 \times 18$ | 19 × 286 × 457 |
| 1 | top | pine | $^3/_4 \times 11^1/_4 \times 19^1/_2$ | 19 × 286 × 495 |

for the top. Yep — in this case, $19^1/_2$" as planned. But you never know.

Cut the top to length at the miter saw and use a sanding block on the ends to remove any mill and burn marks from the saw blade. Then — if like me, you're persnickety — use your combination square to mark a line $^3/_8$" in along each end, and mark nail locations symmetrically along that line, then align the top with the base and drill pilot holes for 6d finish nails.

Drive each nail so it's almost flush to the surface, then use a nail set for the final hammering of each to sink the heads slightly below the top and not damage the wood.

### The Finishing Steps

Sand the top to the same grit as you did the sides and shelves, check the entire build to make sure everything is smooth to your satisfaction, then ease all the edges with sandpaper.

Now break out the stain or paint. I chose a gel stain (in hickory) because gel stain basically sits on top of the surface and thus tends to blotch less on pine than a penetrating stain. And it's the consistency of pudding, so it doesn't drip and run. It also imparts a deeper color than penetrating stain...which is why some people don't like it — it obscures the grain more than a traditional stain.

After donning gloves, rag on a coat (not too thick — but sufficient to cover everything), let it sit for about five minutes, then wipe off the excess with a clean rag.

Wait for the stain to dry (it can take as long as 12 hours), then apply a topcoat (I used a satin polyurethane). After it dries, slide your basket in place, and voilá — an easy contemporary side table for little cash and little time, but with a lot of style.

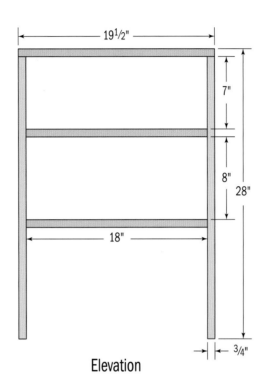

Elevation

# Pirate Chest

**BY MEGAN FITZPATRICK**

Don't let the curved top of this "pirate chest" scare you. It's a lot less tricky than it may appear — and it's excellent practice with your block plane.

For this build, you'll have to venture a bit beyond the home center – but stop there to pick up a 6' 1×12, two 8' 1×8s and 21' of 1½" × 1 slats (though if you have a table saw or band saw with which to rip the slats, that will be more economical). Also get 40 or so upholstery nails, a box of at least 40 6d masonry nails, a hasp, two 4" gate hinges and two handles. Go for the cheap zinc-coated hardware; I'll give you a few options for aging it. Now, you need to visit a "big and tall" clothing department for some 50" (or better, 60") leather belts. At 50" (the largest available where I shopped), I had to cut the belts and nail them at the front and back edge of the bottom. Just 10 additional inches would have meant no cuts — the belts would have wrapped all the way around (and saved a little time and trouble).

## Build the Box First

To make things simple, I used the full width of my stock lumber for the front, back and sides. So I set up a stop at the miter saw and cut the four front and back pieces from the 1×8s to 22" long. Then, I cut the two sides to 14" long — but, because dimensional lumber can vary slightly in width, you should butt the two front pieces (or the two back pieces) against one another, and cut the length of your side pieces to match that measurement.

In other words, it's always risky to rely on the cutlist or drawing for exact dimensions; yours could end being slightly different in any build. Always generate

Curve appeal. This "pirate chest" is really just a simple box. What gives it appeal is the curved top, which is constructed from 12 slats that are shaped with a block plane. (The belts help, too.)

measurements from the actual parts when possible.

Both the front and back have chamfers on the long edges where the two pieces meet in the middle, which serve two purposes: They create a shadow line for a more pleasing aesthetic, and they hide the fact that the two pieces don't form a perfect joint (an impossibility with two home center edges). I simply eyeballed the chamfers using a block plane held at a 45° (or so) angle for each piece, and continued planing until I was content with the chamfer depth. If eyeballing it isn't your style, measure and mark a line across both the face and edge at ⅛" and plane down to your lines.

Now clamp the front and back pieces in place to the sides, then decide on your nail layout (I used on three nails on each plank end: one ¾" from each edge and one in the middle) and drill ⅛" pilot holes — which seems big, but it isn't. In fact, the wood may still split when you

sink the nail — especially if you aren't careful to line it the wide part of the nail in line with the grain. (If you get a split, don't panic. Just pull the nail out and drill a bigger pilot hole.) Masonry nails, like

No wedgies. When using masonry nails (or period cut nails) it's important to align the wedge-shaped nail so that the wide part is going with the grain in the top piece of wood. If you align it across the grain, you'll likely wedge the grain right open and cause a split.

# Parts List

| NO. | PART | STOCK | THICKNESS X WIDTH X LENGTH | |
| --- | --- | --- | --- | --- |
| | | | INCHES | MILLIMETERS |
| 4 | Front/back planks | Pine | $^3/_4 \times 7 \times 22$ | $19 \times 178 \times 559$ |
| 2 | Case sides | Pine | $^3/_4 \times 11^1/_4 \times 14$ | $19 \times 285 \times 356$ |
| 1 | Bottom | Pine | $^3/_4 \times 11^1/_4 \times 20^1/_2$ | $19 \times 285 \times 521$ |
| 2 | Top sides | Pine | $^3/_4 \times 11^1/_4 \times 4$ | $19 \times 285 \times 102$ |
| 12 | Top slats | Pine | $^3/_4 \times 1^1/_2 \times 22$ | $19 \times 38 \times 559$ |

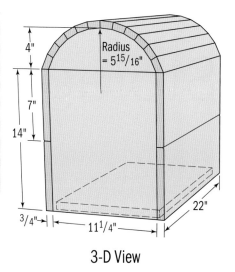

3-D View

period cut nails, are actually wedges, so if you align them incorrectly, you're basically wedging the wood apart — especially in this case, when you're nailing so close to the end.

With the case assembled, cut the bottom to length just a hair undersized at the miter saw, then take a few strokes along a long edge with your block plane. The piece should be a tight fit in the bottom of the case. I knocked it in with a rubber mallet, then put everything on the floor to push the bottom piece firmly in place. Measure, mark and drill pilot holes. I used five nails across the front and back, and three on either side. Locate the side nails in far enough that you won't hit the ones coming in from the front and back.

Do you really need such big nails to hold this small box together? Of course not. And do you really need to use so many of them? Again, no. But the large heads and interesting shape add to the overall look of the chest. It's all about the aesthetics.

Rounding the top. In the story, you discover two ways to fit the slats for this curved top. No matter which approach you choose, you'll need to plane angles on the slat edges with your block plane to get the pieces to fit.

## Make a Curved Top

First, use a compass to mark the two side pieces for the top with a $5^{15}/_{16}$" radius — or just use a 5-gallon bucket to trace the curve. Either way, the apex of the curve is 4" from the bottom center of the pieces.

Before you start attaching the slats to your top end pieces, you'll first have to plane an angle on at least one long edge of each slat (and on both edges as you round the top). What angle? Well, I eyeballed it. I held my first slat in position at the bottom front edge, and marked an angle on the end that looked as if, once the waste was removed, it would allow the slat edge to sit flat to the top edge of the case. Then, I marked the cut along the edges of the slat, clamped it into position, and used a block plane to plane down to my lines.

I temporarily secured the slat in position to the top end pieces with one 2d finish nail at each end, then fit the next slat in the same manner, marking the angle on the edge facing the previous slat while leaving the top edge at 90°, until I came to the two center top pieces. Those must be planed along both long edges. Then, I worked down the other side, with the angle planed on the side facing the back edge of the chest. (Or, you can mark and plane angles on both edges of each piece for a tighter fit, as shown in the drawing.)

Once all the slats are fit and temporarily tacked in place, drill pilot holes for 4d finish nails, mark the order in which each slat is attached to the ends, then pull the slats off. Now apply glue to each long edge as you reattach the slats in order using 4d finish nails. Use a nail set to set each nail well below the wood's surface (and using an oversized nail set will help you jump-start the "aging" process, by making a bigger indentation,

giving the top the appearance of long use and abuse).

Once the glue dries, use your block plane to smooth the arris where each slat meets (double-check first that all your 4d nails are below the surface; if they're not, you'll nick your plane blade).

I painted my piece dark brown, then beat the heck out of it using a bunch of keys and a hammer. This process exposed raw wood in the "wounds," but I added a topcoat of dark Briwax paste wax to simulate years of dirt, working it in well to the newly exposed wood.

To age your hardware, you have a few options. You can soak everything in vinegar to remove the bright coating, or simply paint it black. Or, grab a propane torch and burn the finish off (make sure you do this in a well-ventilated area, and have a bucket of water on hand for quenching).

Attach the hardware, then wrap the belts around the chest, buckle them, drive in a bunch of upholstery nails to effect a studded look (I used them every $1^1/_2$" across the top, and every 2" on the front and back). If your belt is less than 60" long, you'll have to cut it and attach it at the top and bottom edge — I suggest long staples for this, covered with a upholstery nail.

Now load your chest with booty and start talking like a pirate.

# Storage Bench

**BY DREW DEPENNING**

The inspiration for this "I Can Do That" storage bench was simple — I wanted it. Ever since I picked up a king-size bed at a liquidation sale, I wanted a matching bench to hold my shoes at the foot of the bed. After seeing many designs that were running anywhere from $250 to $400, I thought to myself "I can do that" — and with a sheet of plywood and some pocket screws, you can too.

Storage with strength. Hidden pocket screws ensure this handsome bench will grace your home for years to come.

## Cut to Length

For my stock, I used ³⁄₄" Baltic birch plywood. Using your circular saw and a clamped-down straightedge jig to guide the cut, begin ripping your lumber. For tips on using the circular saw and guide, read the Rules for Using Tools section. Start by ripping a 16"-wide panel from which you'll cut both side pieces, then cut them to length. Now rip the bench-top and bottom shelf to 15¹⁄₄" wide to accommodate for the ³⁄₄" thickness of the back panel. Next cut the back panel to match the length of the benchtop and bottom shelf. Finally cut the height of the center divider to set the height of the storage cubbies.

## This is My Good Side

Before cutting the side profiles with your jigsaw, examine your stock to choose the best outside face. With plywood it is more than likely that you'll have patches in several places; so make sure these will not be exposed.

Using a paper pattern for the feet, trace the outline along the bottom, flip the pattern for the opposite foot, then connect the tops of the feet with a square. For marking the notch on the top, trace the inside of a roll of packing tape.

Now you are ready to cut the profile with your jigsaw. (If you haven't picked up any Bosch T380B Xtra-Clean jigsaw blades, we highly recommend them.) First cut the insides of the feet, making sure to stay on the waste side of your line. To connect the feet, start by cutting a gradual curve until you reach the connecting line as seen in the photo below. Then remove the rest of the waste.

To remove the wood for the top corner notch, first make several relief cuts — slice toward the line as if you were cutting a pizza. This will make it easier to

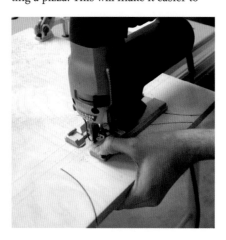

Angle of attack. Your jigsaw can't turn at sharp angles, so make a curved cut to the line.

cut the final curve of the notch with your jigsaw or with a coping saw.

Then grab your rasp and some #120-grit sandpaper to clean up all your jigsaw cuts and you're almost ready for assembly.

## Prepare for Pocket Screws

To make assembly a breeze, it's a good idea to cut all your pocket-screw holes in advance. First examine your stock for the best faces, then use your pocket-screw jig to make four evenly spaced holes along the ends of the three large panels. The faces needing pocket screws are the bottom of the benchtop, the bottom of the bottom shelf and the back of the back panel. The center divider needs only one row of holes along its top edge. Once all of your pocket-screw holes are drilled, sand all your parts up to #150-grit.

## Upside-down Assembly

To assemble, start by placing the benchtop on two 2" blocks of scrap with the pocket holes facing up. Clamping these scrap blocks to the side panels provides a square platform for attaching the benchtop and creates the proper seat depth of 2". After flushing the benchtop to the front of the side panels, attach it with 1¹⁄₄" pocket screws.

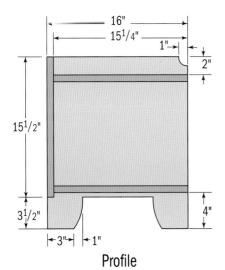

**Profile**

## Parts List

| NO. | PART | STOCK | THICKNESS X WIDTH X LENGTH | |
|-----|------|-------|--------|--------|
| | | | **INCHES** | **MILLIMETERS** |
| 1 | Bench-top | Plywood | $3/4 \times 15^{1}/4 \times 46^{1}/2$ | $19 \times 387 \times 1181$ |
| 1 | Bottom shelf | Plywood | $3/4 \times 15^{1}/4 \times 46^{1}/2$ | $19 \times 387 \times 1181$ |
| 1 | Back panel | Plywood | $3/4 \times 15^{1}/2 \times 46^{1}/2$ | $19 \times 387 \times 1181$ |
| 2 | Sides | Plywood | $3/4 \times 16 \times 19$ | $19 \times 406 \times 483$ |
| 1 | Center divider | Plywood | $3/4 \times 15^{1}/4 \times 11^{1}/2$ | $19 \times 387 \times 292$ |

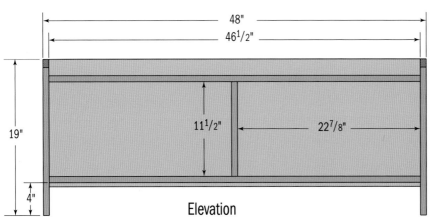

**Elevation**

Next, locate the center of the bench-top and clamp a block in place to keep the center divider square as you drive the screws. Again, keep this piece flush to the front.

To position the bottom of the bench to the sides, clamp two $11^{1}/2$" offcuts to the sides to provide a square platform. This prevents the bottom shelf from rocking on the center divider as you tighten your pocket screws.

After attaching the bottom shelf, mark its center and square up the center divider. Use your countersink bit to drill four holes and secure the bottom shelf to the center divider with #8 $\times$ $1^{1}/4$" flathead wood screws.

To attach the back, flip the bench forward so it is lying on its face, flush the back panel to the top of the sides, then drive home the pocket screws. Then use your countersink bit to drill four evenly spaced holes to secure the back to the benchtop, and repeat to join the back to the bottom shelf.

Now break all the edges with some #120-grit sandpaper and you're ready to finish.

### For that Store-bought Look

To match my bed, I wanted this bench to have a contemporary finish. The goal

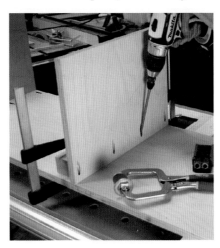

Square with scrap. A clamped block ensures the center divider remains straight as you drive the pocket screws.

was to have a dark mahogany look with a touch of grain showing through, while still masking the plys on the exposed edges.

It sounds like a lot to accomplish, but heavily thinned latex enamel paint works perfectly. To thin the latex enough to allow a gradual build of color, begin by adding the paint to a cup of water. Once it has reached the consistency of chocolate milk, test the paint on an offcut. Once the consistency seems right, build up two to three coats of paint on your bench, until the wood reaches a rich, dark color but still has some grain peeking through.

When painting with this thinned-down latex, don't start at the corners. When you paint the vertical sides, the paint will inevitably run down and fill in the corners. By not painting the corners first, you eliminate this fun "extra" coat and end up with a more even finish all around. For the exposed edges of the plywood, apply multiple coats (it doesn't hurt to use the extra-thick paint at the bottom of your cup — the plys will soak up a lot).

After that, apply two coats of a glossy wiping varnish, sanding with #320-grit between the coats. Finally, buff down any remaining dust nibs with #0000 steel wool then apply a coat of paste wax.

# Country Tool & Toy Chest

**BY MEGAN FITZPATRICK**

This rustic hinged-lid box is a design traditionally used as a basic tool chest, but I thought a scaled-down version would make a great chest for stashing toys (with the addition of a safety hinge) or extra grocery bags in the kitchen. It is adapted from a chest shown in John A. and Joyce C. Nelson's "The Big Book of Weekend Woodworking" (Lark Books).

## A Trip to the Home Center

A trip to the home center is the beginning of every "I Can Do That" project, and there I assessed every #2 pine 1x12 in stock. Because I'd decided to paint the chest, I wasn't concerned with the grain as much as getting the straightest, flattest boards. While two 8'-long boards would have been enough to construct the chest, I purchased an extra, just in case. I also bought a quart of red paint, 6" strap hinges and a box of 4d finish nails. Even with the extra wood, the materials cost was but $50.

## Rough Cut the Pieces

The top and front are the most visible pieces, so I marked these first and rough cut them to length (with a couple inches to spare) using the miter saw. I then selected the next-clearest areas for the sides, then two boards for the back, and finally the bottom. Offcuts were set aside for the battens and cleats.

## Lay Out the Arches

Arched cutouts on the sides dress up the piece a bit. To lay them out, first mark a line on each piece 1¹¹⁄₁₆" up from the bottom, then measure in 4¹⁄₁₆" from each long edge on both pieces and mark the intersections. Then butt the sides against

one another (feet to feet), set the compass to make a 5¼" radius, then place the point on each mark and draw arcs on the opposite piece. The two arcs on each piece will intersect at the center of your board, forming the arch apex. Cut out each arch with your jigsaw, then clamp the sides together and clean them up using a rasp and sandpaper.

## Chamfered Panels

Because the top, front and back of the chest are 13" wide and a 1x12 is narrower than that, you have to rip two boards to 6½" wide to make each panel. It's nigh on impossible to cut a glue-ready edge with a jigsaw, so to help disguise any resulting gaps at the seam, I used my block plane to chamfer the adjoining edges.

Now you're ready to assemble the box. Glue and clamp the back boards in place

on the sides and drill three ¹⁄₈" pilot holes in each board. Drive 4d finish nails into the holes, then repeat this process for the front boards. Leave the nails proud of the surface to avoid dinging the boards with your hammer, then use a nail set to drive them ¹⁄₁₆" below the surface.

## Top & Bottom

To make the battens, cut two 1" x 13" pieces from your offcuts, trim the front edge at 45° but leave a ¼" flat at the top. To make the top, screw the top pieces to the battens. First snug the two top pieces together on your bench, and lay the battens across either end. Drill countersunk clearance and pilot holes, then attach the battens with #8 x 1½" wood screws.

To make the bottom, first cut your

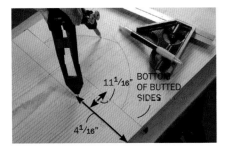

Mark a horizontal line 11$^1/_{16}$" from the bottom of each piece, then measure in 4$^1/_{16}$" from each of the four sides and mark the intersecting points. These are the four points on which you'll place the point of your compass to mark the arches.

Clamp the sides together and use a rasp and sandpaper to clean up the arches. Don't worry if they don't match perfectly; because there's 22" between them on the finished chest, minor differences won't be noticeable.

Hold your plane at a 45° angle to the edge of the board, and shave down the length until you're satisfied with the chamfer. The goal is to draw attention to the "seam," so make sure the chamfer is big enough so that paint doesn't overwhelm it.

After drilling pilot holes, drive 4d nails and leave them a little proud of the surface.

Cut the front and back cleats to size first, then snug the end cleats between them.

cleats to size and nail them around the inside bottom edge of the chest. Now cut the bottom a hair wider than necessary and use your block plane to trim it to fit. Drop the bottom in place, hang the work over the edge of the Workmate so the cleats are supported, then nail the bottom to the cleats from the inside.

## Woodworking Therapy

Sand to #120 grit and apply two coats of bright red paint to the outside and a coat of amber shellac to the interior to seal it. After the paint dries, grab a ring of keys and beat the you-know-what out of the box until you get a lot of lovely dings. Take a rasp to the edges, and for good measure, grab your hammer by the head and use the handle end to whomp the top edge a few times. Once the piece looks distressed (and you feel de-stressed) apply a coat of any dark gel stain over the entire thing. Work the stain into the dings, dents and raw edges. Wipe it off, and voilá – a century of age in just minutes. After the stain is completely dry, apply a coat of paste wax.

## The Finishing Touches

To attach the strap hinges, measure in 4" from the battens on the top, mark the holes with an awl, and drill pilot holes for the screws. The screws that came with the hinges were too long, so we used some we had on hand. You can color the heads black with a Sharpie if you want everything to match. I also attached a length of chain, leaving a few extra loops so the open angle of the top can be easily adjusted.

## Parts List

| NO. | PART | STOCK | INCHES | MILLIMETERS |
|---|---|---|---|---|
| | | | THICKNESS X WIDTH X LENGTH | |
| 4 | Front/backs | Pine | $^3/_4 \times 6^1/_2 \times 22$ | 19 × 165 × 559 |
| 2 | Top | Pine | $^3/_4 \times 6^1/_2 \times 23^1/_2$ | 19 × 165 × 597 |
| 2 | Sides | Pine | $^3/_4 \times 10^3/_4 \times 17$ | 19 × 273 × 432 |
| 1 | Bottom | Pine | $^3/_4 \times 20^1/_2 \times 10^3/_4$ | 19 × 521 × 273 |
| 2 | Battens | Pine | $^3/_4 \times 1 \times 13$ | 19 × 25 × 330 |
| | Cleats* | Pine | $^3/_4 \times 1 \times 72$ | 19 × 25 × 1829 |

* Cut to fit.

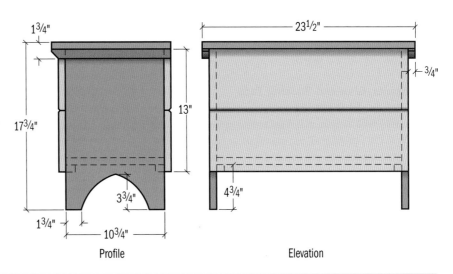

Profile

Elevation

# Mitered CD/DVD Rack

**BY ROBERT W. LANG**

Learning a new skill is often a matter of getting past the scary part. If you can reduce the number of things that can go wrong, you become comfortable enough to push past what once seemed an insurmountable obstacle. Miter joints are never a walk in the park, but they don't have to be a middle-of-the-night trip through the cemetery.

A four-sided frame or box is the usual starting point for mitered joinery. In this scenario, the beginner will likely be frustrated by tiny errors in the degree of angle or the length of the parts. Any errors made will show up in the last joint to be closed.

At this point errors aren't tiny any more. On a square frame with 12" sides, even with only ¹⁄₁₀° of error, the gap at the last corner will still be ⅛". The degree of perfection required is obtainable, but there are two other hurdles to overcome for successful mitering.

This I Can Do That project addresses the two problems that can cause even perfectly cut miters to fail: Getting a strong glue joint and clamping the corners together. There is a simple solution for each, and knowing these will make getting perfect corners easier.

## Two Sticks, Glue and Packing Tape

One 6' length of 1×2 (actual size ¾" × 1½"), and one 2' length of 1×4 (actual size ¾" × 3½") provide all the material. These were available in red oak at our local home center. Look for the straightest pieces in the pile. If you don't have yellow wood glue at home, pick up a small bottle before you leave the store. And while you're there, purchase a roll of clear packing tape.

No other joint looks like a miter. Miter joints allow the wood grain to flow around a corner, without exposing any end grain. Good miters aren't always easy, but a few tricks make them manageable.

Begin by cutting two pieces of 1×2 to 22⅝" long. This length isn't critical, but both pieces should be the same length, and both should have two square ends. Sometimes the material you buy has a ragged end, so I usually cut ¼" or so off the end of a new piece to make sure it's square and clean.

Make a mark on the edge of one of these pieces that's 4½" from the end, and with your combination square draw a line at a 45° angle back toward the end. Only mark one piece — you will use that to set up the miter saw to cut identical lengths.

Swing the miter saw to the right and lock it in at 45°. Without turning on the saw, put your marked piece below the blade and bring the blade down until a tooth of the blade is on the pencil line, with the blade to the left of the line. Let the saw swing back up out of the way and without moving the workpiece, draw a pencil line on the back fence of your miter saw at the end of the workpiece.

When you cut each piece, line up a square end of the 22⅝" pieces with the pencil line, hold the work with your left hand well away from the blade and make the cut. You don't want to clamp a stop-block to the fence because the short piece will be trapped, and the blade could send it flying. Make the cut in one smooth motion and leave the blade all the way down until it stops spinning.

Flip the piece over, and make certain that the angle you just cut is pointing in the opposite direction of the next cut. Line up the square end with the pencil line and make the cut. This procedure will yield all six pieces of the upper part of the rack, with only four saw cuts, and your hands will stay safely away from the blade at all times.

Swing the saw to the 22½° setting to make the cuts for the feet and middle rail. Cut one end of the middle rail, then turn the rail around, measure, mark and cut the other end. The feet can be cut the same way as the short uprights, but it will be better to return the saw to the 90° stop, and tilt the head 22½° to the left.

Bevel cutting the flat face will keep the work on the saw table. There is a chance if you cut it on edge that the short piece could fall into the blade. The two ends of the rail are angled in opposite directions, but the ends of the feet are parallel. Make a pencil line on the fence, and slide the stock up to the line, holding on to the long end of the board as you make the cuts.

## Two Ways Tape Makes it Easy

Sand all the pieces, except the mitered ends with #120-grit sandpaper before assembling. To put the top parts together, lay the three pieces of each section end to end. Hold the ends together with a piece of tape, as seen in the photo below left, then flip the taped pieces over.

Smear some glue on each side of the joints and walk away for about five minutes. The glue will wick up into the short grain, and if you try to put it together now, most of the glue will disappear from the joint, leaving it weak. When you come back, apply more glue and fold the joints together. The tape will act as a hinge, keeping the pieces from sliding apart and holding the ends tightly together.

Flip the pieces over, and use another piece of tape to hold them in position while the glue dries. The tape will stretch, so be careful not to pull it too tight. You should see some glue squeezing out of the joints. Wipe off the excess with a wet rag.

Mark the top of each foot 1½" in from each end and put some glue in between the pencil marks. Again this is a short-grain surface, so let the glue soak in for

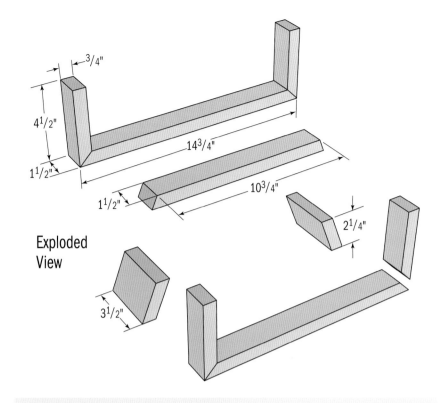

Exploded View

## Parts List

| NO. | PART | STOCK | THICKNESS X WIDTH X LENGTH | | COMMENTS |
| --- | --- | --- | --- | --- | --- |
| | | | INCHES | MILLIMETERS | |
| 2 | Rails | Oak | ¾ × 1½ × 14¾ | 19 × 38 × 375 | 45° miter both ends |
| 4 | Uprights | Oak | ¾ × 1½ × 4½ | 19 × 38 × 115 | 45° miter one ends |
| 1 | Bottom | Oak | ¾ × 1½ × 10¾ | 19 × 38 × 273 | 22½° bevel both ends |
| 2 | Feet | Oak | ¾ × 3½ × 2¼ | 19 × 89 × 57 | 22½° bevel both ends |

five minutes before assembling. Use tape to hold the ends of the center rail to the tops of the feet and allow the glue to dry overnight.

The last step before finishing is to glue the two outer assemblies to the middle rail and feet. Apply some glue to the exposed top of each foot, let it soak

in, then apply more glue to those spots, and along the length of the middle rail. Put the edges of the three rails together, centering the middle rail end-to-end. Use a couple small clamps to hold them in place, or you can wrap some tape around all three instead.

Let the glue dry overnight, remove the tape or clamps and lightly sand the entire project with #150-grit sandpaper. Round the sharp edges slightly and you're ready for a finish. We used an oil-based stain followed by Danish oil to obtain a dark brown satin finish.

Tape as a hinge. Clear packing tape holds the ends of the joints together, and it lets you see what is happening as you assemble the joints.

And as a clamp. Fold the ends up and use the tape to hold the parts in place while the glue dries.

# Canted Wall Box

**BY MEGAN FITZPATRICK**

Adapted from an 1840s piece, this canted wall box is scaled up from the one you'll find in John A. & Joyce C. Nelson's *The Big Book of Weekend Woodworking* (Lark). Making it just a wee bit bigger allowed me to make use of $\frac{1}{2}$" × 6" poplar (which is actually only $5\frac{1}{2}$" wide) without having to make any rip cuts.

## Cut Your Pieces

First, cut the two sides to length with your miter saw, then draw the side pattern on one piece. Clamp the side pieces together, then clamp them flat to your workbench so the offcut area is overhanging the edge. (To help control the two pieces from slipping, you could use carpet tape to help keep them together.) With a jigsaw, carefully cut to the pattern, leaving your lines intact. (If you need instruction on proper jigsaw use or any other step to construct this project, read the Rules for Using Tools section.)

Unclamp the sides from your workbench, but not from one another. Clamp

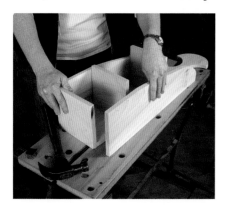

Fit before nailing. Dry fit your pieces before cutting the shelves and bottom to final size. Notice that the sides overlay the bottom and back, and that the back sits on top of the bottom piece.

them cut-edge up in your Workmate then use a rasp, file and sandpaper to refine and smooth the curve, then set them aside.

Now cut the back to length and lay it flat on your bench. Lay out the arcs using the pattern to the right, or mark them out with a compass. Each arc is a half circle; the top radius is $2\frac{3}{4}$", the side radii are 2". Cut with a jigsaw then refine and smooth the arcs.

While you can certainly cut the shelves and bottom to depth according to the cut list, it's beneficial to first cut them a little oversized (the shelves should for now extend past the front of the piece), then do a dry fit of your pieces as shown in the picture at left, and carefully mark the final size. That way, you'll get a custom fit; your shelf edges will match with the front edge of your box. You'll need to do this for the top shelf anyway because you must mark the angle on the front edge to match the side curves. Cut the angle with a jigsaw, then refine the cut as necessary. Use a file to clean up your saw marks. You could, however, forgo the jigsaw altogether for this cut, and instead use a rasp or block plane to establish the angle, then refine it with your file and sandpaper.

## Dry Fit Your Assembly

Now that all the pieces are cut and shaped, do your final sanding prior to assembly. Then dry fit the pieces together as shown, with the back flat on your workbench. Glue isn't necessary for this project because it's small and nails will provide sufficient hold, but you can use glue if you wish. Clamp across the sides at the bottom and at each shelf, snugging the bottom and shelves into place. Be careful not to move the pieces as you tighten the clamps, especially the bottom.

This 19th-century primitive wall box is a perfect place to display some of your treasures … or a hang it by a door for use as a handy receptacle for mail, keys and other small items.

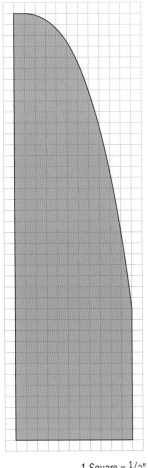

1 Square = $^1/_2$"

**Side Pattern**

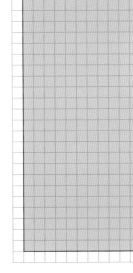

1 Square = $^1/_2$"

**Back Pattern**

## Parts List

| NO. | PART | STOCK | THICKNESS X WIDTH X LENGTH | |
|---|---|---|---|---|
| | | | **INCHES** | **MILLIMETERS** |
| 1 | Back | Poplar | $^1/_2 \times 5^1/_2 \times 25^1/_2$ | 13 × 140 × 648 |
| 2 | Sides | Poplar | $^1/_2 \times 5^1/_2 \times 19^1/_2$ | 13 × 140 × 496 |
| 1 | Bottom | Poplar | $^1/_2 \times 5^1/_2 \times 5^1/_2$ | 13 × 140 × 140 |
| 1 | Middle shelf | Poplar | $^1/_2 \times 5 \times 5^1/_2$ | 13 × 127 × 140 |
| 1 | Top shelf | Poplar | $^1/_2 \times 4^1/_4 \times 5^1/_2$ | 13 × 108 × 140 |

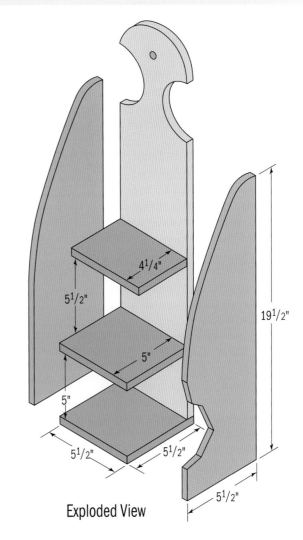

**Exploded View**

It's crucial that the bottom piece be situated properly, as it determines the fit of the back piece.

Using a $^1/_{16}$" standard twist bit, drill pilot holes for 4d nails through the sides and into the back. Be very careful to keep your drill steady; $^1/_2$" stock has little forgiveness for sloppy drilling. Now drive your nails through the sides. Then, drill pilot holes through the sides and into the bottom, and through the bottom into the back, and drive your nails.

Before attaching the shelves, make sure they're exactly where you want them. If they've moved, simply unclamp the workpiece and resituate the shelves. With the back, bottom and sides already nailed in place, you needn't worry about reclamping; you can simply hold the shelf in place with one hand as you drill your pilots through the sides then drive the nails. Once that's done, for added strength you may also wish to drill pilots and drive nails through the back into the shelves.

Now, drill a hanging hole centered 1¾" down from the top edge (I used a ¼" bit), then prime and paint the wall box the color of your choice.

# Pleasant Hill Firewood Box

**BY CHRISTOPHER SCHWARZ**

The buildings at the Shaker Village in Pleasant Hill, Ky., are filled with handy firewood boxes. After a few visits to the colony, I concluded that this example is the best one.

Tucked into a room in the Centre Family Dwelling, this firewood box represents what I like about the Western Shaker furniture styles. This box has a few graceful and unexpected curves, yet it still looks decidedly Shaker.

Building this box is simple. With the exception of the curves on the sides, all the cuts are straight. With the exception of the hinged lid, all the joinery on the box is glue and nails.

The biggest construction challenge is gluing up narrower boards into the panels that make up the box's sides, front and bottom. I glued these up using pocket screws as clamps, however, because this project is painted, there's an easier solution at the home center. In the lumber section of the store you'll likely find wide laminated pine panels that are pieced together at a factory from narrow strips. If you purchase this material, you won't have to glue up any panels and can go right to cutting.

The other option is to buy No. 2 common 1×12s. I bought five 8'-long 1×12s so I could cut around knots. I also bought a small piece of ¼"-thick Masonite. Why? Read on.

## Make a Template

When you're working out a complex design or need to make multiple and identical parts, a full-size template is handy.

With this project, a full-size template helps you get the curves just right and

Repurposed. While originally designed to be used to hold firewood and kindling, this Shaker piece also can be pressed into service as a recycling bin.

helps you fit the pieces to the hinged kindling box. Plus, if you ever need to make more of these boxes, the template will give you a good head start.

Use the illustration to draw your template on the Masonite using a ruler and a compass. All the curves are a 7" radius, so the layout work is easy. Cut the template to shape using a jigsaw and sand the edges until the template looks good and has smooth edges. If you want

to adjust the design, here's your chance to alter it and see how it looks. Glue up all the panels you need and get ready to cut the sides.

## Construction

Trace the template's shape on your side pieces and cut them with your jigsaw. Clamp the two sides together and shape the curves with a rasp and sandpaper so the two are identical. Using the side pieces as a guide, determine the actual width of the box's bottom, the width of the bottom of the kindling box and the width of the front of the kindling box. Cut these three pieces to finished size. Glue and nail them between the sides.

Now work on the front of the box. Cut this panel as close to size as possible — I like to leave it a hair long. Glue and nail the front to the carcase. Trim any overhang with your block plane or #100-grit sandpaper.

Now repeat the same process with the back pieces. I used three horizontal boards for the back. Two of the boards were 1 × 12s. The third one was ripped to fit just right. If you like, you can plane a small chamfer on the back boards' long edges as a decorative detail. This adds a shadow line where the backboards meet one another.

Crosscut the hinge rail and lid at the same time so they are the same length. Your miter saw is an excellent tool for this

sort of operation. Screw your hinges to both the hinge rail and the lid. Then glue and nail the hinge rail to the carcase.

The last bit of construction is the box's front edge. I took the difficult route to fit this piece in place. I notched out the underside of the workpiece with a handsaw and chisel so the notches nest neatly over the curve on the sides. You can fit the piece any way your skills or tools allow.

Disassemble the lid and hinges and sand the project up to #150-grit. Break all the sharp edges of the piece by hand with a piece of old sandpaper. The finish is simply three coats of semi-gloss paint. As shown, this piece is a little more barn red than the original. But it is still a red that is consistent with the original Shaker paint recipes. You should, of course, finish yours to suit your decor.

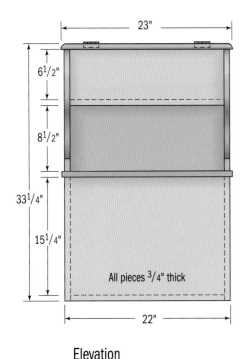

Elevation

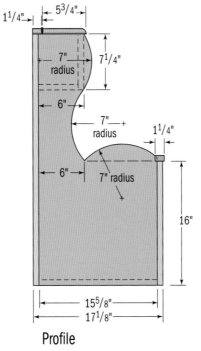

Profile

Watch those curves. A full-size template helps in many ways. It allows you to refine the design details, determine the finished sizes of key components and to lay out your cuts.

## Parts List

| NO. | PART | STOCK | THICKNESS X WIDTH X LENGTH | | COMMENTS |
|-----|------|-------|------|------|----------|
| | | | INCHES | MILLIMETERS | |
| 2 | Sides | Pine | $3/4 \times 15^5/8 \times 32^1/2$ | 19 × 397 × 826 | |
| 1 | Front | Pine | $3/4 \times 16 \times 22$ | 19 × 406 × 559 | |
| | Back | Pine | $3/4 \times 32^1/2 \times 22$ | 19 × 826 × 559 | Three boards |
| 1 | Bottom | Pine | $3/4 \times 15^5/8 \times 20^1/2$ | 19 × 397 × 521 | |
| 1 | Kindling box bottom | Pine | $3/4 \times 5^1/4 \times 20^1/2$ | 19 × 133 × 521 | |
| 1 | Kindling box front | Pine | $3/4 \times 7^1/4 \times 20^1/2$ | 19 × 184 × 521 | |
| 1 | Kindling box lid | Pine | $3/4 \times 5^3/4 \times 23$ | 19 × 146 × 584 | |
| 1 | Hinge rail | Pine | $3/4 \times 1^1/4 \times 23$ | 19 × 32 × 584 | |
| 1 | Front edge | Pine | $3/4 \times 1^1/4 \times 22^1/2$ | 19 × 32 × 572 | Notched around sides |

# Painted Cupboard

**BY GLEN HUEY**

Small cupboards fit anywhere in your home. This piece can hang in the kitchen to catch any pantry overflow or it can look equally impressive hanging in your living room showcasing your collectibles. Hey, you may even want to build two when you see how easy this cupboard is built.

This project will also serve as an excellent teaching tool for a dramatic finish. Once I walk you through the basic steps, you'll not only find out how much fun it can be to beat-up a finish (I'm not kidding), but you'll definitely say, "I can do that!"

Start by selecting and cutting to length the material for your shelves and the cupboard sides. The shelves will need to be ripped from the purchased stock. Draw a line on each piece that is 4¾" from one edge and make the cut along that line with the jigsaw.

If you're like most of us the cuts will need to be straightened up with your hand plane. Make sure that you keep the edge squared to the face of the piece and trimmed to the layout line.

Next, pull out your pocket-screw jig and place two holes at each end of the shelves. Since these will be inside the cupboard there is little need to select the top or bottom of each piece, however, you should study the case sides in order to place the best face toward the outside of the piece.

## The Box is Formed

The building of the box begins with attaching the top and bottom shelves to the case sides. Make sure to align the front edges and install the pieces with the holes facing outward.

Next, lay out the location of the middle shelf and attach it as well. You'll find it

Most of the construction on this piece is done with pocket screws. This mini-pocket guide makes the work easy, allows you to work in tight spaces, and best of all, it's affordable!

easier to drive the screws for the shelf if you cut a scrap to fit between the top shelf and the middle shelf. With pieces positioned as shown in the photo below, it would be impossible for the shelf to move as the screws are installed.

Flip the assembled portion of the case and install the second case side the same way. The only tricky spot might be adding the screws to the middle shelf because your drill may not fit in the open space.

Select and cut the case front stiles from your stock, position the box on its back and attach the pieces so that the edges of the stiles are flush to the sides of the box. Add a thin bead of glue for reinforcement and make the connection with flat-head woodscrews that are driven into holes made with a ⅜" countersink. You'll want to fill those holes with a matching ⅜" plug, then sand the assembly with #150-grit sandpaper.

## Build the Flat Panel Door

The door is made from bead board tongue-and-groove panelling, but I found it in the home center stores referred to as reverse flooring. Call it what you want, it makes an easy frame for a frame-and-panel door. First you need to rip the tongue portion from three 24" pieces. Use the same process for this operation as you did to rip the shelves to width. Draw in the cut line, cut close with the jigsaw and clean up the cut with the hand plane.

Next, take the measurements for the four pieces that will make up the door's frame. Measure from top to bottom and subtract ⅛" to arrive at the length of the stiles. To get the length of the rails repeat the same step beginning with the width of the door opening.

There are two stiles and two rails. Off to the miter saw to make 45° cuts on both ends of all pieces. Cut the angles so that the groove is on the inside after the angles are added. You'll need that groove to hold the plywood panel. Either set up a stop block to ensure that the two stiles match in length as do the rails or, align the rails and cut both pieces at the same time. Repeat this step for the two stiles as well. Once cut, arrange the pieces to check the fit.

When assembling the case, it's always smart to work down towards the bench, rather than trying to balance the sides on top of the shelves. Note the spacer I'm using to keep the shelves aligned accurately.

Rather than juggle the pieces to keep things flush, put a clamp across the piece and save the frustration.

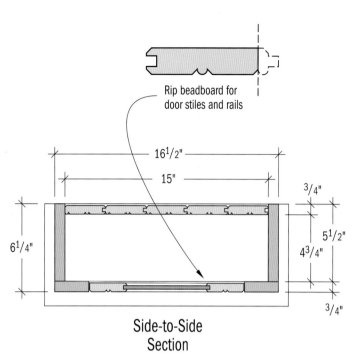

Rip beadboard for
door stiles and rails

16$\frac{1}{2}$"

15"

$\frac{3}{4}$"

5$\frac{1}{2}$"

4$\frac{3}{4}$"

6$\frac{1}{4}$"

$\frac{3}{4}$"

### Side-to-Side
### Section

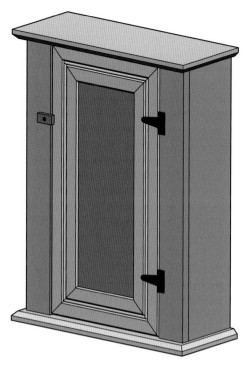

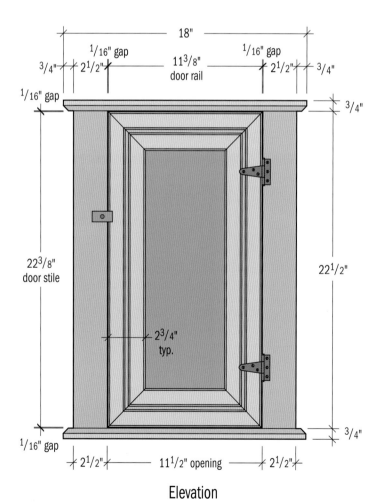

18"

$\frac{1}{16}$" gap

$\frac{1}{16}$" gap

$\frac{3}{4}$"

2$\frac{1}{2}$"

11$\frac{3}{8}$"
door rail

2$\frac{1}{2}$"

$\frac{3}{4}$"

$\frac{1}{16}$" gap

$\frac{3}{4}$"

22$\frac{3}{8}$"
door stile

22$\frac{1}{2}$"

2$\frac{3}{4}$"
typ.

$\frac{1}{16}$" gap

$\frac{3}{4}$"

2$\frac{1}{2}$"

11$\frac{1}{2}$" opening

2$\frac{1}{2}$"

### Elevation

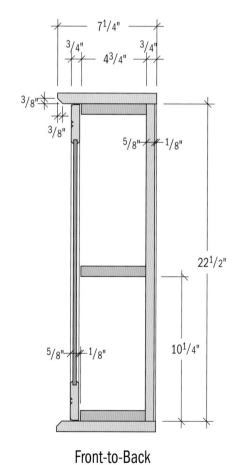

7$\frac{1}{4}$"

$\frac{3}{4}$"

4$\frac{3}{4}$"

$\frac{3}{4}$"

$\frac{3}{8}$"

$\frac{3}{8}$"

5$\frac{8}$"

$\frac{1}{8}$"

22$\frac{1}{2}$"

10$\frac{1}{4}$"

5$\frac{8}$"

$\frac{1}{8}$"

### Front-to-Back
### Section

The case front stiles define the space that the door will fit within. Hold the pieces flush to the case sides and fit the door to the space, rather than trying to allow the space for the door and trim the stiles. It's just easier. Countersunk flat head screws hold the stiles in place, and a little putty and sanding make them invisible once the piece is painted.

To make the connection of the angled pieces you are again going to use the pocket screw. Add the pocket-screw holes to the stiles of the door only and position the pocket-screw jig so that the pocket does not show from the edge of the door (next page bottom left photo). Prepare two pocket holes per corner of the door.

Driving the screws for the doorframe can be fussy. Position the pieces face down on your bench and add a clamp to the piece accepting the screws (next page top photo). Hold the matching piece in position and carefully drive the screws home. The accurate cutting of the angles will bring the frame into square as you attach the final corner.

With the frame assembled, take the measurement for the plywood or flat panel. You need to get accurate measurements then add ¼" to the overall sizes to both the length and width. Cut the panel

I'm particularly proud of using bead board material to create the door frame, though it does require a little extra ripping.

One trick with the frame is making sure that all of your cuts leave the bead detail on the frame matching at the corners. It doesn't take much to kick the pattern out of whack.

## Parts List

| NO. | PART | STOCK | THICKNESS X WIDTH X LENGTH | |
|-----|------|-------|----------------------------|--|
| | | | INCHES | MILLIMETERS |
| 2 | case sides | paint grade | ¾ × 5½ × 22½ | 19 × 140 × 572 |
| 2 | case top and bottom | paint grade | ¾ × 7¼ × 18 | 19 × 184 × 457 |
| 2 | case front sides | paint grade | ¾ × 2½ × 22½ | 19 × 64 × 572 |
| 3 | shelves | paint grade | ¾ × 4¾ × 15 | 19 × 121 × 381 |
| 2 | door rails | flooring | ⅝ × 2¾ × 11½ | 16 × 70 × 292 |
| 2 | door stiles | flooring | ⅝ × 2¾ × 22½ | 16 × 70 × 572 |
| 1 | flat panel | plywood | ¼ × 6¼ × 17¼ | 6 × 159 × 438 |
| 1 | turn button | paint grade | ¾ × 1½ × ⅜ | 19 × 38 × 10 |
| - | back boards | flooring | ⅝ × 14⅞ × 22½ | 16 × 378 × 572 |

to size with the jigsaw and clean any cut marks with the plane. In crosscutting the plywood, if you score the line with a utility knife, you can reduce possible splintering and obtain a cleaner cut.

Remove all screws from one stile to allow the panel to slide into the frame. After the panel is installed, add the screws back to the frame and your door is built.

## Adding the Crowning Touch

The case is topped (and bottomed) with a separate piece of stock. Cut both pieces to size according to the cut sheet. In order to dress up the cupboard a bit, add a beveled edge to three sides of these pieces.

Draw a line on the ends and the front of both the top and bottom that is half the thickness of the stock or $3/8$". Next, draw a line that is $3/8$" in front the edges on those same three sides. A hand plane will remove the material between the two lines, creating the bevel.

Position the box onto the top and align the back edges. Slide the box along the top until the overhang is equal on both ends. Once set add screws through the box into the top. It's best to prepare these holes with a countersink bit. Repeat the steps to attach the bottom, also using four screws, one at each corner area. Clamps will keep everything held tight during this operation.

The back boards for the cupboard are the same material that is used for the door frame. Take the measurements for the pieces and cut them to length. It is

To hold the door frame together, I'm once again using pocket screws. The pockets need to be oriented across the corner joint, but drilled so that the pocket isn't visible from the edge of the door frame. Both the pieces in this picture are stiles. Don't cut any pockets in the rails, or you'll have twice as many holes as you need.

Clamping the door rail to your bench during assembly makes things easier to handle. Nothing like an extra hand to help.

Don't forget to slip the panel into the frame before attaching the last stile.

necessary to fit the first four pieces, position them into the case and find the correct width for the final piece of the back then reduce the measurement by ⅛". This will help with seasonal adjustments of the back due to humidity changes. It will need to be ripped to the final size.

Mark the exact width of the final piece beginning from the existing grooved edge of the stock. You'll cut the tongue area to complete the fit. Use the jigsaw to make the cut and straighten the cut with your hand plane. Remember this is the back and it fits tight to the sides as viewed from the interior of the case.

After finishing, nails are driven through the boards and into the shelves to install the back.

## The Stain, Paint, Rub Finish

The finishing process for the cupboard starts with staining the piece. Use an aniline dye stain that is mixed to the manufacturer's directions. It doesn't really matter what the exact color is, so long as it is a shade of brown.

A simple chamfer on the front and both side edges of the top and bottom pieces adds a simple, but effective detail to the finished look. Mark the defining edges of the chamfer in pencil on the pieces and then use your block plane to remove the material. It sounds a little tedious, but it's actually fun to add a hand-crafted detail to your piece.

The case is centered on both the top and bottom pieces, and they are attached using flat head screws in countersunk holes.

The first four pieces of the back remain full-width, and only the last piece is trimmed in width to fit the case.

Applying the stain could not be easier. Paint the stain onto the cupboard with a foam brush. Make sure that the entire piece is coated, with stain dripping from the wood. Allow that to sit for five minutes then wipe any excess away with a dry cloth.

Once the stain is dry, in about 6 -8 hours, lightly sand the cupboard with a #400-grit paper to knock down any raised grain (water will raise the grain of wood).

The next step is to add a coat of shellac. The best way to do this is with an aerosol can of shellac. With the can about six inches from the piece, add a single coat of sprayed shellac. The idea is to apply a level coat without any runs or drips, so keep the can moving. When you stop without stopping the spray, you will get runs. When the shellac is dry lightly sand the surface with #400-grit sandpaper.

Choose a paint color for the inside of the piece and paint the interior with two coats. Use an acrylic latex paint and don't forget the backboards. I like to select a color that is bold and will almost shock when the door is opened. The color should bounce off of the mellow painted exterior. Of course, you can pick and choose which colors you like best. The paint process is the same with each color.

Next, apply the paint to the exterior of the cupboard. Use an acrylic latex paint — I chose an off white, almost crème color. Work with small areas at a time because if the paint dries too quickly you won't be able to add the wear to the piece.

As the paint dries it will reach a point where it is dry enough to allow manipulation of the paint without smearing the surface. This is when you spring into action. Rub areas that will simulate ages of wear. Work around the turn button — this is where the greatest amount of wear would be in an antique piece. Create wear at the corners, along the top and bottom of the cupboard and lightly on the sides of the piece.

Create as much wear as you like, but don't overdo it. It's easy to pass the antique look and get into the beaten up stage. The great thing about this process is that you can always go back and add paint to cover overly worn areas without it being obvious in the finished piece.

With the paint complete and dry add a coat of paste wax to the cupboard then in-

Apply the stain liberally using a foam brush. Let the stain penetrate the wood for about 5 minutes, then wipe off the excess using a dry cloth.

After the stain is dry, apply a coat of shellac. Keep the can moving while you're spraying to prevent the shellac from running or dripping.

Apply the paint with a foam brush. Let the paint dry for a few minutes, then begin rubbing the paint off in some areas. This will create wear areas and give the piece an old, used look.

stall the hinges. I've darkened the regular strap style hinges from the home center with gun bluing that is used to color the steel on gun barrels.

Place the hinges and screws into the solution until they're black, remove them and allow all to dry. Always use rubber gloves and avoid letting the bluing mixture touch your skin.

The turn button is made from scrap. Begin with a 1½" wide portion chopped from one of the leftover pieces. Next spin the cut off at the miter saw and slice away the ⅜" thick piece that is the button. Smooth any sharp edges and add the screw into the center of the button. The turn button mounts ⅔ up the edge of the door on the case stile where it can spin to lock the door.

Add the backboards by nailing them with 4d finish nails, one nail per piece, located just off of the grooved edge, and the cupboard is ready for placement in your home.

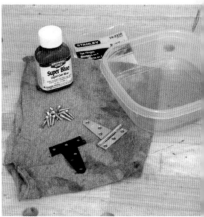

Gun bluing will turn off-the-shelf hinges black, giving them the look of iron.

# Gent's Chest

**BY MEGAN FITZPATRICK**

Common in the 19th-century, a "Gentle-man's Tool Chest" typically contained a set of fancy household tools including the first "multi-tools" — a handsome handle into which a variety of tools including gimlets, drivers, chisels and the like could be fitted. The chest might also include a small brass-backed saw, a filigreed square, dividers, a brass ham-mer and more — "showcase tools" for the squire who simply liked to putter around the house.

This project is an adaptation of a 19th-century example, made simpler by the use of dimensional lumber, nailed butt joints and applied moulding – and it was built using a small set of tools (though a powered miter saw was certainly not found in the gentleman's tool set!).

## A Basic Box

The basic box construction couldn't be simpler. Cut two 18"-long pieces of 1x8 (which is, of course, actually 7$\frac{1}{4}$" wide) and two 7$\frac{3}{4}$"-long pieces at the miter saw. Clamp them into a box shape with the front and back overlapping the ends. Drill three pilot holes through the long grain of the front and back and into the end grain at each corner, eyeballing the location at the top, middle and bottom of each corner. There's no need to be persnickety about a symmetric layout — the joint will be covered with moulding. Sink 4d finish nails in your pilot holes to secure the box parts together.

Glue cleats at the bottom edge of the front and back (nail them — or clamp them in place until the glue dries).

To fit the bottom to size, cut a 16$\frac{1}{2}$"-long piece of 1x10, then clamp

a straightedge to guide your jigsaw's shoe, and cut it to 7$\frac{3}{4}$" wide (or just a hair under), and use your block plane to trim it to the perfect width and length to drop snugly onto your cleats. Nail it in place.

The lid is an 18"-long piece of 1x10 (9$\frac{1}{4}$" wide), attached with two butt hinges mortised into the back and lid.

## Gussy it Up

With the basic box built, let's make it look better. That's going to involve a lot of 45° miter cuts of what my local home center calls "outside L" (a.k.a. "corner mould-ing"). You'll need at least 12' or so (but you might want to buy a little extra).

Mitered moulding gets wrapped around the entire bottom; on the lid, the two front corners are mitered while at the back of either side the cut is at 90°.

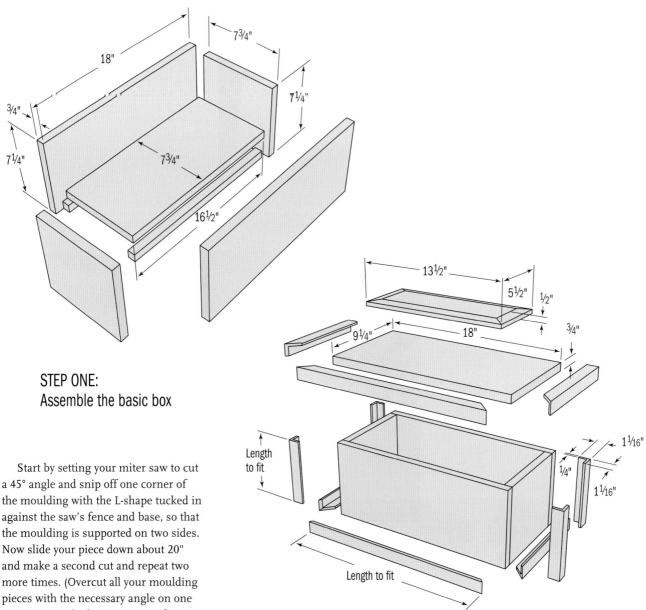

**STEP ONE:**
Assemble the basic box

**STEP TWO:**
Apply moulding & panel

Start by setting your miter saw to cut a 45° angle and snip off one corner of the moulding with the L-shape tucked in against the saw's fence and base, so that the moulding is supported on two sides. Now slide your piece down about 20" and make a second cut and repeat two more times. (Overcut all your moulding pieces with the necessary angle on one corner.) Now do the same to cut four 11"-long pieces (two for the top, two for the bottom).

Slide one 20"-long piece of moulding over the front edge of the top, line up the cut at the corner, then use a pencil to mark at the back where your cut for the other corner begins. Do the same with all your pieces – and mark the correct cut direction for the second angle (just to keep things straight — er, angled).

Back at the miter saw, reset for 45° in the other direction, make the cuts for the other ends of your mitered pieces, then reset to 90° for the lid's two side pieces.

With the pieces cut and fit, glue and nail the long piece to the front of the box lid. On the lid sides, apply glue at the front; use nails at the front and back (to accommodate seasonal movement and

## Parts List

| NO. | PART | STOCK | THICKNESS X WIDTH X LENGTH | |
|---|---|---|---|---|
| | | | INCHES | MILLIMETERS |
| 2 | front/back | pine | $3/4 \times 7^1/4 \times 18$ | 19 × 184 × 457 |
| 2 | ends | pine | $3/4 \times 7^1/4 \times 7^3/4$ | 19 × 184 × 197 |
| 1 | bottom | pine | $3/4 \times 7^3/4 \times 16^1/2$ | 19 × 89 × 419 |
| 1 | lid | pine | $3/4 \times 9^1/4 \times 18$ | 19 × 76 × 457 |
| 2 | cleats | pine | $3/4 \times 3/4 \times 16^1/4$ | 19 × 19 × 413 |
| 1 | top panel | poplar | $1/2 \times 5^1/2 \times 13^1/2$ | 13 × 76 × 343 |
| 1 | outside L moulding | pine | $1/4 \times 1^1/16 \times 144*$ | 6 × 27 × 3,658 |

* Rough total length needed; it's a good idea to buy a little extra when working with miters.

The trickiest part of this build is getting all the miter joints to fit snugly. I find it's easiest to hold one 45° corner in place while I mark the moulding at the inside back corner for the second cut (no measuring). And I always mark an angled line on the top of the moulding in the direction my second cut needs to go.

cross-grain construction). Attach the bottom pieces in the same way.

With your miter saw set for 90°, set a stop 6$\frac{1}{8}$" to the left of the blade and cut the four pieces that wrap the corners, then nail them in place butted against the bottom moulding.

## Top Panel

To dress up the top more, cut a $\frac{1}{2}$" x 5$\frac{1}{2}$" x 13$\frac{1}{2}$" piece of poplar (or whatever $\frac{1}{2}$"-thick stock is available at your home center). Set a combination square to 1" and mark a line in from each edge of the top face. Use a block plane to cut a bevel from the edge to your lines. Center the panel inside the moulding on the top, then glue and nail it in place.

## Finishing Touches

The hinges are 2"-long brass butt hinges with $\frac{5}{8}$"-wide leaves, mortised into the underside of the lid and the back. I used my combination square to mark the depth and width for each mortise, defined those extents with a chisel, then removed the waste with a series of chisel cuts.

The finish is mahogany gel stain on the inside, and two coats of dark green latex paint on the exterior.

This "gent's box" is now ready to be loaded with my (not-so-fancy) set of household tools.

When cutting the hinge mortises on the top edge of your back, clamp an offcut on the backside; the narrow piece of stock that forms the back of the mortise is fragile.

# Shaker Carry Box

**BY MEGAN FITZPATRICK**

This form is typically called a Shaker silverware tray — but it comes in handy for ferrying all sorts of things hither and yon.

I got lucky at the big box store in finding some perfectly straight, flat and clear $1/2$"-thick white pine with a bird's-eye-like pitch-pocket pattern.

At my home center, thin stock is available in nothing longer than 3' lengths. So to be sure I'd have plenty of that pretty "bird's-eye" for all my parts, I picked up three 3'-long and two 2'-long $1/2$" x 6" boards.

A design note: The dovetailed piece that inspired this version (which can be found in the October 2007 issue of *Popular Woodworking Magazine*, #164) has half-pins at the bottom (and top) of the ends, which helps to support the sides as you lift. And for the notched construction shown here, it would arguably be a bit stronger to have the joints reversed so that notches on the ends support the front and back when you pick up the box.

But reversing the notches would mean two more shoulder cuts to bring the box ends flush with the outside faces of the front and back — technically, you would be cutting one box joint by hand at each corner (and a box joint is typically a machine joint). Those additional shoulders would make the pieces harder to fit well so I elected to keep it simple. Besides, I'm not planning to put anything heavy

in the piece; the nails will hold it together just fine.

You could also choose to simply reverse the joints and inset the ends so as to avoid a box joint — but I don't think that looks as clean (you'll find a bonus SketchUp drawing online for this approach).

Whichever approach you choose, the size of the workpieces remains constant; only the joint layout changes.

**First Cuts**

The ends are $5^1/2$" wide — which is the actual width of 6"-wide dimensional lumber — so those two pieces need only be cut to their final $9^1/2$" lengths, which I did at the miter saw.

The front and back are 16$\frac{1}{2}$" long but only 4" wide. So before cutting them to length, mark out the cutline and use a jigsaw to cut them to width. If you have a little practice under your belt, you don't really need to set up a straightedge for this rip cut. Yes, you need the cut to be straight — but you can arrange the factory edge at the top and turn your cut to the bottom (and of course, you can quickly clean up your cut if necessary using a block plane). Now cut the front and back to length.

## Joinery Layout

Set your adjustable square to $\frac{1}{2}$" — or for more precise work, set it to the actual thickness of your wood. Put your wood face-down (or up) on your Workmate, then set the square's stock on the wood and drop the rule down over the edge of your workpiece until it meets the table surface. Then tighten the thumbscrew to lock the rule in place.

Using that setting and a pencil, mark (or scribe with an X-Acto knife) a layout line on both faces and the top and bottom edges of both end pieces and the front and back. This is more easily accomplished with a marking gauge if you have one.

The notched cutouts are all 2" x $\frac{1}{2}$". Reset your adjustable square for 2", then on each workpiece, mark a line from your first layout line to the edge of the piece on both faces, and across the end. It doesn't matter off which long edge you register the square for the front and back; the layout line is at the centerline of the board. On the end pieces, register off the bottom edge.

## Time to Saw

We recommend a dozuki as your first handsaw, in large part because you can get a decent one at the home center. This Japanese saw cuts on the pull stroke, and the one in our kit has a back that stops short of the end of the sawplate, as you can see in the picture on the previous page. That's important, because the 2"-deep shoulder cuts can't be made if you don't have 2" of sawplate under the back — and this saw doesn't. So as I finish each long cut, I nibble away my cutline with the toe of the blade.

To make these cuts, pinch across the work with your off-hand using the pads

of your fingers to align the sawplate with your cutline. With your index finger extended toward the end of the saw, grasp the handle just enough to keep it from flying out of your grasp.

To start the cut, "hover" just barely on the work and pull the saw toward you. Align your body so that you can pull the saw straight back (and push it forward) using your shoulder to supply a locomotive-like motion. Saw straight down to your baseline, then make the shorter cut — and on to the next one.

After all your notches are cut, dry-fit the pieces to ensure that you've sawn the mating surfaces on each one flat and straight. If necessary clean up your cuts with a sharp chisel.

Once your joints are fit, lay out the curve across the top and the handle holes on the two end pieces. Cut the top curves

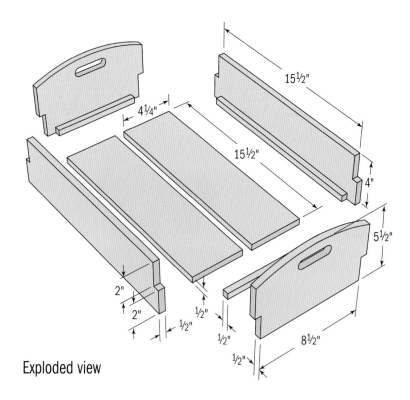

Exploded view

with a jigsaw. Then drill a hole inside the handle waste on each end piece, into which you can insert your jigsaw blade, then cut those, too. If clean-up is required, use a rasp, file and/or sandpaper.

## Hammer Time

It's almost time to nail everything together. But first, cut cleats to fit inside the joined pieces, and glue and clamp them in place aligned with the bottom edge of both sides and the front and back. The notches make it easy to properly align the workpieces while you clamp them square. Drill two pilot holes through the long grain and into the end grain of each joint, then sink 5d finish nails to secure it together. Rip your bottom boards and cut them to length then drop them in place. A coat or two of clear Watco, and you're done.

## Parts List

| | | | THICKNESS X WIDTH X LENGTH | | |
|---|---|---|---|---|---|
| NO. | PART STOCK | | INCHES | MILLIMETERS | |
| 2 | ends | pine | $\frac{1}{2} \times 5\frac{1}{2} \times 9\frac{1}{2}$ | 13 × 140 × 241 | |
| 2 | front/back | pine | $\frac{1}{2} \times 4 \times 16\frac{1}{2}$ | 13 × 102 × 419 | |
| 2 | bottom boards | pine | $\frac{1}{2} \times 4\frac{1}{4} \times 15\frac{1}{2}$ | 13 × 108 × 394 | |
| 4 | cleats | pine | $\frac{1}{2} \times \frac{1}{2}$ | 13 × 13 | *cut to fit |

Just shy of your cutline, pinch with your fingers to form a guide for the cut. Slight changes in finger pressure will micro-adjust where the sawplate falls.

Hold your chisel at 90° to the work and gently pare toward the shoulder to create a flat mating surface for your joint. If you need to pare the end-grain surface, take lighter cuts — and use a sharp chisel.

# Egg Crate Shelves

**BY ROBERT W. LANG**

The premise for our "I Can Do That" column is that you don't need a lot of tools or experience to make a good-looking, functional project. For these shelves, we decided to put our theory to the test, and dragged the non-woodworkers on our staff out to the shop. In an afternoon, they were nearly ready to assemble a set of egg crate shelves.

The name for these shelves comes from the simple joint that holds them together, also called a half-lap joint. Each half of the joint is a notch that fits over the other piece. When put together, the two notches interlock, making a very strong and stable structure. The good news for the beginner is that these don't have to fit perfectly to work effectively.

While this isn't the fanciest joint in woodworking, it's strong and forgiving, and a good opportunity to learn about laying out and cutting joints. But before we get to cutting the joints, let's look at the design.

The material is 1 × 6 poplar, which actually measures ¾" × 5¼". All of the parts for a set of shelves as shown can be cut from two 8'-long pieces. This width of material is good for holding CDs, DVDs, paperback books or small objets d'art. Some of our staff members chose to use wider 1 × 8 material to better hold larger books. In either case, using the width as it comes from the home center or lumberyard greatly simplifies the work.

The shelves can be adapted in size for different purposes. A simple version with just two uprights and two shelves works well in the bathroom or as a desk

accessory, while a larger version can be hung on a wall. You can tailor the depth, height and width to suit your needs or sense of style.

Leave at least 2" of board length past any joints; there is a chance that the wood beyond the joint can split when put together. To make assembly easier and prevent sagging, keep the space between joints less than 24".

The two key elements for success in this project are getting the notches in the proper place, and making them the correct size. We have a trick to make each of those easier, and there are enough joints to give you plenty of practice. Our beginners struggled with the first few cuts, but by the end of the day they were getting good results quickly.

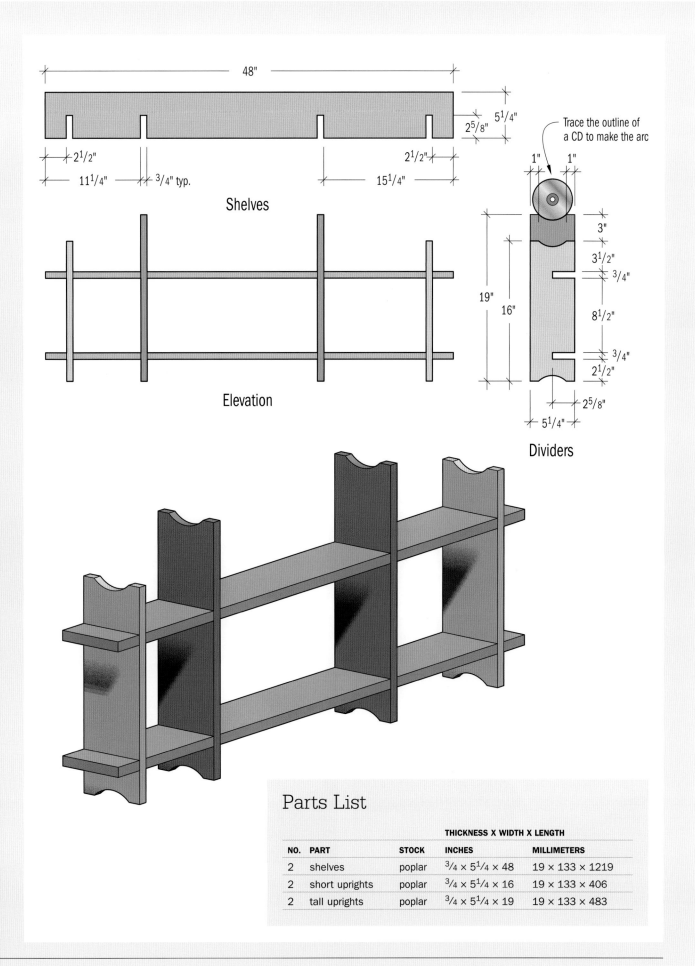

48"

5 1/4"

2 5/8"

2 1/2"

11 1/4"   3/4" typ.

2 1/2"

15 1/4"

Shelves

Elevation

Trace the outline of
a CD to make the arc

1"   1"

3"

3 1/2"

3/4"

19"   16"   8 1/2"

3/4"

2 1/2"

2 5/8"

5 1/4"

Dividers

## Parts List

| | | | THICKNESS X WIDTH X LENGTH | |
| NO. | PART | STOCK | INCHES | MILLIMETERS |
|---|---|---|---|---|
| 2 | shelves | poplar | 3/4 × 5 1/4 × 48 | 19 × 133 × 1219 |
| 2 | short uprights | poplar | 3/4 × 5 1/4 × 16 | 19 × 133 × 406 |
| 2 | tall uprights | poplar | 3/4 × 5 1/4 × 19 | 19 × 133 × 483 |

Measuring isn't always the best way to work accurately. Holding a block of scrap against the blade of the square guarantees that the line drawn will represent the thickness of the piece that will fit in the notch. It's much more important that the slot and the shelf be identical in size than it is to know the exact thickness of the shelf. Every time you measure and mark something you introduce the opportunity to make a mistake. I consider measuring to be a last resort, and avoid it when I can.

## Layout

Long before the term ergonomics was invented, the combination square was designed to neatly fit the hand. In the egg crate shelf project, the square is used in several different ways, many of them with the left hand holding the square. Once you get used to using it and the way it works, you can use it as an all-purpose layout and marking guide. Find a comfortable way to hold it firmly against the edge of your material.

We want the joints to be in the same place on all the parts, even if our measurements are off a little. By clamping all of the uprights together, we can measure and mark the locations of joints only once, then use the square to transfer the marks to all the pieces by drawing a line across the edges of the boards. This saves time, and it also guarantees that the locations marked are in the same place on each piece.

Next we want to be sure that the slot we cut is the same size as the thickness of our wood. It isn't safe to assume that the ¾" material really is that size, so use a piece of scrap to get the size right, even if the material is too thick or too thin. Draw a line to represent one edge of the notch, and slide the blade of the square over to barely cover the line.

Holding the square firmly in place, the scrap is placed against it, and a pencil line is drawn against the scrap's edge as seen in the photo (top). After drawing the line, you can remove the square and look down on the scrap and the two lines. If you can see both lines against the edge of the scrap, your layout is accurate.

If we're confident that the shelf will fit between the lines, then we can preserve the lines until the final fitting, cutting inside of them, and trimming down to them. The lines will let us know if our cuts are straight, and show how much more material we have left to remove.

The ends of the notches need to be marked, and we'll use the end of the blade of the square as our guide after we adjust it to be centered in the width of the board. Measuring will get us close, but not exactly there. Make your best guess as to the center measurement, and make a mark with your pencil.

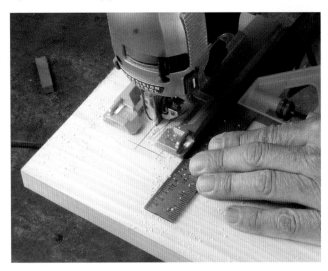

Clamp the board to your workbench, hold the square with one hand and jigsaw in the other and cut on the inside of the lines.

Move the square and make the second cut on the inside of the line.

Adjust the blade of the square to meet that mark, and draw a short line against the end of the blade. Now, flip the square over so that it's against the opposite edge of the board, and make a second mark. If these two lines coincide, you got lucky and hit the center on your first try. Chances are there's a gap between the two. Adjust the blade again, trying to place the end of it between the two marks. When you have it set, make a

mark from each edge as you did before. You should be able to get the lines to meet in a couple of attempts.

We can also use the square to guide the jigsaw (opposite page, bottom photos) to make straighter cuts than we could make if we were trying to saw freehand. Clamp the board down, and with the square in one hand, and the jigsaw in the other, line up the saw so that the blade is just inside one of the lines.

## Cutting Joints

Back the saw away from the line while holding the square firmly against the edge of the board. Turn on the saw and push it in against the blade of the square to make the cut. Hold the base of the saw flat, and release the trigger when you get to the line at the end of the notch.

Making the square cut at the end of the notch seems impossible. There isn't a way to start the cut on the line, so you need to create some space for the blade. Run the sawblade down one of the previously cut lines, and aim for a corner. After the waste piece falls away, you have room to turn the saw as you head to the other corner. It may take a few times going back and forth, but eventually you can cut to the line. If you go too far, or end up with some ugliness, don't worry. This end of the joint will be covered up when you put the pieces together.

## Fitting Joints

We used a rasp to clean up the saw cuts, removing material back to the pencil lines. Holding it in both hands as shown (lower left) helps to keep it square to the face of the board. When you get close, take a piece of scrap and see if you can fit it in the notch (lower right). If you can get it in with the pressure of your hand, you're ready to move on to the next joint.

If the scrap won't fit with hand pressure, take a close look at the joint and

With the waste piece cut away, it's a simple matter to come back and nibble away the end of the cut to leave a square end to the notch. After a little practice with the jigsaw, this technique will be second nature to you.

Using both hands helps to keep the rasp in a vertical position. Remove material evenly with long strokes of the rasp until you are down to the layout lines. Working to the lines will help you to keep the edges of the notches straight.

Test fit each joint as you go by fitting a piece of scrap wood. Take note of where the joints are too loose or too tight and correct your technique when you cut the next joint. Don't worry if the first joints have some gaps. The project will still come together if you're not perfect. The idea is to practice and get better with each attempt.

One simple joint is all it takes to build these shelves. The decorative cut is laid out by tracing the edge of a CD.

layout lines. Take a few more strokes with the rasp and try again. By checking the fit of each notch as you cut it, you will increase the chances of the entire project fitting together, and you will get instant feedback on your sawing technique.

The arched cutouts at the top and bottom of the upright pieces were marked, then cut with the jigsaw. Make a pencil mark 1" in from each edge, line a CD up to the pencil marks, and draw the curved line. (If you're building wider shelves, choose an item with a larger radius to guide your line, such as a gallon paint

can.) Cut just shy of the line, and use a rasp and sandpaper to smooth the curve.

When all the notches are cut, sand the wide surfaces of the parts, and make a test fit of the entire assembly. The pieces should slide together by pushing them by hand. If they stick somewhere, take a close look at the location and make a pencil mark along the intersection. Take it apart, and with the rasp trim down to your pencil marks.

When you're satisfied that you have a good fit, pull the joints apart about half-way, spread some glue carefully on the

inside surfaces of the joints, then put the joints back together.

The shelves shown in the photo were stained with gel stain then sprayed with lacquer from an aerosol can. Some of our staff opted to paint their shelves. Like the layout, the finish is up to you.

# Whale Tail Shelves

**BY MEGAN FITZPATRICK**

These classic shelves are easy to build thanks to the pocket-hole joints that attach the shelves to the sides. While pocket holes aren't a traditional joint, they allow you to build pieces that might otherwise be too complex. (If so inclined you could even build a kitchen using pocket-hole joinery, but the screws would add up in cost).

To build these shelves, based on a design from Contributing Editor Troy Sexton, buy two 8'-long 1 × 6s (which actually measure approximately ¾" × 5½"). Sight down the boards to check for cupping or twisting. And while you're at the home center, pick up a couple of hangers so you don't have to make a second trip (at least it got me out of the office).

Before you start cutting, make a pattern for the sides. Cut a piece of cardboard to 5" × 26" (just a wee bit bigger than the shelf side) and draw a 1" grid on it. Using the grid as your guide, copy the curve from the pattern (page 142) onto your full-size grid. Use a utility knife to cut out the pattern, employing a fluid hand motion. It's better to make a few light cuts than to try to cut through several paper layers in the cardboard all at once.

Now use your miter saw to crosscut three 27" pieces of wood for the shelf sides (it's always good to have a spare).

Put double-sided tape on two of the boards (this will help keep them from slipping) then clamp them together and trace the pattern on top. Use your jigsaw to make a few relief cuts at the top and bottom of the curves, as shown (page 143), then cut along the edge of the pattern. When finished, clean up the edges with your rasp, file and sandpaper.

Next, cut the four shelves to final length on the miter saw. Test-fit the shelves between the two sides, and mark the width in relation to the curve of the sides, as shown (page 143).

Set your jigsaw's blade to the angle that matches the line, and rip each shelf to width. Clean up each cut as necessary with a block plane or a rasp and sandpaper.

Next, mark the placement of the pocket holes on the bottom of each shelf,

¾" in from each long edge. Set the jig for ¾"-thick material, and make a few practice holes in scrap material. When you feel confident, line up the mark on the shelf with the mark on the jig as shown, secure the shelf in the jig, and drill your pocket holes using the bit provided in the kit. For the best result, keep the angle of your drill in line with the angle of the hole, and squeeze the trigger while the bit is at the top of the hole to allow it to

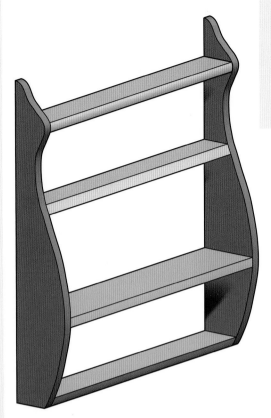

## Parts List

| NO. | PART | STOCK | THICKNESS X WIDTH X LENGTH | | |
| --- | --- | --- | --- | --- | --- |
| | | | INCHES | MILLIMETERS | COMMENTS |
| 2 | sides | pine | $3/4 \times 4^7/8 \times 25^1/4$ | $19 \times 107 \times 641$ | |
| 4 | shelves | pine | $3/4 \times 5^1/4 \times 23$ | $19 \times 134 \times 584$ | trim to fit |

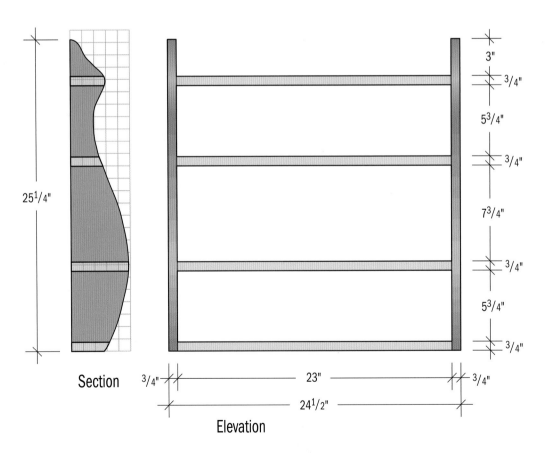

$25^1/4$"

3"

$3/4$"

$5^3/4$"

$3/4$"

$7^3/4$"

$3/4$"

$5^3/4$"

$3/4$"

Section

$3/4$"  23"  $3/4$"

$24^1/2$"

Elevation

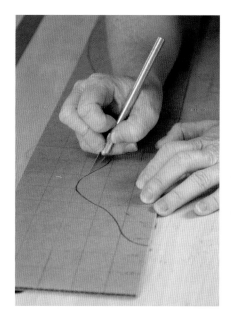

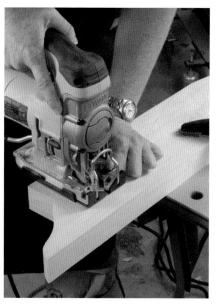

Fit the shelves against the two side pieces, and carefully mark the width in relation to the curve of the side. Then cut with your jigsaw.

After transferring the pattern at the left to a piece of craft paper, use a craft knife to trace the pattern onto the side pieces. This will give you an easy line to follow with the jigsaw.

Use double-sided tape and clamps to keep your side pieces firmly together as you make your relief and curve cuts.

get up to speed before making contact with the wood. Now drill the remaining fifteen pocket holes.

Before assembly, sand all the parts to #180-grit (stop at #120 if you plan to paint).

Using a scrap piece of material as a clamping block to help secure the shelf to the side as shown at far right, clamp the top shelf to the top of one side and drive pocket screws through the two pocket holes and into the side, using the driver provided in the kit. For the best result, set your drill on a low speed and clutch setting, to help avoid stripping the screws.

Now, attach the three remaining shelves to that side. Then attach the other side to the unit.

As shown, the whale tail shelf has three coats of brushed-on amber shellac. Sand between your coats with #320-grit stearated paper. Wipe off the dust with a tack cloth, and add a couple of coats of aerosol lacquer before attaching hangers to the back.

After securing the board firmly in the jig, squeeze your drill's trigger and allow it to get up to speed before drilling into the wood.

An offcut makes a handy clamping block to help you keep the shelves in place as you drive the pocket screws.

# Stacking Bookcases

**BY ROBERT W. LANG**

The typical bookcase is a good example of poor design. We make them that way because that's the way we've always made them; almost every plan you see is 12" deep, yet few books require that much space. Most bookcases are heavy and a pain to move. These stacking bookcases solve those problems, and won't take long to build.

Before you begin, assess your library. The three sizes shown here are based on common lumber sizes, and typical sizes of books and video cases. If you stay with standard 1× lumber, you won't be able to change the depth, but you can change the height and width.

An inch or two higher than your tallest book is a good inside height, but don't go too wide; beyond 36" and the shelves may begin to sag. Also consider how the parts of the sizes you are planning will fit the available lengths of material; an inch or so of adjustment may save you from buying another board.

## Get Ready to Rabbet

The individual boxes could be just glued and nailed together, but the rabbet joints shown here will be stronger, and the boxes will be easier to assemble. I used a ³⁄₈"-wide rabbeting bit that uses a ball bearing below the cutter as a guide.

You may find a cheaper version of this bit with a solid piece of steel instead of the bearing. Don't give into the temptation to save a few dollars. The solid guide spins at the same speed as the cutter, fast enough to burn the edges of your wood.

Plan on making at least two passes with the router to reach the final depth. In theory that should be ³⁄₈", but your wood might be a bit thinner or thicker.

In reality, the depth is half the thickness of your material, and you can use an adjustable square to quickly find that dimension and set your router to the exact center of the wood.

If you're new to routing rabbets, make a few practice cuts in scrap to get the feel of it. The router will behave differently when you move it in different directions. When you move from left to right, the cutting edge of the bit is moving into the work. This is more efficient and gives you greater control — but when you reach the edge of a board, it tends to break a chip out of the edge.

Moving from right to left is considered backward, and is called "climb-cutting." If you move the router backward into what would normally be the end of a cut before you make the cut, you can prevent blowing out the wood. You should only climb-cut for a short distance after the cutter enters the wood.

Keep the base of the router flat on your work while you press the guide bearing against the edge. Be careful at the start and end of a cut that the bearing doesn't go around the corner and on to the adjacent edge.

## In This Corner

Before you put the boxes together, sand the inside surfaces with a random-orbit sander or by hand. It is difficult to sand into the corners after the boxes are assembled. The vertical pieces go outside

Made to order. Fit the cases to your books to avoid wasting space, lower your material costs and make moving easy.

the horizontal pieces, hiding the end grain when viewed from the side.

Put a bead of glue on the end-grain surfaces of the sides and spread it across the entire surface. Let it soak in for about five minutes before applying glue to the

# Parts List

| NO. | PART | STOCK | THICKNESS X WIDTH X LENGTH | |
|-----|------|-------|---------------------------|---|
| | | | INCHES | MILLIMETERS |
| 2 | Narrow sides | 1×6 pine | $^3/_4 \times 5^1/_2 \times 10^1/_4$ | 19 × 140 × 260 |
| 2 | Medium sides | 1×8 pine | $^3/_4 \times 7^1/_4 \times 12$ | 19 × 184 × 305 |
| 2 | Wide sides | 1×10 pine | $^3/_4 \times 9^1/_4 \times 14$ | 19 × 235 × 356 |
| 2 | Narrow tops & bottoms | 1×6 pine | $^3/_4 \times 5^1/_2 \times 23^1/_4$ | 19 × 140 × 590 |
| 2 | Medium tops & bottoms | 1×8 pine | $^3/_4 \times 7^1/_4 \times 23^1/_4$ | 19 × 184 × 590 |
| 2 | Wide tops & bottoms | 1×10 pine | $^3/_4 \times 9^1/_4 \times 23^1/_4$ | 19 × 235 × 590 |
| 1 | Narrow back | Plywood | $^1/_4 \times 5^1/_2 \times 23^1/_4$ | 6 × 140 × 590 |
| 1 | Medium back | Plywood | $^1/_4 \times 7^1/_4 \times 23^1/_4$ | 6 × 184 × 590 |
| 1 | Wide back | Plywood | $^1/_4 \times 9^1/_4 \times 23^1/_4$ | 6 × 235 × 590 |
| 2 | Base ends | 1×4 pine | $^3/_4 \times 3^1/_2 \times 9^5/_8$ | 19 × 89 × 245 |
| 1 | Base front | 1×4 pine | $^3/_4 \times 3^1/_2 \times 24^3/_4$ | 19 × 89 × 629 |

Router rules. Clamp the work securely before routing the rabbets and keep the base firmly on the surface.

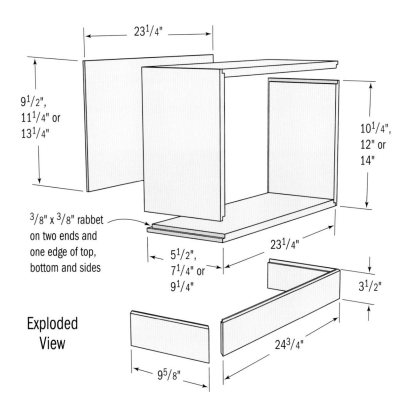

23¹/₄"

9¹/₂", 11¹/₄" or 13¹/₄"

10¹/₄", 12" or 14"

$^3/_8$" x $^3/_8$" rabbet on two ends and one edge of top, bottom and sides

5¹/₂", 7¹/₄" or 9¹/₄"

23¹/₄"

3¹/₂"

24³/₄"

9⁵/₈"

**Exploded View**

Nice and square. Clamp a square in the corner to hold the boards in position while you drive and set the nails.

## Off the Floor

Cut a rabbet along one long edge of the piece for the base before mitering the corners. Size the mitered ends with glue, as was done with the end-grain of the rabbets. Assemble the three parts of the base with more glue and nails. Clear packing tape at each corner will hold the pieces in position while you nail.

I used clear shellac as the finish, brushing on two coats. Before finishing, I mixed some dust from the collection bag of the sander with a dollop of shellac to make a filler for the nail holes, and any gaps on the edges of the joints. This takes a while to dry, but the price is right, and the color will match the surrounding wood.

After finishing, the boxes are stacked on top of one another and on the base. Drive a couple 1¹/₄" drywall screws from the top of one box into the bottom of the next to keep the assembled bookcase stable.

other joint surfaces. This allows the glue to soak into the end grain and makes for stronger joints — it's called "sizing."

Put the corners together and use clamps to pull them tight. Clamp a Speed Square (or a square block of wood) in each corner as you nail to keep the entire assembly square. I used 3d finish nails, and set them slightly below the surface of the wood. When the nails are in, the clamps can be removed and you can move on to the next box.

Let the glue dry overnight, and remove any excess wood at the joints with a block plane or a random-orbit sander. When all the corners are flush, sand the outside surfaces and break the sharp corners with sandpaper.

Cut the backs to fit the openings, but finish the bookcases before attaching them permanently. You can hold the backs in place with either 3d finish nails (quick, but be careful with your aim) or #6 × ⁵/₈" wood screws.

# Contemporary Shelves

**BY ROBERT W. LANG**

For sturdy, attractive and affordable material to build these shelves, bypass the fancy stuff at the front of your local home center and head for the back where they keep the lumber intended for use as rafters and floor joists.

In my neighborhood the available wood is Southern yellow pine. In other parts of the country you might find Douglas fir, spruce or another species. When logs are milled for construction lumber, this is where the good stuff goes.

Three 12'-long 2×12s will provide enough material to build the shelves as shown. You may have to cut them (or have them cut) to get them home, but longer lengths will be straighter and of better quality than short stuff. Pick through the stack and select the straightest, nicest-looking pieces.

Look at the ends of the boards, and avoid any with a tight circle in the rings in the middle of the board, which tells you that the board came from the middle, or heart, of the tree. As the wood dries and shrinks, this is the most likely part to cup and split. These boards will likely be relatively damp, and you should expect some movement as they dry.

You can hasten the drying process by cutting the boards to rough lengths. Let them sit for a while to acclimate to your environment. The parts don't need to be perfect for this project to be a success, but the straighter they are, the easier it will be to put your shelves together.

## Everything but the Sides

Cut the top, bottom, shelves and uprights to length, but leave the ends long for now. It is important that all of the uprights be square and the same length.

Double-check the length of these short pieces, and the thickness of the horizontal parts. Lay out the locations of the shelves on the sides based on the actual size of the parts.

You only need to make the layout on one of the side pieces. Rather than measure and mark a second time, transfer the shelf locations by placing both sides next to each other. Use a square to mark the shelf locations from one side to the other.

The uprights are centered in the width of the top and bottom. Measure from both ends, and again transfer the layout marks from one piece to the other. Stack the four shelves on the bottom piece, with the ends flush. Use your square to mark the upright locations on each of the shelves.

## You Know the Drill

All the parts of this shelf unit are held together with screws. If you're going to paint the shelves, the screws can run from the outside in. Countersink the screw heads and plug the holes before priming and painting. If you want to use a clear

Humble origins. The thick, wide planks used to construct this set of shelves are framing lumber — 2x12s normally used for floor joists. Select the best of the lot and let them be seen.

finish as shown in this article, some of the screws should be discretely placed.

The first and last short uprights connect to the top and bottom with 3" deck screws from the outside in. Drill three clearance holes on the centerline of the top and bottom. You can also attach one end of each upright to a shelf with the same method. Use pocket screws at the opposite end of the uprights, and at the ends of the top, bottom and shelves.

When you assemble the shelves, put the pocket screw holes facing down so they won't be visible. Drill the pocket screw holes in all the parts before doing any assembly. After all the holes are drilled, sand the pieces with #100-grit paper on a random-orbit sander.

The edges of the material will be rounded from the machining process. This is a problem where the ends of pieces meet the faces of other pieces. You can use a router equipped with a chamfer bit to turn this drawback into a design feature.

Set the depth of the router bit so that it cuts about ³⁄₁₆" deep on the edge of a piece of scrap. The exact distance isn't important; what's important is that all the edges are chamfered the same. Think about how the parts will go together, and use a crayon or chalk to mark the edges you don't want to rout.

All the long edges of all the parts should be chamfered. The edges on the ends of the top, bottom, shelves and uprights are also chamfered, but only on the short ends at the front and back. The ends of the long sides that go against the faces of other parts should remain square.

After routing, sand all the parts again, this time with #150-grit paper on your sander. If there are any areas where the grain broke out during routing, you can blend them in to the surrounding area with some judicious sanding.

## Give Me Some Room

Screws will hold the shelves together, but the assembly will be stronger if you also glue each joint. Use yellow or white wood

Make it a feature. Chamfering the edges add a design highlight — and helps to cover up any slight misalignment.

Square to start. Square subassemblies will make the overall structure easier to put together.

glue, and smear some glue on the end-grain surfaces of each piece. Let this soak in for a few minutes, then apply additional glue to both surfaces when you assemble.

Screw one upright to each of the four shelves, using the through-holes in the middle of each shelf. Set these aside and find a large, flat area to assemble the rest of the shelf unit. You'll probably need to work on the floor to have enough room. Screw the top and bottom to the sides using 2½"-long pocket screws. Take the last upright and screw it to the bottom, coming in from the outside of the case.

Work up from there. Attach a shelf assembly to the cabinet side, and the upright to the bottom of the shelf with the long pocket screws. Remember that every other shelf attaches to the opposite side. If you need to, use clamps to help position the pieces to the appropriate layout lines.

You can buy special plugs to fill the visible pocket screw holes in the uprights, or you can use short lengths of ³⁄₈"-diameter dowel. Glue them in place. When the glue is dry, cut off the protruding part of the dowels then sand them flush to the surface.

Cut the three feet from your leftover material, chamfer the edges with the router and attach the feet to the bottom. Go over the assembly, clean off any excess glue and sand any spots that may have been missed or dinged during assembly. Now you're ready to finish; I used two coats of clear shellac.

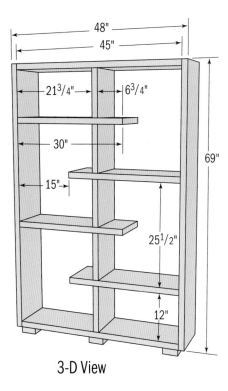

3-D View

## Parts List

| NO. | PART | THICKNESS X WIDTH X LENGTH | |
|-----|------|------|------|
| | | INCHES | MILLIMETERS |
| 2 | Sides | 1¹⁄₂ × 11¹⁄₄ × 69 | 38 × 285 × 1753 |
| 2 | Top & bottom | 1¹⁄₂ × 11¹⁄₄ × 45 | 38 × 285 × 1143 |
| 4 | Shelves | 1¹⁄₂ × 11¹⁄₄ × 30 | 38 × 285 × 762 |
| 5 | Uprights | 1¹⁄₂ × 11¹⁄₄ × 12 | 38 × 285 × 305 |
| 3 | Feet | 1¹⁄₂ × 11¹⁄₄ × 4 | 38 × 285 × 102 |

# Simplified Stickley Bookcase

**BY GLEN D. HUEY**

This piece originally appeared in our *Woodworking Magazine* using traditional joinery techniques. We did a bit of construction modification to allow the design to better fit the "I Can Do That" concept, and that design is presented here. And that's something you should be on the lookout for as you read woodworking articles or skim the pages of your favorite catalogs. Find a piece you like and see what changes can be made to match the construction to your skill set and tools.

For this piece, we eliminated the complicated shelf joinery, and we adjusted a few sizes to better accommodate the lumber dimensions found at home centers. But by and large, this bookcase is close to our original project and a great piece to build.

For material, you'll need an 8' piece of 1 × 10 for the sides and one shelf, and a 1 × 10 × 4' for two shelves, the braces and one toe kick. Crosscut the material to the required length, then rip the braces and toe kick.

## Add Design to the Sides

The bookcase sides require the most work, so begin at the handle area. Measure down from the top 1¼", then square a line across the grain. Also, find the top center of the sides then square a line off the top edge that extends just across the first line.

The next layout step is to grab a compass that's set for a 2½" radius, position the point of the tool at the intersection of the two lines and mark a half-circle with the flat side parallel with the top edge of the sides. To soften the look, round the sharp corners of the handle area. I used

Look at projects with a different eye. Find a piece with great design, such as a Stickley No. 79 bookcase, then make adjustments to the construction to better match your skill set.

a pair of nickels placed at the corners to establish the radius.

To create the handle opening, use a ¹³⁄₁₆" bit to drill holes at each corner (the bit closely matches the diameter of the nickels). With the two difficult-to-cut areas done, use a jigsaw to remove the balance of the waste. Insert the blade

through one of the holes then cut on the line from hole to hole. After that's complete, pivot the saw to cut the half-circle line. Stay close to the line, take your time as you cut and slow the blade speed if possible — a slower blade increases your control as you cut. Then clean up your cuts with a file and sandpaper.

Next, make the cutout at the base. This, too, is a half-circle with a 2½" radius. Because you can start the cut from the bottom edge of the sides, there's no need to drill a hole. Use your jigsaw to cut the area, then smooth the cut as you did before.

The last shaping step is to round the top corners. This step is a bit more expensive; use quarters as a template. Draw the profile on your sides, then remove the material with your jigsaw, or use a file and sandpaper.

The only other shaping work required is on the toe kick. Make a mark 1" in from both ends along the bottom edge of the piece. At the top edge, find the center of the piece then add a vertical pencil line across the toe kick. Move down that line 1¼" and mark the location.

Next, instead of finding the appropriate radius with a trammel, bend a ruler or thin stick to create the curve. Hold the ruler at the two points at the bottom edge as you bend the piece to reach the center point of the curve. With the bend set as you like, have a friend mark a line following the bend in the ruler. Cut on the waste side of your line with your jigsaw, then smooth the curve with your file and sandpaper.

## No Complex Joinery

Pocket screws make the joinery for this project a snap. Each shelf is drilled for four pocket screws, two at each end,

It's just pocket change. Quarters and nickels make great templates for rounding off corners. The larger the coin, the bigger the radius.

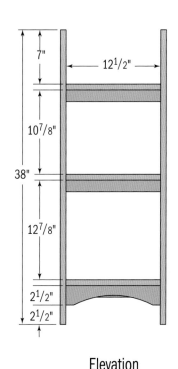

Elevation

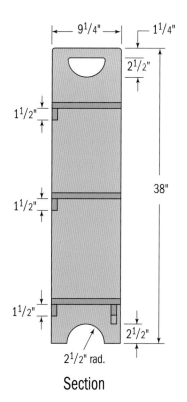

Section

spaced 1½" from the edges. The toe kick is drilled for two screws at both ends as well. And the support braces have one hole per end (with the braces held tight to the bottom of the shelves, you need only the two screws for a secure connection).

Set up your pocket-screw jig as directed and drill the pockets. Use 1¼" screws for this project; fine threads are better because you're working with hardwood. Note: As you drill in your toe kick, stay toward the top edge of the workpiece. If you bore near the curved portion, it's possible to have a pocket extend into the curve and be visible in the finished bookcase.

## Curtail Creepy Movement

As you install pocket screws, it's possible for your pieces to creep slightly. To reduce that possibility, use a stop block and a clamp to keep things in place. To begin, do a simple layout of the shelf locations on the inside face of your sides (a couple short lines set in from the edges is all that's needed).

STOP BLOCK

Stop the creep. Use a clamp and stop block, or in this case one of the bookcase sides, to keep your shelves from inching forward as screws are driven.

## Parts List

| NO. | PART | STOCK | INCHES | MILLIMETERS | COMMENTS |
|---|---|---|---|---|---|
| | | | THICKNESS X WIDTH X LENGTH | | |
| 2 | Sides | Red oak | ¾ × 9¼ × 38 | 19 × 235 × 965 | |
| 3 | Shelves | Red oak | ¾ × 9¼ × 12½ | 19 × 235 × 318 | |
| 3 | Support braces | Red oak | ¾ × 1½ × 12½ | 19 × 38 × 318 | |
| 1 | Toe kick | Red oak | ¾ × 2½ × 12½ | 19 × 64 × 318 | Curved lower edge |

Next, clamp a wide cutoff at a layout line that is the top edge of a shelf's location. As shown in the photo below, with the shelf pressed against that clamped-in stop block there is no problem with creeping pieces. Install the screws to affix all the shelves to one side of the bookcase, then align the second side and add the screws to complete the installation of the shelves.

One support brace fits tight to the bottom edge of each shelf and flush with the back edge of the bookcase. Align the pieces, then drive the screws to lock the braces in place. The toe kick also sits under the bottom shelf but is held back ½" from the front edge. A clamp added after the toe kick is positioned holds the piece secure and tight to the shelf as the screws are installed.

## A One-Two-One Finish

With the construction complete, take the time to knock off any sharp edges (especially around the handle area) and sand the piece to #120-grit. The finish is a coat of "Dark Walnut" Watco Danish Oil followed, when the oil is dry, by two coats of amber shellac. To complete the bookcase, lightly sand the piece with #320-grit sandpaper then apply one layer of paste wax for protection. All that's left is to put books, family photos or other knickknacks on display.

# Shaker Shelves

**BY MEGAN FITZPATRICK & GLEN HUEY**

Basic skills are all it takes to create this graceful set of shelves, so with this project we'll teach you a few clever tricks to draw arcs without a compass, and to straighten twisted boards — which is often a problem when working with wider pieces of wood.

This modified Shaker design, downsized from a set of creamery shelves, is adapted from a Shaker Workshops catalog. To ensure our ¾"-stock would not bow under the weight of even the heaviest items, we decided to make these shelf pieces a bit shorter than those on the company's web site (shakerworkshops.com).

Many home centers carry only pine, poplar and oak (you may also find maple or aspen, depending on your region). We decided on oak because we think it has the best natural appearance.

One of the biggest challenges you'll have with this project is finding wide boards that are straight and flat ... and that remain straight and flat after you cut them to size. Take time to look through the racks for the best boards — and if at all possible, avoid shrink-wrapped boards, no matter how pretty. You'll need two 6' and one 4' 1 × 12s (or one 10' and one 8' length). You'll also need a 6' length of 1 × 4 for the supports.

Once you're back in the shop, your first step is to cut the sides to length on your miter saw. If you have a 10" miter saw, your crosscuts on the sides (and shelves) will be a two-step process because the diameter of the saw blade limits the width of the cut. You'll need to first cut on one side of your board, then flip it over and carefully line up the kerf with the saw blade before completing the cut.

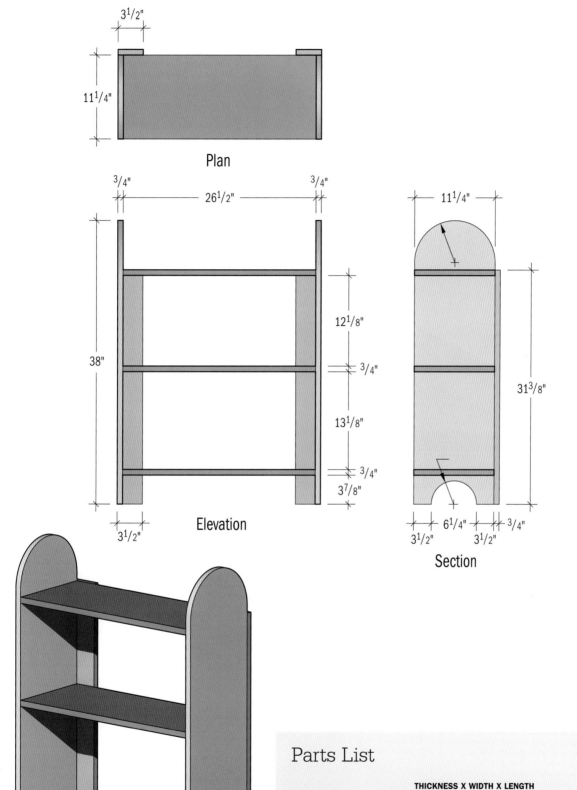

3 1/2"

11 1/4"

Plan

3/4"    26 1/2"    3/4"

38"

12 1/8"

3/4"

13 1/8"

3/4"

3 7/8"

3 1/2"

Elevation

11 1/4"

31 3/8"

3 1/2"    6 1/4"    3 1/2"    3/4"

Section

## Parts List

| NO. | PART | STOCK | THICKNESS X WIDTH X LENGTH | |
|-----|------|-------|----------------------------|--|
| | | | INCHES | MILLIMETERS |
| 2 | sides | oak | $3/4 \times 11^1/4 \times 38$ | $19 \times 286 \times 965$ |
| 3 | shelves | oak | $3/4 \times 11^1/4 \times 26^1/2$ | $19 \times 286 \times 673$ |
| 2 | supports | oak | $3/4 \times 3^1/2 \times 31^3/8$ | $19 \times 89 \times 797$ |

Because the wood for the sides and shelves is 11¼"-wide and your miter saw is likely a 10" model, you'll have to cut the pieces in two steps. Measure and make the first cut. Then flip the board over and line up the saw blade to the existing kerf, and make the second cut.

A thin piece of scrap, a nail and a drill are all it takes to make this simple compass jig.

Now, you're ready to lay out the arched top and cutout at the bottom. Align the top edges of the sides and stick the faces together with double-stick tape to keep them from slipping, then clamp both pieces together flat to your workbench. Now, measure across the width to find the center of your board, and make a mark. That measurement is the same distance you'll measure down from the top edge to mark the intersection of the two points (5⅝" unless you've resized the plan, or used different-sized stock). This point is where you'll place your compass point to draw the half-circle arch across the top.

And if you don't have a compass, it's no problem. It's easy to make a compass jig. Simply grab a thin piece of scrap and drive a nail through the middle near one end. Now, using the same measurement you already established to find the compass point (again, it's 5⅝" on our plan), mark and drill a hole that distance from the nail, and stick a pencil point through it. Voilà — a compass jig.

You can use that same jig for the bottom arched cutout. Simply drill another hole 3⅛" away from your nail. Set the nail as close to the center of the bottom edge as possible and mark the cutout arch. Or, mark the arch with a traditional compass.

Now use your jigsaw to cut as close to the lines as possible, and use a rasp and sandpaper to clean up the cuts. If you keep the pieces clamped together during this process, you should end up with nearly identical arches. If you're not confident in your jigsaw skills, practice making curved cuts on some scrap pieces before moving on to the real thing.

Now cut the shelves to length.

Set up your pocket-hole jig for ¾"-thick material. Mark the placement for three pocket holes on each end of each shelf, two of them ¾" from each long edge, and one in the center of the end. Drill the holes.

Cut the back supports to length, and sand all pieces to #150-grit before assembly (#120 if you're planning to paint).

Now you're ready for assembly, and the second trick we promised. Lay one side flat on your bench and mark the location of the top shelf at both sides. You may not be able to line the shelf up with your marks because of cupping in the wide board; that's where the trick comes in. Position the back support (or any straight piece of scrap) along the bowed side of the shelf, if there is one, and use clamps to bring the edges of the shelf flat to the support or straight scrap. Slide the clamped unit to the layout lines, hold or clamp it in place then use screws to attach it. This trick will work to pull the bow from any of the shelves.

Attach all three shelves to both sides, straightening the pieces where necessary.

Now lay the assembly face down, line up the support with the top of your top shelf. Drill countersunk holes at the top shelf, at the bottom shelf, and at the inside edge where the support meets the middle shelf. Be sure to hold your drill at 90° to the sides; because you're drilling into ¾" stock, you could easily drill through the side if you're not careful.

Attach the uprights with #8 × 1¼" screws (rubbing the threads on some wax will help them seat more easily). Pay particular attention at the top and bottom as the stock can easily split. If it does crack, stop your drill immediately —but don't panic. Just back the screw out a tiny bit, and the split will close up.

Finish the shelves with two coats of wiping varnish.

To get matching shapes on the two top radii, I clamped both pieces into the Workmate and used a rasp and file on both surfaces at the same time. Not only did this make the two pieces identical in shape, it gave me a more broad surface to work on which made it easier to keep the edges flat.

You can pull a cup out of a board by clamping the piece to a straightedge and pulling it tight with clamps before screwing it down.

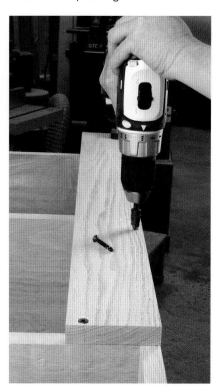

Make sure your drill is at a 90° angle to the most narrow stock through which you're drilling — in this case, the ¾" edge of the side beneath the support.

# Library Magazine Rack

**BY GLEN D. HUEY**

I might be going out on a limb, but I'm willing to bet that if you visit the library or special reading room (also known as the potty room) of most woodworkers, you'll find scads of magazines for occasional perusal. At one time in my bathroom I had a basket filled to the brim with periodicals. Some dated as far back as June 1991.

After my basket collapsed, I began to stack my collection in a corner on the bathroom floor. So when this project presented itself, I gladly stepped forward. A wall-hung magazine rack is just what I need.

A trip to the store to pick up materials is always the first step for "I Can Do That" projects and with only two pieces of stock, the material is not only easy to carry, it's also light on your wallet. One 6' piece is cut for the sides and one 10' piece provides all the face pieces, shelves and the hanger support. I opted to combine two wood species for a non-traditional design — aspen for the sides and red oak for everything else.

## A Stop-block for Consistency

Begin by cutting the sides to length. I've seen many woodworkers stack two or more pieces together in preparation to cut parts identical in length. While you sometimes can get away with this shortcut, it's better to add a stop to your miter saw setup if you have an extended table — or accurately measure, mark and cut your material.

After crosscutting the sides, the remaining parts for the rack are all cut to the same length. For this operation, set up a stop-block. This is easily done on most miter saws even if there is no

In the round. Slightly rounded edges soften the overall look of a linear design.

extended table, and it's worth the effort to do so. Seven of the 10 pieces are their finished size, but three pieces need additional work. Those pieces are the shelves and each needs to be ripped to fit.

To measure the width of the shelves, position a front piece face down and snug it against a rack side that's set on its edge. Set the body of a combination square flat on the rack's side with the ruler extending to just touch the front piece. Lock the square.

Next, use your combination square setup and a pencil to mark a cut line on each of the three shelf pieces. Hold the pencil at the end of the square and slide the unit along the shelves. Use a jigsaw to make these cuts and stay just to the waste side of each line. A block plane trims the shelves to their final width. A couple passes should be all that's needed.

Although the pieces for the magazine rack are all at final sizes, additional shaping of the stock is required to soften the look. It's sometimes difficult to perfectly flush the face of the fronts with the front edge of the sides. Any variation is noticeable and would need to be sanded flush. To hide any slight variations, lightly round over the edges of the fronts and sides.

This is easily done with your block plane and sandpaper. Set your plane for a light cut and make several passes along the edges of the fronts. Begin on the end-grain edges. Cutting across end grain is a snap, but it's possible to blow out the long-grain edges as you work. By rounding the ends first, you remove any possible long grain tear-out as you plane the remaining edges. After your edges are rounded with a plane, finish the process with #150-grit sandpaper. A couple quick passes per edge is all it takes.

## How to Connect

All horizontal pieces of the magazine rack are joined to the sides with pocket screws. Create four pocket-screw holes in the back face of each front piece and the hanger support (two per side); choose your ugliest piece for the support. If you

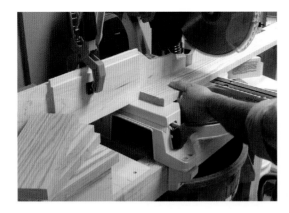

SPACER BLOCKS

Consistent lengths. A stop-block and your miter saw work in unison to provide pieces that are equal in length — no matter the number of parts needed.

Appropriate spacing. Lay out the locations with pencil marks — these have to be sanded out prior to adding any finish — or you can use spacer blocks to locate the front positions.

wish to reduce the pocket-screw work, drill only two holes in the front pieces that connect to the shelves. While this saves six holes, I didn't find the additional holes that much of a burden.

The shelves need only three pocket-screw holes drilled, one for a screw into each side and a third — centered in the shelf — to affix the shelf to the adjacent front. Finish-sand all the parts before moving forward.

With the pocket holes drilled and parts sanded, you're ready to begin assembly. It's important to stand the side piece on its edge on a flat work surface, and to position the front piece face down with its end tight to the rack's side. Attach the front pieces to one side at this time. Begin at the top. Drive the screws while keeping the front flush with the end and front edge of the side.

**Block Out the Locations**

Each front piece is spaced either $2^{1}/4$" or $3^{1}/2$" from the piece attached directly above it. Cut a spacer block for each size. Set the narrow block just below the intersection of the front piece and side, then slide the next front piece into position. Drive screws to secure the front piece. Position the wider spacer block below that front piece to locate the third front. This pattern is repeated along the entire height of the magazine rack.

After the fronts are connected to one side, add the second side to the assembly, then drive the screws to secure those connections. The width of the unit makes this part of the build rather tight, but a standard pocket-screw driver in your drill does the job.

Now that the fronts are in place and attached, slip the shelves into position. Drive the center three to lock the shelf to the corresponding front, then drive the remaining two screws.

Add the hanger support with the pocket-screw holes facing the back of the rack — the hanger support acts as a spacer to keep the upper part of the sides aligned. Sand again as needed and you're ready to apply a finish.

I used shellac and wax as my finish. Purchase a spray can of shellac and the task becomes toolless. After a couple coats of shellac, sand the entire piece with #320-grit sandpaper and apply a coat of paste wax.

Add brass hangers to the back — make sure you find at least one stud in the wall for needed support — then have a friend hold your rack in place as you complete the installation. Store your most treasured *Popular Woodworking* issues, then enjoy your solitude.

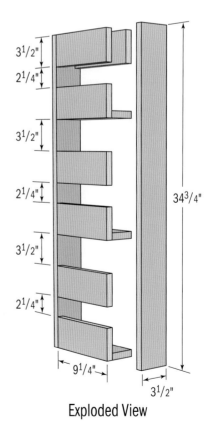

$3^{1}/2$"
$2^{1}/4$"
$3^{1}/2$"
$2^{1}/4$"
$3^{1}/2$"
$2^{1}/4$"
$34^{3}/4$"
$9^{1}/4$"
$3^{1}/2$"

**Exploded View**

## Parts List

| NO. | PART | STOCK | THICKNESS X WIDTH X LENGTH | |
| --- | --- | --- | --- | --- |
| | | | INCHES | MILLIMETERS |
| 2 | Sides | Aspen | $^{3}/4 \times 3^{1}/2 \times 34^{3}/4$ | 19 × 89 × 883 |
| 6 | Fronts | Red oak | $^{3}/4 \times 3^{1}/2 \times 9^{1}/4$ | 19 × 89 × 209 |
| 3 | Shelves | Red oak | $^{3}/4 \times 2^{3}/4 \times 9^{1}/4$ | 19 × 70 × 209 |
| 1 | Hanger support | Red oak | $^{3}/4 \times 3^{1}/2 \times 9^{1}/4$ | 19 × 89 × 209 |

# Corner Shelf

**BY MEGAN FITZPATRICK**

This simple and casual storage unit offers a choice when it comes to stock selection. In the Shaker Step Stool project on page 186 we offer an easy way to glue up panels using pocket screws. So you might wish to follow the steps outlined there to make panels for the backs, top and shelf.

But, you can also buy already glued-up panels of pine at the home center for just a little more cash outlay, so that's what I did for this project. My shopping trip for this corner shelf was quick and easy. I picked up two 24" × 48" pine panels, one pine 1" × 8" × 3' for the sides, one pine 1" × 2" × 2' for the rail, and two double hooks with a rubbed-nickel finish.

Start by cutting your top to the proper-sized square; the rest of the pieces simply need to fit under it, as shown below. While the top in my version is 23½" square, you can easily makes yours smaller (or larger), and base the size of your other pieces off the top, calculating in a ¾" overhang.

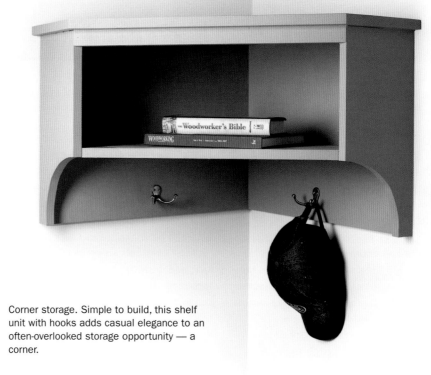

Corner storage. Simple to build, this shelf unit with hooks adds casual elegance to an often-overlooked storage opportunity — a corner.

To cut all the panels to size, I clamped a straightedge with a beefy edge to the piece, 1½" to the left of my cutline, and used that as a rail along which to guide the jigsaw. (Note that one back piece is 21¼" wide, the other is 22" wide because they overlap.) Depending on the width of your jigsaw (or circular saw) base, your setup may vary. To set your straightedge location, simply measure from the edge of the blade to the outside of your baseplate. That's the offset for your guide.

To join the two back pieces, lay the narrow back piece face down on a table,

Cut to size. Cutting your top to size first allows you to easily fit everything that goes under it, even if you change the dimensions to suit your specifications.

Straightedge jig. A straightedge with a beefy edge makes a good guide for making straight cuts with a jigsaw or circular saw.

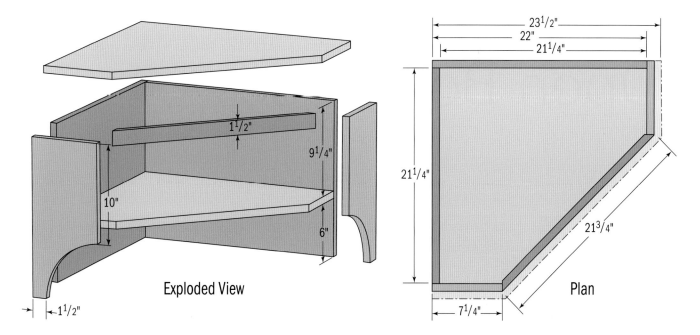

Exploded View

Plan

## Parts List

| NO. | PART | STOCK | THICKNESS X WIDTH X LENGTH | | COMMENTS |
|---|---|---|---|---|---|
| | | | INCHES | MILLIMETERS | |
| 1 | Narrow back | Pine | $3/4 \times 21^{1}/4 \times 16$ | 19 × 539 × 406 | |
| 1 | Wide back | Pine | $3/4 \times 22 \times 16$ | 19 × 559 × 406 | |
| 2 | Sides | Pine | $3/4 \times 7^{1}/4 \times 16$ | 19 × 184 × 406 | |
| 1 | Top | Pine | $3/4 \times 23^{1}/2 \times 23^{1}/2$ | 19 × 597 × 597 | |
| 1 | Shelf | Pine | $3/4 \times 21^{1}/4 \times 21^{1}/4$ | 19 × 539 × 539 | |
| 1 | Top rail | Pine | $3/4 \times 1^{1}/2 \times 21^{3}/4$ | 19 × 38 × 552 | 45° on both ends |

line up a thick caul (a piece of 2×4 works well) across the edge, and clamp it in place. This allows you a flat reference surface against which to balance the wide back piece as you drill holes and screw the pieces together (I used $1^{1}/2" \times$ #8 screws). Set the back pieces aside, and move on to the top and shelf.

To make the 45° cuts across the top and shelf, use the same jig setup as for the panels. On the top, the angle begins 8" from the back corners; on the shelf, it's at $6^{1}/2"$.

The sides were simply chopped to $7^{1}/4"$ length from the dimensional stock to 16" at the miter saw.

Then, I measured in $1^{1}/2"$ from the bottom edge, grabbed a handy bucket off our shop shelves, and used that to draw my arcs. The arc ended at 6" from

What's on hand. You don't need a compass to draw an arc. Just grab whatever's handy around the house. I used a bucket with an 11" diameter to its outer rim.

the side's bottom edge, so that's where I installed the shelf later in the process. The position of your shelf can vary based on your radius — or based on what you think looks most attractive. There's no structural reason that the shelf be aligned with the curve.

After marking and cutting one side with a jigsaw, I used that cut to mark the second side. I then cut it, clamped the two together, and did the final shaping and smoothing with a rasp and #120-grit sandpaper. I also sanded to clean up saw cuts and break the edges.

Now it's time to put it all together. First, position your shelf and mark on the back of both back pieces the location for your screw holes (I used five screws across each back piece). Drill pilot holes at the marked locations into the positioned shelf, then sink your screws.

Position your side pieces with the top edge aligned with the top of the back

pieces, and drill pilot holes and countersinks to attach the sides to both the backs and shelf (I used four screws along the side, and two to hold the sides tight to the shelf).

Nail (or screw) the top in place after drilling pilot holes, making sure you have an even overhang on both sides.

The last step is to measure across the front edge just under the top, and cut your rail to length. So that it fits snugly into the angled opening, cut 45° angles on both ends. Now run a bead of glue along the top edge, position it, drill pilot holes and nail it in place.

Now that everything is assembled, fill your screw and nail holes, then paint, add the hooks where you like them, and you're done.

# Open Bookcase

**BY A.J. HAMLER**

Ah, wonderful plywood! Good quality oak is expensive. In fact, if you were to make this bookcase with solid ¾"-thick oak you'd easily spend over $125 for the wood — probably more — at home center prices.

On the other hand, a single 4 × 8 sheet of ¾" oak veneer plywood will create all the components for this project for about $40, with plenty left over for future projects. (You can also buy oak ply in 2 × 4 and 4 × 4 sheets.) As a bonus, plywood at home centers is generally far straighter and flatter than dimensional oak, which is prone to severe warping in the storage racks. Plywood has an unattractive edge, but we'll fix that with iron-on oak edge-banding for a finished appearance.

Can't handle a big sheet of plywood in your car? No problem. They'll cut it to a more manageable size for you on one of their big panel saws, killing two birds with one stone: Not only does it make transporting it home easier, but having the sheet ripped to width before leaving the store will save a lot of time and effort over doing it with a jigsaw. However, plywood is notorious for tear-out when crosscutting, so only have them do the ripping; crosscut the pieces to length yourself when you get home. Your best bet is to have them cut enough 10"-wide stock to create the four shelves and the six main vertical pieces, plus one 4' length each of 3½" wide and 6½" wide stock for the base and divider sections. Leave the rest uncut for future use.

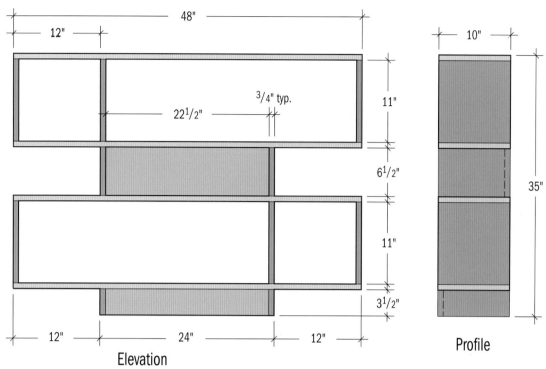

48"

12"

$3/4$" typ.

$22^1/2$"

11"

$6^1/2$"

11"

$3^1/2$"

12"  24"  12"

Elevation

10"

35"

Profile

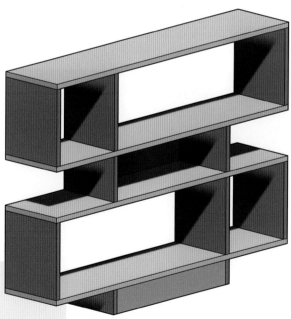

## Parts List

| | | | THICKNESS X WIDTH X LENGTH | |
| NO. | PART | STOCK | INCHES | MILLIMETERS |
| --- | --- | --- | --- | --- |
| 4 | shelves | oak plywood | $3/4 \times 10 \times 48$ | 19 × 254 × 1219 |
| 6 | main verticals | oak plywood | $3/4 \times 10 \times 11$ | 19 × 254 × 279 |
| 1 | base front | oak plywood | $3/4 \times 3^1/2 \times 22^1/2$ | 19 × 89 × 572 |
| 2 | base sides | oak plywood | $3/4 \times 3^1/2 \times 10$ | 19 × 89 × 254 |
| 1 | divider back | oak plywood | $3/4 \times 6^1/2 \times 22^1/2$ | 19 × 165 × 572 |
| 2 | divider sides | oak plywood | $3/4 \times 6^1/2 \times 10$ | 19 × 165 × 254 |
| Oak iron-on edge-banding $3/4$" (19mm) | | | | |

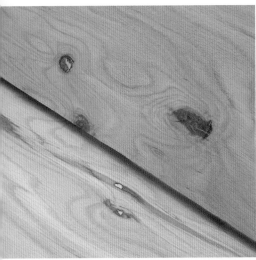

One face of a plywood sheet is typically better than the other. Orient components with face blemishes so they're not easily seen.

To prevent tear-out when crosscutting, score the cut line with a utility knife or razor blade.

Although both faces of the plywood are oak, one side is usually better than the other. Sometimes, the occasional knot can be an interesting detail, but examine your components for undesirable surface flaws and orient them so they'll be less visible in the finished piece — such as the underside of shelves, or facing inward where they'll likely be hidden by books.

Measure and mark each of the 10"-wide pieces to length for the shelves and verticals, but before cutting, score along the cut line several times with a utility knife. This will help prevent tear-out as you cut. With the jigsaw's orbital action on the lowest setting for a cleaner cut, crosscut your pieces to length. Clean up the cut if necessary with a piece of sand-paper wrapped around a wooden block, but leave the edges sharp for now.

Do the same to cut the 3½" and 6½"-wide components of the base and divider sections to length. Depending on its capacity, you may be able to cut these narrower pieces on your miter saw. No scoring is necessary here, but use a piece of scrap underneath to prevent tear-out on the underside.

With all the components cut, organize and mark them with a pencil according to face appearance. Again, less attractive faces should orient either down, inward or to the back.

### Getting the Edge

The only drawback of using plywood for furniture is that the raw edges don't match the oak faces, but you can correct that easily with oak edge-banding. Furniture manufacturers use huge, ridiculously expensive automated machines to apply hundreds of thousands of feet of edge-banding for furniture components. Fortunately, there's an easy, inexpensive home shop option for doing the same thing.

Iron-on edge-banding can be quickly applied — it comes with hot-melt glue already on the contact surfaces — and once trimmed will give plywood edges the look of solid wood. Oak edgebanding is readily available at home centers, usually in 25' rolls for about $6. You'll want to apply it to all visible edges, so you'll need about 30' for this project, plus a bit extra

Cut carefully up to the cut line, with the jigsaw's orbital action on the lowest setting for a cleaner cut. When crosscutting, keep these less-attractive faces up — jigsaws tend to tear out on the top surface when cutting.

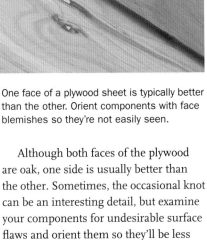

for trimming purposes, so you may have to buy two rolls. If you plan to use your bookcase against a wall, there's no need to put it on the back; for a freestanding bookcase, apply it to the rear edges, too.

Cut all the edge-banding pieces to length with scissors, allowing an extra inch on each end, but handle it carefully as it's easy to get splinters. Be sure to refer to the packaging for specific iron settings.

Edge-banding is quite thin, but you'll still want to apply it before assembly so all components go together flush. Hold the edge-banding in place with one hand while running the iron carefully along the length. Check frequently to be sure it's adhering and continue until the entire piece is securely attached. Mistakes are easy to fix: Just reheat with the iron and correct it. When cool, trim the ends flush with a utility knife.

Because plywood is slightly thinner than the nominal thickness — ¾" ply is really about ²³⁄₃₂" thick — the edgebanding will overhang the edges a bit. This can be trimmed with a knife or a small block plane to almost flush. Take it down the rest of the way with a sanding block, but leave the edges sharp for now; we'll soften those edges after assembly. Put edge-banding on all components except the front edges of the center divider. We'll do that later.

## Putting It Together

Assembly is easiest if you put the components together in sets, starting with the base section and working from the ground up. Line up the components so that the front piece is flush with the edge-banded sides, and drill countersunk pilot holes at the screw locations. I use a combination drill/countersink that leaves perfect ⅜" holes above the screw head, just right to accept an oak plug that hides the

A miter saw makes short work of crosscutting the narrower piece. Put a piece of scrap beneath the workpiece to prevent tear-out on the underside.

An ordinary household iron can apply edge-banding quickly and easily. (Get permission *before* borrowing the iron for shop use.)

Since edge-banding is slightly wider than the plywood edge, trim the excess with a knife or a small block plane. If using a razor knife (left), keep the blade parallel to the wood's surface, or slightly canted edge-up. It's very easy to gouge the veneer if you get distracted. Sand edge-banding smooth and flush with a sanding block (above).

The type of plug you use determines how your project will look. The face-grain plug on the left (inset) will hardly be noticed; the end-grain plug on the right will add a contrasting detail. Put a small amount of glue in the countersunk hole with a nail or toothpick, insert the plug (left) and tap gently into place. Sand plugs flush with the surface when dry.

screw. Plugs are available in a variety of wood species at your local hardware store or home center, or from any woodworking supply catalog. Plugs come in two types: end grain and face grain. End grain plugs accept stain more readily, making for a darker finished plug which can be a nice accent. For something more subtle (in fact, almost invisible) use face-grain plugs. Put a bit of glue in the countersunk hole, drop in a plug, set it in place

with a few light taps from a hammer, and sand flush with a sanding block.

Note that the interior vertical pieces in the shelf sections are offset and line up exactly on one side with the base and divider sections, so center the finished base on the very bottom shelf and trace the outline on one side as a guide for locating the vertical piece in the bottom. Set the base aside and assemble the lower shelf section.

To attach the base to the bottom shelf section, flip everything upside down. I simply drove a few screws up through the base into the bottom of the shelf section, using the drill from my pocket-screw set for pilot holes. Measure the drilling depth carefully and wrap masking tape around the bit to mark the depth. Drill your holes, apply a bit of glue to the mating edge of the base, and screw it into place.

As with the base, use the assembled divider section to mark locations of the interior vertical piece. There's no vertical piece on the left side, so just drive screws up from underneath and plug them, but the vertical will limit access to the lower shelf unit on the right side. Solve this by driving screws at a 45° angle through the front and back of the divider section, using your pocket-hole bit to make the pilot holes. (That's why we didn't put edgebanding on the front of the divider section.) You'll find that this is easier to accomplish if you clamp the section together before drilling so that the parts remain aligned.

Repeat the process with the top shelf section. As before, you can drill and plug on one side, and screw at a 45° angle on the other. When completely assembled, cut edge-banding to fit the front edges of the divider section, and iron in place to hide the angled screws.

With the bookcase assembled, check for any bits of tear-out that may have

Before assembling, mark the locations of the vertical components so they can be lined up accurately.

Build each of the four sections of the bookcase — base, divider and the two shelf sections — separately, then assemble them.

To prevent drilling pilot holes too deeply (and risking drilling through the workpiece) measure the depth carefully, marking the drill bit with some masking tape.

occurred when crosscutting and fill with wood filler. Ease all the edges with fine sandpaper. Good oak plywood doesn't usually require a lot of sanding, but you may want to go over the whole piece for a uniform smoothness.

Stain the bookcase if desired — I used a golden oak stain on this one — and top it off with a few coats of satin polyurethane.

When assembling the four sections, clamping them together will keep everything aligned when drilling and driving screws.

# Contemporary Bookshelves

**BY MEGAN FITZPATRICK**

Inspired by a design in the February 2008 issue of the German magazine *Selbst*, this "I Can Do That" project commenced (as always) with a pilgrimage to the home center, where I picked up four 6' 1×12s and one 6' 1×6 of red oak, and a bag of red oak plugs.

Because there are no curves and no long rip cuts, this piece is ultra-simple to build. The trickiest operation is notching out the upright that will be stained black ... and that's not tricky at all.

It's always a good idea to ensure the ends of your boards are square, so first trim a small amount off one end of all your pieces at the miter saw, and mark the cut ends.

Now you're ready to get started. Set up a stop 31½" to the left of the saw blade as shown in the picture on the next page. Butt the trimmed end of one 1×12 against the stop, cut your first shelf, then repeat three times. Move the stop to 37½" and cut the matching top and bottom pieces. Your final crosscuts are on the two side pieces, at 58" (again, butt the ends you've trimmed against the stop so that both ends will be square after the cuts).

Lay the 1×6 (which is actually 5½" wide) flat and mark the four notches for the shelves. Theoretically, each notch should be ¾" thick (the thickness of your stock), but because you still need to sand the shelves, you may want to cut the notches a hair under that — or sand all your pieces to #120-grit first, and use the final thickness as your marking guide. Each notch is 1¼" deep, marked per the drawing.

Now clamp the 1×6 flat to your Workmate and use a jigsaw to cut out the notches. To minimize blade deflection, use a heavy blade for the 1¼"-deep cuts, then switch to a fine, narrow blade to make the ¾" cuts at the end of each notch. You may have to use a rasp to clean up the cuts after jigsawing, as you need them to be flat on all sides, and fit snug to the shelves. (For more information on cutting notches with a jigsaw, see the Egg Crate Shelves project on page 136.)

Lay the notched side piece atop the interior face of the wide side piece with the top and bottom aligned, then mark the notch locations on the wide side to show the location for the screws. Set the notched piece aside. Use a combination square to mark the shelf lines across the wide piece and mark for three screw holes across each shelf location. Drill the clearance holes with a ⅛" bit, then flip the piece over. Using your already drilled holes as a guide, drill countersinks at each hole location on the outside face.

Now find a flat surface on which to rest one end of the wide side piece, then clamp a shelf into your Workmate and lay the side piece across it (interior down),

Two-toned appeal. Different colors of wood, simple lines and sharp, square edges give these easy-to-build bookshelves a contemporary flair.

carefully lining up the shelf with the lines you've marked on the side. The side piece serves as a location guide to drill ⅛" pilot holes into the shelf. Now sink 1¾" screws into each hole, securing the shelf

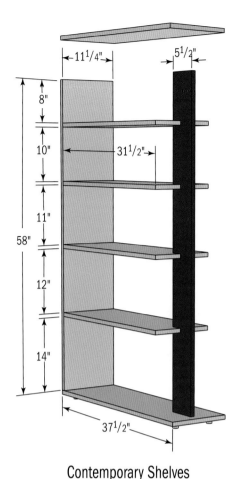

**Contemporary Shelves**

Dimensions shown: 11¼", 5½", 8", 10", 31½", 11", 58", 12", 14", 37½"

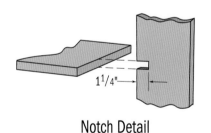

1¼"

**Notch Detail**

## Parts List

| NO. | PART | STOCK | THICKNESS X WIDTH X LENGTH | |
| --- | --- | --- | --- | --- |
| | | | INCHES | MILLIMETERS |
| 1 | Top | Oak | ¾ × 11¼ × 37½ | 19 × 285 × 953 |
| 1 | Bottom | Oak | ¾ × 11¼ × 37½ | 19 × 285 × 953 |
| 4 | Shelves | Oak | ¾ × 11¼ × 31½ | 19 × 285 × 800 |
| 1 | Wide side | Oak | ¾ × 11¼ × 58 | 19 × 285 × 1473 |
| 1 | Narrow side | Oak | ¾ × 5½ × 58 | 19 × 285 × 1473 |
| 4 | Feet | Scrap | ½ × 1 × 1 | 13 × 25 × 25 |

to the side. We recommend McFeeley's or Spax "premium" wood screws; both are available at mcfeelys.com or 800-443-7937.

Attach the remaining three shelves in the same manner. (You may need help to reposition the workpiece as you add the shelves; it gets heavier with each one.)

After the four shelves are attached, lay the piece on its side on a table (shelves pointing up), and scoot it to the end of the table so you have room to easily manipulate your drill. Balance the top piece at the top edge, and drill three pilot holes through the top and into the side. Then drill countersinks into the pilot holes in the top, and set the screws. Do the same at the bottom.

Line up the notched side at the center, drill two pilot holes and countersinks at the top and bottom, and set the screws.

Once you're sure everything fits together well, remove the notched piece and finish as desired. I used two coats of Cabot's ebony stain. After the stain was completely dry, I reinstalled the notched side, glued and tapped in plugs to cover

Countersink bit. The top of this countersink bit drills a hole with angled sides, into which a screw head seats so that it's flush with or below the surface of your work, depending on how deep you drill the countersink.

the screw holes on top and sanded them flush, then finished the entire piece with two wiped-on coats of Watco Danish Oil in natural.

Unless your notches are very snug, you'll need to "toenail" the shelves from the undersides to the notched side piece, to keep each shelf firmly in place. (Toe-nailing is simply a nail set at an angle through two pieces.)

Finally, make four 1" × 1" feet out of pieces of scrap (I used ½" plywood) and nail them to the bottom, about 1" in from the corners.

A final note: With any heavy and tall piece, it's necessary to secure it to the wall before loading it up.

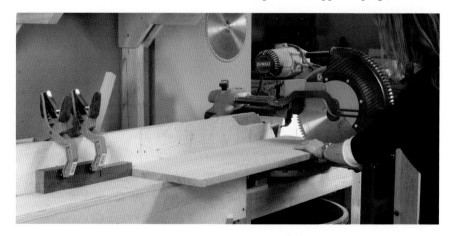

Clamped stop. Making multiple cuts of equal length at the miter saw is made easier by measuring just one piece then clamping a stop-block to the fence. Then, instead of measuring and marking each cut, you can simply butt the squared stock against the stop.

# Shaker Shelf

**BY GLEN HUEY**

In the 1989 edition of the Willis Henry Shaker auction of ephemera, wooden-ware and furniture, this Canterbury, New Hampshire, shelf immediately caught my eye. I've incorporated a few size and construction variations from the antique in my version, but this design is true to the spirit of the original.

You'll find a use for those scraps from earlier projects if you decide to paint this piece. Mixed woods are often found in antique furniture. Don't be afraid to try it (if you don't have enough scraps, head to the home center).

Building the drawer for this shelf is a new technique, but don't freak on me! It appears more complex than it is and your list of must-do projects will grow once this skill is in your arsenal.

## Curvy Bottoms Add Appeal

Each side of the shelf has three curves or arc cuts. Each arc evolves from the previous arc, starting with the smallest radius at the lower, rear corner of each side.

Crosscut the sides to length and draw the pattern on the pieces. The size of each radius is called out on the illustrations and can be easily transferred to the side using a compass. You could also choose to lay out the curve on a piece of cardboard, or scrap piece of 1/4" plywood. Either will give you a chance to get the shape perfect before transferring it to the actual piece of wood.

Cut the profile with the jigsaw then clean up any rough edges with a rasp and

# Parts List

| NO. | PART | STOCK | INCHES | MILLIMETERS |
|---|---|---|---|---|
| | | | THICKNESS X WIDTH X LENGTH | |
| 1 | top | poplar | $3/4 \times 9^1/4 \times 22^3/4$ | 19 × 235 × 578 |
| 2 | sides | poplar | $3/4 \times 7^1/4 \times 17^1/2$ | 19 × 184 × 445 |
| 1 | top face rail | poplar | $3/4 \times 3^1/2 \times 17^1/4$ | 19 × 89 × 438 |
| 1 | bottom face rail | poplar | $3/4 \times 2^1/2 \times 17^1/4$ | 19 × 64 × 438 |
| 3 | internal rails | poplar | $3/4 \times 2^1/2 \times 17^1/4$ | 19 × 64 × 438 |
| 2 | drawer sides | poplar | $3/4 \times 3^1/2 \times 6^1/4$ | 19 × 89 × 159 |
| 2 | drawer front/back | poplar | $3/4 \times 3^1/2 \times 15^3/4$ | 19 × 89 × 400 |
| 1 | drawer face | plywood | $1/4 \times 3^3/4 \times 17^1/4$ | 6 × 95 × 438 |
| 1 | drawer bottom | plywood | $1/4 \times 6^1/4 \times 17^1/4$ | 6 × 159 × 438 |
| 1 | case back | plywood | $1/4 \times 8 \times 17^1/4$ | 6 × 203 × 438 |
| 1 | bed moulding | pine | $9/16 \times 2^1/4 \times 48$ | 14 × 57 × 1219 |
| 2 | wooden knobs | | $1^1/2$in (38mm) diameter | |

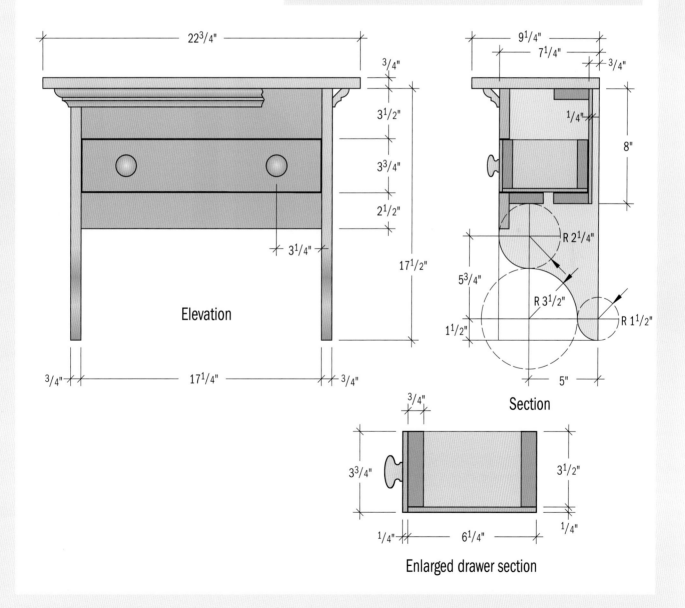

Elevation

Section

Enlarged drawer section

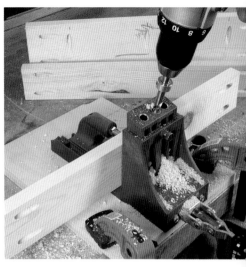

Take a minute to mark out the location of all your pocket screws. Some of the rails will have four pockets, some will have more.

When drilling a pocket on the end of a tall piece, such as this side, make sure that the clamp is very secure and be conscious of the potential of the piece to rock side-to-side as you drill.

I've always felt that it seemed easier to cut a curved line with a jigsaw rather than a perfectly straight one. But don't get too comfortable when cutting these curves. Stay close to the line, but still on the waste side and take it slow so you'll have time to react if you cut too close.

sandpaper. Since you have two sides with identical shapes, it makes sense to gang the two sides together as you clean up the edges. This allows you to make sure that both shapes will be identical, even after filing and sanding.

Next, square one end of the stock and crosscut the five rails that fit between the sides. Position and clamp a stop block at the miter saw to cut each piece to the same length. Then pull out the pocket-screw jig. You have holes to drill.

Each rail requires two pocket-screw holes per end. Also, the top face rail needs three extra holes, spaced evenly and along the grain, to attach the top.

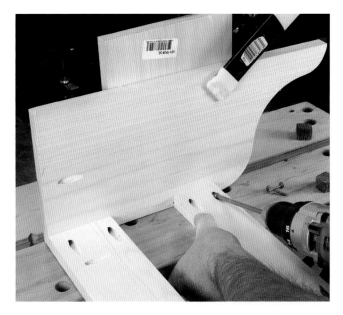

The first assembly step is to attach the top and lower face rails to the sides. Start with one side first, then spin the piece and attach the rails to the second side.

The partially assembled case is attached to the top. Make sure the case is centered from left to right on the top before putting in the screws. The nailing rail (not shown) is next attached to the sides.

The front drawer rail is next. It attaches to the sides and the front rail. A clamp makes it much easier to flush up the top edge of the front rail to the drawer rail as it's attached.

With the rear drawer rail in place, you're ready to attach the ¼" back to the nailing rail and the rear drawer rail.

The drawer rail will need one hole that is centered, also along the grain, to hold the drawer rail flush with the lower face rail. It's a good idea to mark all of your boards before you start, to avoid any mistakes.

## Step to Successful Assembly

The steps to assemble the case need to be completed in a specific order to allow you access to the pocket-screw holes. Follow the photos on this page to get the order right.

First, attach the top face rail and lower face rail flush with the front edge of the sides. Next, cut the top to length and position the partially assembled case on the underside of the top. Make sure the case is centered on the top and flush at the back edge. Add the screws and the top is attached.

Now attach the top nailing rail to the sides, holding it in ¼" from the back edge of the sides. Then attach the front

drawer rail to the lower face rail and the sides, followed by the rear drawer rail which is attached only to the two sides.

All that's left to assemble the case is to nail the back in place. Now for the crown.

## The Crowning Moment

To fit the mouldings to the case, position the project on its top with the front facing toward you as you work.

Set the miter saw at 45° to the right and position the moulding to the saw with the two flat areas on the back against the fence and table as shown above. Make the first cut leaving the side moulding extra long.

To make the second cut you need to swing the saw to 45° in the opposite direction, or to the left. Holding the moulding on the left side of the blade, make a cut that fully establishes the new angle on the stock.

Match those cuts to form the left-front corner. Hold the front moulding tight to the case and move to the right corner of the project and find the cut line.

Mark the cut line for the second cut on the front moulding as well as the angle of cut. Head back to the miter saw to complete the first cut for the right corner.

With the remainder of the stock you'll need to change the angle of the saw again and make a cut that mimics the second cut of the left corner. This gives you all the necessary pieces for your project.

Back at the project, position the first corner as before and add a 3d finish nail to the front moulding. Check the fit of

the corners then complete the installation of the front moulding by driving nails into both the top and bottom of the profile as shown in the photo below left.

Position the side mouldings and mark a line at the back edge of the shelf (see photo below). The 90° cut is made with the moulding flat against the miter saw's table and tight to the fence.

Add glue to the miters for a bit of insurance to hold the miter joints tight, and attach the side mouldings with 3d nails too.

Use a nail set to set the heads of the nails just below the surface of the moulding — sometimes you can use a second nail for this step.

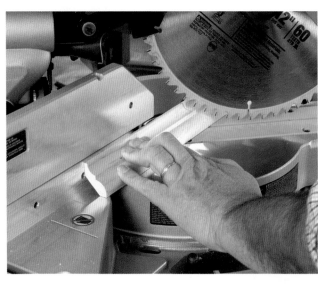

The best way to cut crown moulding at the miter saw is to position the moulding upside down to how it's installed on your project. As you mark the cut line, also note the direction of the 45° cut.

Marking the cut line for the second cut on moulding requires an exact layout. A ruler or straightedge held tight to the sides will reveal the location for the cut.

Two nails per corner, per piece will keep the corners tight. Pilot drilling for the nails will help avoid splits at the ends of your moulding.

After placing the return moulding tight against the corner miter, mark for the square cut, flush at the back of the case.

Building the drawer with pocket screws is a simple task. But, it is necessary to achieve a flush fit between the front and sides. The level joint makes the best connection when attaching the drawer face with glue.

Your jigsaw will do a decent job of cutting out the ¼" plywood drawer face and drawer bottom, but a little clean up will be required. A block plane does a nice job on this thinner material.

Nails hold the bottom in place on the drawer. Center the nails carefully on the drawer sides or you might add an extra hole to the inside or outside of your drawer.

The aesthetics of the drawer, which shows no screws during normal use, is achieved by turning the pocket screws toward the outside of the drawer box and covering the front with the drawer face. Cut the face oversized and trim it flush with your plane.

## Building an Inset Drawer

You already have the skills to build a drawer. You just need to know how to cut with a jigsaw, drill pocket-screw holes and hammer nails.

To properly fit an inset drawer, the front should be about ⅛" smaller than the opening — ¹⁄₁₆" on either edge. Measure the opening from side to side and subtract ⅛". Then subtract the thickness of the two sides (1½") to arrive at the cut length of the front and back of the drawer box. Drill two pocket-screw holes at each end of the these pieces.

Next, cut the drawer sides to size and attach the front to the sides with pocket screws. Careful alignment of the joint makes attaching the drawer face easier. Complete the drawer box by installing the back piece.

The drawer bottom is ¼" plywood. Measure the footprint of the box then cut the bottom with the jigsaw. Smooth rough cuts with a plane and attach the bottom with 3d nails.

Measure for the drawer face, including the thickness of the plywood bottom. Cut the plywood a little oversized, then

add glue to the front rail of the drawer box, position the box onto the drawer face and add clamps as shown above.

Once the glue is dry trim the face with your plane, making the box and face flush on all sides. Finally, install store-bought wooden knobs.

To complete the shelf, knock off any sharp edges with #100-grit sandpaper, apply two coats of your favorite paint color, then cut and install the plywood back with 3d finish nails. Your Shaker-inspired shelf is ready to hang.

# Hanging Shelves

**BY MEGAN FITZPATRICK**

The inspiration for this small hanging set of shelves is a late 18th- to early 19th-century (circa 1775-1825) English dovetailed version in oak with a dark finish. I wanted to replicate the look as much as possible using the I Can Do That tool set and big-box stock, so I adjusted the dimensions to fit dimensional lumber, and, after the construction was done, sanded the edges heavily to impart a well-worn look. I then applied a somewhat distressed finish (more on that later).

## Lumber Choices

The inspiration project is 8" wide and appears to be made of stock slightly thicker than $1/4$". But at the big box store, the thickness choices are $1/4$" and $1/2$", and I dithered between 4"-wide and 6"-wide stock.

Because I knew I'd be using nails rather than dovetails for the box's joints, I opted for $1/2$" stock to allow for a bit of forgiveness for slightly off-kilter drilling. And, I decided on the 4"-wide nominal lumber (which, as you know, is actually $3^1/2$" wide) because $5^1/2$" wide (the 6" nominal stock) simply looked too bulky. So, after crosscutting and gluing up two 19"-long pieces, the overall width of my back piece ended up 7" wide.

## Add Curves

After the glue on the back dries, use the glue line as your centerline, and set your dividers (basically, a compass without a pencil) to a $7/8$" radius, then scribe a circle at the center top of the back.

Then, measure down $4^1/2$" from the top edge and mark a pencil line across the width. At either edge, that

line locates the terminus of the arcs.

Now measure down $1^1/2$" from that line, and at $7/8$" to either side of the centerline, make a pencil mark.

Reset your compass or dividers to a $4^1/2$" radius, set the point on one of those marks, then strike the arc from the bottom of the small circle to the edge of your back; repeat on the other side of the centerline. (This is not exact; please your eye.)

Use your jigsaw to cut the curves. Typically, we recommend the Bosch X-tra Clean for Wood blades, and I used that blade to cut the large arcs on either side. But when it came time to cut the tight circle at the top, I switched to the narrowest blade I could find, with lots of fine teeth, and cut slowly to overcome blade deflection. Once all the curves are cut, smooth them as needed with sandpaper.

## Five Easy Pieces

The box is simply five pieces of 4" nominal lumber, nailed together. The two sides are each $14^1/2$" in length; the three shelves are $5^1/2$" in length. Make all the cuts at the miter saw, and set a stop so the two side pieces are exactly the same length. Set the stop again so all three shelves will match one another perfectly. While you can measure and mark each cut individually, why would you? That simply opens the door to error.

It doesn't matter if the sides are dead-on 19"; it does matter that they match — and the same is true for the shelves. If everything matches and is cut square, clamping up a square box is a breeze. But before assembly, sand all the pieces to #120-grit.

If you can't find a compass, dividers work just fine for marking out circles — and the resulting tool marks add an air of period flair.

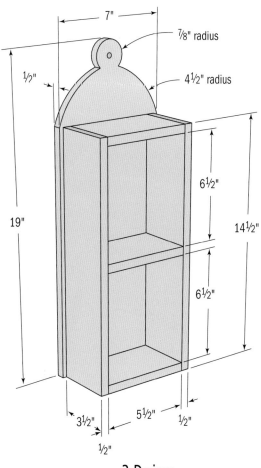

**3-D view**

After you've clamped the five pieces in position, drill three pilot holes at each joint location, then hammer in 1" finish nails to hold the pieces together. (I recommend checking twice to make sure your clamps are tight before you start to hammer.)

### Attach the Back

On the back face of the back piece, center your shelf assembly side to side and flush with the bottom, and trace around the shelf assembly inside and out. (You'll drill your pilot holes centered between those lines.)

Now flip the back face up, and again center the shelf assembly side to side and flush to the bottom, then clamp the two workpieces together with a clamp or two — make sure to locate the clamps to leave access to drill your pilot holes. Now drill pilot holes through the back and into the shelf assembly. As always, drill pilot holes that are slightly smaller

in diameter than the shaft of your nails, and be cognizant that the shelf assembly is only $1/2$" thick; there's little room to wander off course with your drill bit.

To attach the back, I used roofing nails to add a little mechanical strength to the joints. Unlike finish nails, roofing nails have wide, flat heads that aren't easily pulled through — though it's unlikely anything small enough to fit on these shelves will impart enough weight to cause that problem.

### A Fun Finish

To give this piece a well-worn look, I attacked the edges with #80-grit sandpaper, creating a few divots to emulate a century or so of wear and tear, and I softened the crisp 90° angles of the shelves' butt joints the same way. I also hit the project a few times with the claw end of a hammer, and threw my keys at it repeatedly for a couple minutes.

After slaking my appetite for destruction, I went over the surface with

## Parts List

| NO. | PART | STOCK | THICKNESS X WIDTH X LENGTH | |
| | | | INCHES | MILLIMETERS |
| --- | --- | --- | --- | --- |
| 1 | back | poplar | $1/2 \times 7 \times 19$ | $13 \times 178 \times 483$ |
| 2 | sides | poplar | $1/2 \times 3^{1}/2 \times 14^{1}/2$ | $13 \times 89 \times 368$ |
| 3 | shelves | poplar | $1/2 \times 3^{1}/2 \times 5^{1}/2$ | $13 \times 89 \times 140$ |

While you could try to hold adjacent pieces in place while you drill pilot holes, it's much better to clamp everything together first — just be sure to keep the clamp pads clear of where you need to drill!

#120-grit sandpaper, and painted on two coats of Benjamin Moore "Bittersweet Chocolate" latex. After the paint was completely dry, I sanded it almost all the way through in a few places. Then, I rubbed on a coat of ebony Briwax, making sure to fill the nail holes and purposeful imperfections I'd created (and perhaps some not-so-purposeful ones, too).

Typically, we use finish nails in our projects, but in this case, I chose roofing nails because their wide, flat heads will help keep the shelves firmly attached to the back for years to come (copper roofing nails are also available — and those would look great on a nice wood with a clear finish).

# Message Center

**BY STEVE SHANESY**

The kitchen is the crossroads for today's busy family. And while we have high-tech gadgets to text messages, take notes and keep a calendar, I've found a kitchen message board has helped to keep my family organized for 30 years. Three decades ago, I made several message centers as gifts and can report that some are still in use — a testament to their utility.

My concession to "high-tech" materials and woodworking methods for this updated version are a dry-erase writing surface instead of chalkboard, and pocket screws instead of dowel joints. Both make an easy project even easier. And as with all I Can Do That projects, the materials come from your local home center and the tools used are all from the modest I Can Do That kit.

## Round up Your Materials

I found $1/8$"-thick dry-erase board in the paneling section of the store. It was offered in 32" x 48" for just more than $10. That's worth mentioning because you could make two message boards from this one piece of dry-erase board. The other materials needed, an 8' length of 1x2 pine and an 8' length of half-round pine moulding, came to another $7. If you buy one more length of 1x2, you'll have enough material to make two message boards with a total outlay of about $28.

Take your time and select your 1x2 pine carefully. Look for pieces that have few large or loose knots (or better yet, none). If there are knots, you can cut around them and get clear workpieces. Also, check that the wood is reasonably straight and flat.

## The Importance of Square

In woodworking, the principle of "square" is fundamental to satisfactory results. Slight deviations, even one degree, can play havoc with your results and leave a twisted mess. Keep this principle in mind while building. Use your combination square to check the setup of your miter saw and circular saw. Check your 1x2 pine. Are the faces and edges square? Make sure your crosscuts are square to both the width and thickness of your workpieces. Get in the habit of "working square" and your projects will have fewer problems.

## Cut Parts to Size

Cut the two vertical pieces, called stiles, to length using your miter saw. If you're starting from the end of the board as it came from the store, first trim off the end. Cut the top horizontal piece (the

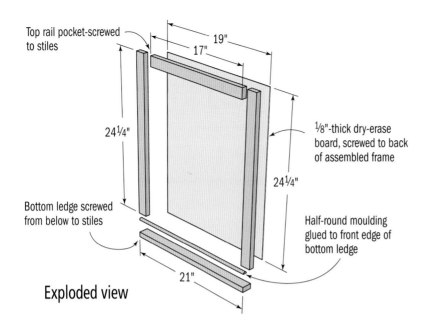

Top rail pocket-screwed to stiles

19"

17"

24¼"

24¼"

⅛"-thick dry-erase board, screwed to back of assembled frame

Bottom ledge screwed from below to stiles

Half-round moulding glued to front edge of bottom ledge

21"

### Exploded view

upside-down in your Workmate. Position the bottom piece and check that it over-hangs the outside edge of the stiles $1/2"$ on each side. Drill a pilot hole in the end grain of the stile so the part doesn't split when screwed. To mark the hole location, push the point of a screw though the bot-tom holes to make a mark, then drill the hole. Set the bottom in place and screw it to the frame.

Now remove the bottom piece because there's a bit more work on the three-sided frame. Use your router and a $1/4"$ round-over bit to ease the frame's edges. Rout this profile on all long edges on the face side of the frame. Clamp the work to the bench while routing and move the clamps as needed. On my router setup,

rail). Cut the bottom piece as well. Again, make sure your cuts are square.

You can arrange these pieces and verify that your dimensions are accurate. Then go ahead and cut the dry-erase board. To make this cut, use a circular saw and a straightedge jig to guide the saw (more information on this jig can be found on page 17). For support, set up a pair of sawhorses and place a couple plywood strips across the horses to sup-port the dry-erase board. Mark the panel to width and set the jig so the saw cuts to the mark. Now clamp the jig to the ply-wood strips and check to be sure nothing has moved. Set your depth of cut so you barely cut into the plywood strips, then make your cut. Repeat the process to cut the panel to length.

### Assemble the Frame

The upper rail is joined to the stiles using two pocket screws at each joint. Remem-ber, the rail goes between the stiles. After checking the drill depth on your pocket-hole jig, space the pocket holes in about $1/2"$ from the edge of your 1x2 and drill them. When done, screw the three parts together. Keep the top edge of the stiles flush to the top edge of the rail.

The bottom is screwed on to the ends of the stiles from below, with one #8 x1⅝" screw at each side. Drill and countersink a hole that's 1¼" in from the ends and ⁵⁄₁₆" in from the back edge. Now clamp your three-sided frame

Use a straightedge guide with your circular saw to guarantee an accurate, straight cut. You'll use this jig over and over in future projects.

## Parts List

| NO. | PART | STOCK | THICKNESS X WIDTH X LENGTH | |
|-----|------|-------|------|------|
| | | | INCHES | MILLIMETERS |
| 1 | top rail | pine | $3/4 \times 1^{1/2} \times 17$ | 19 × 546 D |
| 2 | stiles | pine | $3/4 \times 1^{1/2} \times 24^{1/4}$ | 19 × 508 D |
| 1 | bottom ledge | pine | $3/4 \times 1^{1/2} \times 21$ | 19 × 89 × 292 |
| 1 | half-round moulding | pine | $5/16 \times 5/8 \times 21$ | 19 × 76 × 610 |
| 1 | back | dry-erase board | $1/8 \times 19 \times 24^{1/4}$ | 19 × 89 × 292 |

In any project, parts must be square or problems will arise. Use a combination square to check all perpendicular faces.

the bottom of the bit was above the surface of the benchtop.

The half-round moulding is glued to the top surface of the bottom piece; it keeps your markers and eraser from falling off the ledge. Carefully cut the moulding to the same length as your bottom piece. Apply glue to the moulding and lightly clamp for 45 minutes. Wipe off any glue squeeze-out with a wet rag. After the glue has set, reattach the bottom to the frame.

Before screwing the dry-erase board to the frame, sand and finish the pine. I used a random-orbit sander and #120, then #150-grit sandpaper. Next, I sprayed a clear lacquer finish from an aerosol can. Spray only in a well-ventilated space and away from open flames — think water heater and furnace!

The dry-erase board is easily attached to the back of the frame with countersunk flat-head screws.

When you decide where you want to install your message board, use picture hanging hardware.

You can fit two pocket screws in each corner of the stile-to-rail joints. Snug the screws tight — but be gentle because pine is soft.

# Tool Rack

**BY CHRISTOPHER SCHWARZ**

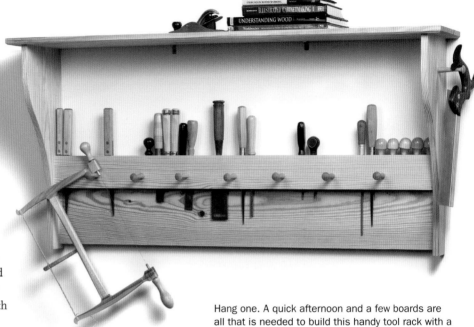

It's good to keep your tools protected (think: tool chest). But it's also good to keep them handy (think: at arm's reach). My favorite way to accomplish both goals is a stout tool rack.

I've made many tool racks since I became a woodworker, most of them crude affairs that were cobbled together in a few minutes. I've always wanted a rack that both looks good and is easy to build. Then, while browsing a French book on vintage handplanes, I saw it.

In a 19th-century engraving of a French workshop, the back wall was covered with a rack very much like this one. Finding it and drawing it to scale were the hard parts. Building it took just a few hours.

### You Know the Drill

The project is assembled using pocket screws, dimensional pine and some Shaker pegs I found at our home center (will wonders never cease?).

You are going to need at least 12' of 1×12 and 4' of 1×4 pine to build this rack. Once you have the wood in hand, the first step is to cut all the parts to length. Then rip the back and top pieces to width. Use a circular saw with an edge guide to make the rips, or use a jigsaw to make the rips then remove the saw blade marks with your block plane.

Next work on the ends with their ogee shape. I used the SketchUp drawing (available for free on our web site) to create a full-size paper template. I stuck the paper to one of the end pieces using 3M spray adhesive. Then I cut the ogee shape using a jigsaw and cleaned up my curves with a rasp and sandpaper.

Hang one. A quick afternoon and a few boards are all that is needed to build this handy tool rack with a shelf above.

Then I used the finished end piece as a pattern to make the second end.

### Everything is in Pocket

All the joinery for this rack is screws. Bore three pocket holes on each end of the 1×4, which is the front of the tool rack. Then drill five pocket holes on each end of the back piece of the rack.

You are just about ready to assemble the bulk of the rack, but first clean off all the tool marks using a block plane or sandpaper.

You have to assemble the rack's parts in a certain way for everything to go together. The first job is to screw the front 1×4 to the end pieces.

The position of this part is critical because it will determine how much of a gap you will have between the front and the back of your rack. And this gap is what holds your tools. After much experimentation, I have found that a ½" gap is ideal for handling about 99 percent of my tools. However, you should take a close look at the tools you are going to store on your rack before you imitate me.

Use my drawing (or your own modified drawing) to mark a line where this front piece will join the ends. Clamp the front piece in position and screw it down.

The entire project is assembled with pocket screws. Here I'm boring five pocket holes on one end of the back piece.

Screw the other end in place using the same procedure.

Now you can screw the back piece in place. You should be able to squeeze it between the two ends, tap it gently in place, then screw it tightly to the ends.

Now you can turn your attention to the top piece. I cut a ¼" × ¼" chamfer on the underside of the top using a block plane. This is easy to do freehand — just use your combination square to lay out the pencil lines for the chamfer and plane the corner down to them. A little irregularity is OK.

The top of the rack is screwed to the ends. It's not done with pocket holes — just six simple countersunk No. 8 × 1¹/₄" wood screws.

## I've Got You Pegged

The Shaker pegs on the front of the rack give you more places to hang your tools. The seven pegs are spaced every 5¾" across the front of the rack. The center of each hole is 2¼" down from the top edge of the front of the rack.

The pegs I bought needed ½"-diameter and ½"-deep holes. Drill the holes, dab in some glue and knock them home. I had an extra peg left over from the package from the home center and put it on one of the ends to hold my shop apron (our photographer hung a backsaw on it for the photo at left).

## Finishing & Hanging

My first instinct was to paint this rack, but the pine I found was clear enough to use without paint. So the finish for this rack is the same I use for all my shop furniture. I thin down satin spar varnish with paint thinner at 3:1. I wipe on three

Don't forget the little L-brackets under the top. These prevent the top piece from sagging.

coats, sanding between each coat with a #320-grit sanding sponge.

Hanging the rack is simple. Find the studs in your shop wall. Drive No. 8 × 3" screws through the back of the rack and into your studs. Then purchase two simple L-brackets. Screw them to the underside of the top and into your studs. That should do the trick.

Though this rack is intended for the shop, several people who have seen it insist they are going to build one for the kitchen and put their knives in the rack, hang pots on the pegs and put cookbooks on the top shelf. As the French are both expert craftsmen and chefs, this is entirely appropriate.

## Parts List

| NO. | PART | STOCK | THICKNESS X WIDTH X LENGTH | |
|-----|------|-------|------|------|
| | | | INCHES | MILLIMETERS |
| 2 | Ends | Pine | ³/₄ × 9 × 23 | 19 × 229 × 584 |
| 1 | Back | Pine | ³/₄ × 10¹/₄ × 46 | 19 × 260 × 1168 |
| 1 | Front | Pine | ³/₄ × 3³/₄ × 46 | 19 × 95 × 1168 |
| 1 | Top | Pine | ³/₄ × 10 × 50¹/₂ | 19 × 254 × 1283 |

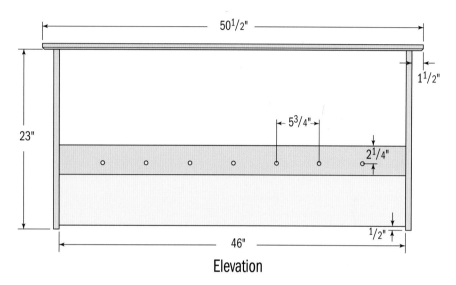

**Elevation**

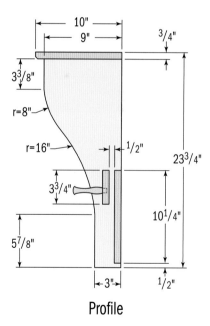

**Profile**

# Step Stool

**BY GLEN D. HUEY**

You may not remember when you looked up at the sink, or when you climbed up to the potty — but if you'd had a few extra inches on your legs, things would have been so much easier. This stool can do that for youngsters — and help you clean out your scrap bin, too.

This column generally begins with a trip to buy lumber, but you probably have the needed material — scraps — floating around your shop. This especially holds true if you paint this piece instead of go all wack-nutty with figured maple like I did. But if you need wood, simply head off to the store with your cut sheet in hand.

On this project, you can cut the pieces to size at the beginning of the build (most times it's better to cut to length and width as you need the parts in case things change). Once the parts are cut, the majority of the work is on the sides; they get laid out, drilled and shaped.

Find and mark the locations for the holes prior to any shaping work and make sure you have mirrored layout images. Keeping the drill square to the workpiece, bore the two ¾"-diameter holes and one ¼"-diameter hole in both sides.

Next, align the bottom edges of the two sides then lay out the centered arched cutout. To do that, set your compass at 2½" then find the location where the compass hits the marks along the bottom edge (3¾" from the outside edges) and 1¼" of height at the center — the compass point rests on the opposing workpiece when drawing the arch.

The photo at right shows how to lay out the side's curved shape. Clamp a workpiece to your bench, clamp a thin strip of wood to the bench just in front of the workpiece then bend that strip to

For tails, it's up. This stool transforms from a step stool into a chair with a simple flip of the step. As it increases the reach of your children, it reduces the materials in your scrap bin.

the 2⅞" layout mark along the top edge to get a pleasing shape. The radius of the line should be around 9¾".

With the strip bent to position, transfer the line to your side with a pencil. Use your jigsaw to cut close to the line and finish smoothing the curve with a rasp and sandpaper. This is the only time that you'll need to use this setup. The remaining layouts are transferred from this one curve.

## A Choice of Power Tools

Align the sides to transfer the layout from the first side workpiece to the second

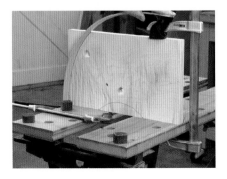

Fairing a curve. A thin strip of wood makes the perfect tool for designing a curve.

side, then flip the shaped side and repeat to add the second curve to second side. There's one curve yet to add, but that comes after you shape the second side.

You could use a jigsaw to cut the curve to the final dimension, but a router with a pattern bit installed does the job in a flash — then, rasp cleanup isn't necessary and final sanding is minimal. (For more information on using a router, refer to the Rule for Using the Tools section.)

Use a jigsaw to rough-cut and stay about ⅛" from the layout line. (This allows the bit to cut exactly to the line.) Fit the sanded curve to the rough-sawn curve, clamp the pieces to your bench so the clamps are out of the path of the router's base as the cut is made, and you're ready.

Adjust the router bit so the bearing rides along the sanded curve while the bit's cutting length is aligned to remove waste material. Make the cut moving the router from left to right, or with the direction the router bit is spinning. After routing the curve, flip the top board and repeat the steps to complete the work on that side.

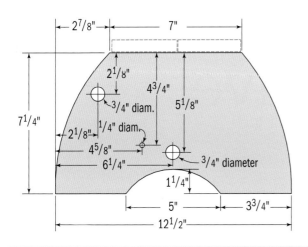

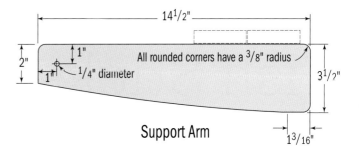

2" · 1" · 1" · 1/4" diameter · All rounded corners have a 3/8" radius · 14 1/2" · 3 1/2" · 1 3/16"

**Support Arm**

**Side Elevation**

## Parts List

| NO. | PART | THICKNESS × WIDTH × LENGTH INCHES | MILLIMETERS |
|-----|------|------------------------------------|-------------|
| 2 | Sides | 3/4 × 7 1/4 × 12 1/2 | 19 × 184 × 318 |
| 2 | Seatboards | 3/4 × 3 1/2 × 16 1/2 | 19 × 89 × 419 |
| 1 | Long dowel | 3/4 dia. x 1819 dia. x 457 | |
| 1 | Short dowel | 3/4 dia. x 16 1/2 | 19 dia. x 419 |
| 2 | Step supports | 3/4 × 3 1/2 × 14 1/2 | 19 × 89 × 369 |
| 4 | Dowel pins | 1/8 dia. x 2 | 3 dia. x 51 |
| 2 | Steps | 3/4 × 2 1/4 × 18 1/8 | 19 × 57 × 460 |
| **HARDWARE** | | | |
| 2 | Carriage bolts, 1/4" × 2" | | |
| 2 | Nuts, 1/4" | | |
| 4 | Washers, 1/4" | | |

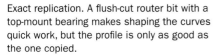

Exact replication. A flush-cut router bit with a top-mount bearing makes shaping the curves quick work, but the profile is only as good as the one copied.

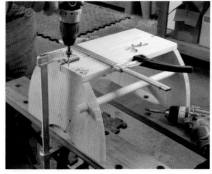

Arrange and attach. The seat boards, as are the steps, are spaced with pennies, clamped together and clamped to the frame prior to drilling for screws.

### On to Assembly

The seat boards, with the edges rounded with a block plane, are taken from standard-width stock, but the steps need to be ripped to width. Use your jigsaw to make the cuts and clean the sawn edges with a block plane. Sand all the parts, including the dowels, to clean up the surfaces and you're ready to assemble.

Position the dowels: The short dowel fits toward the bottom center of the sides with the ends flush with the exterior face of the sides. The longer dowel acts as a stop when the step is flipped up and the stool is in seat mode. This dowel extends 3/4" beyond the exterior faces of the sides. After the dowels are positioned, drill 1/8" cross holes through the edge of the sides and into the dowels. Glue in a dowel pin to secure everything.

The seat boards and the steps are attached with countersunk and piloted screws. Plug the screw holes then sand the areas smooth and it's time for finish, be it paint, or stain and topcoats.

With the finish complete, attach the step support assembly to the main stool assembly using lag bolts, washers and nuts (slip an extra washer between the support and side to keep the parts separated) then take the stool into the house and watch your youngsters reach new heights.

Switch the sides then lay out, rough-cut and rout the remaining curved edge. The sides are complete after a bit of sanding.

If you want to bypass the router work, jigsaw, rasp and sand those three curved profiles.

There's a bit of layout and shaping work done to the step supports. Make sure to locate the 1/4" holes prior to any shaping. The bottom edges of the supports have gentle curves and the corners are softened, or rounded. Make the cuts with your jigsaw, then use a rasp and sandpaper to finish the shaping. Or use the router setup to complete this work, like you did on the sides.

# Fish Sticks Trivet

**BY MEGAN FITZPATRICK**

A fishy project. This trivet is a quick, easy and fun project for kids of all ages.

This simple trivet is incredibly easy to make, and very inexpensive. I spent $16.44 (including tax) for four ½" × 2" × 4' pieces of red oak stock at the home center (and if you happen to have scraps and a table saw, well, this fun project is basically free).

Begin by clamping a stop-block 8" to the left of your miter saw blade (if you're right-handed), then proceed to cut 15 8"-long pieces. The stop block keeps you from having to measure and mark each piece — butt the end of the stock against the block for each cut and hold the workpiece with your left hand.

Now grab a small piece of scrap (or use the end of one of your 8"-long pieces) to serve as a stand-off block for the next cuts. A stand-off block is basically just a spacer that's used to set up a cut, then removed before the cut is made, to keep little pieces from getting trapped against a fence and perhaps rubbing up against the saw blade, which could cause the piece to go flying (possibly into your face — ouch). Now clamp your stop-block to the fence to the right of the blade at 2¹/₄" plus the width of your stand-off block, hold the stand-off block against your stop-block, and butt your stock against it. Hold the workpiece in place as you remove the stand-off block, then make the cut. Repeat this nine more times.

## Make a Sandwich

Now sandwich two sets of three 8" pieces, using glue on both sides of the center pieces, then clamp them together until the glue sets. These will be your head and tail pieces.

With those dry, start stacking your pieces, alternating between long and short. Drill two pilot holes near the center of all pieces other than the two sandwiches using a ¹/₃₂" bit, and drive a ³/₄" brad into each of those holes until the pointy ends are just emerging from the

Stand off for safety. With small workpieces, it's a good idea to use a spacer (also called a stand-off block) between the blade and fence to keep the cut piece from getting trapped.

STAND-OFF BLOCK

A fish ladder. Keep stacking until all your pieces are used, then cap with one of the "sandwiches."

A cleaning rule. A damp rag over the end of a 6" rule is handy to get in between the pieces for glue cleanup.

other side. (If you've a pinner or 18-gauge nailer, eschew the pilot holes and make quick work of the build.)

Now, set your combination square to $2^7/8$", grab one of the sandwiches and reference off the end to find the edge placement for the first "spine" piece. Add glue to the backside of the spine piece, and drive the brads home. You'll have to tilt your square slightly to register it against the first long piece as you find the placement of the second long piece. Repeat until all the single pieces are used up. Try to avoid too much glue squeeze-out — and if (when) you do get squeeze-out, wrap a damp rag around a 6" steel rule to get in between the pieces and clean it up while the glue is still wet. The final piece (the head or tail, depending on how you look at it), is simply glued in place, then the entire piece is clamped until the glue is dry.

### Choose Your Animal

Now trace the fish pattern (or whatever shape you like) on top, and cut it out with a jigsaw. Clean up the cuts with sandpaper, drill a hole for eyes (and hanging), and you're done.

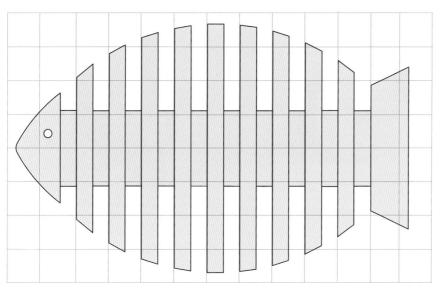
1 square = 1"

**Fish Sticks Trivet**

Jigsaw to shape. To keep yourself from having to do too much end-grain sanding (not fun), use a good jigsaw blade to cut down on blow out. (We recommend Bosch "Xtra-clean for Wood" blades.)

## Parts List

| NO. | PART | STOCK | THICKNESS X WIDTH X LENGTH | |
| --- | --- | --- | --- | --- |
| | | | INCHES | MILLIMETERS |
| 15 | Cross pieces | Red oak | $1/2 \times 2 \times 8$ | $13 \times 51 \times 203$ |
| 10 | "Spine" spacers | Red oak | $1/2 \times 2 \times 2^1/4$ | $13 \times 51 \times 57$ |

# Knife Block

**BY CHRISTOPHER SCHWARZ**

When we build an "I Can Do That" project we buy all the materials from a home center. For this project, however, I also had to stop at the grocery store on the way back to the shop.

That's because this knife block holds all your cutlery in an array of bamboo skewers — the kind you use for kabobs. Though you're not going to believe me, you need more than 1,000 ⅛"-diameter skewers to do the job. Good thing skewers are cheap — about $1.80 for 100.

In addition to cleaning out your supermarket of bamboo skewers, you're going to need some ½"-thick wood. You need about 4' of a board that's about 10" wide. I lucked out. Our Lowe's happened to have one piece of ½"-thick quartersawn red oak.

Begin by crosscutting your parts to length with your miter saw and ripping them to width with your jigsaw. The next step is to cut the finger joints with the jigsaw.

Flexible protection. This simple knife block allows you to store any size knife.

## Jigsaw Joinery

A jigsaw that's fitted with a quality blade can make cuts that require only a little tweaking with a chisel. The trick is to work against a fence.

First you need to figure out the exact distance from the edge of your jigsaw's shoe to one side of the blade. I made a test cut in some scrap to figure this out. Your blade might not be exactly centered so you'll want to check against the left and the right sides of the jigsaw's shoe.

Lay out all the cuts on the side pieces using the construction drawing. Then make the short ⅝"-long rip cuts that define all the fingers on the side pieces.

To remove the waste between the fingers, clamp a straight piece of scrap to your workpiece that will act as a fence for the shoe of the jigsaw. This fence will guide the jigsaw to make a straight cut as you saw out the waste. First remove the waste from the ends.

To cut the waste from between two fingers you'll have to make several cuts. Break up the waste with short cuts, then swoop in with the saw. A couple swoops and you can maneuver your jigsaw's shoe against the fence to make your finished

cut. If you take off too much your blade can deflect.

## Transfer the Shape

Now use the shape of the side pieces to mark the complementary shape on the ends. See the photo at the far right on the next page for details. Mark the waste then remove it from the ends using the same techniques (and the same fence) you used to cut the sides.

Now clean up the joints with a sharp chisel until the sides and ends fit together

Short cuts first. Define the fingers of the joints with these short rips.

Set the fence. With the fence in place remove the easy bits from the ends.

Swoop in. Remove the waste between the fingers in stages. Here's the first swooping cut.

A little tracing. Use the cuts on the sides to mark the shape on the ends.

## Parts List

| NO. | PART | STOCK | THICKNESS X WIDTH X LENGTH | |
| | | | INCHES | MILLIMETERS |
| --- | --- | --- | --- | --- |
| 2 | Sides | Oak | $1/2 \times 9 \times 7^3/_4$ | 13 × 229 × 197 |
| 2 | Ends | Oak | $1/2 \times 9 \times 5^1/_4$ | 13 × 229 × 133 |
| 1 | Bottom | Oak | $1/2 \times 4 \times 6^1/_2$ | 13 × 102 × 140 |
| 1,200 | Skewers | Bamboo | $1/8$ dia. x 8 | 3 dia. x 203 |

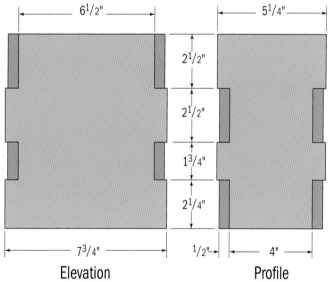

Elevation — 6½", 7¾", 2½", 2½", 1¾", 2¼"

Profile — 5¼", ½", 4"

snugly. Sand your pieces and ease all the edges of the finger joints with sandpaper.

**Assembly**

To glue the sides and ends together, apply yellow glue to the mating surfaces and clamp things together. Check your assembly with a small square and adjust as needed.

Now measure the opening for the bottom. Cut a piece that fits snugly and nail it in place with a new finish nails.

Finish the exterior of the knife block with a clear semi-gloss spray lacquer.

The bamboo skewers need to be 8" long. Don't cut them on the miter saw — that's risky. Bundle them up with tape and do the operation with a fine handsaw.

To keep the bamboo skewers in place, squirt two 25 ml vials of epoxy into the bottom. Mix the epoxy with a long stick then drop the skewers in place.

After the epoxy cures you're ready to pack as many knives as you can between the skewers.

# Shaker-inspired Step Stool

**BY MEGAN FITZPATRICK**

Inspired by a typical Shaker step stool, this version employs pocket screws to join both the side panels and the supports. To cut down on the number of rip cuts, I used three pieces of 1×6 dimensional lumber to form the side panels (1×6 actually measures ¾" × 5½"), so this version also ends up a bit deeper than a traditional Shaker stool — and thus a little sturdier and beefier looking.

First, use your miter saw to cut the 1×6 pieces to length for the side panels. You'll need two each at 20¼", 13¼" and 6¼".

Now, clamp one of the 20¼" pieces flat to your bench (face side down), and drill holes for two pocket screws along the edge that will meet the middle piece. Place one hole 2" from the bottom edge,

Shaker-inspired step stool. Don't let the panel glue-up scare you. This step stool (useful in just about any room of the house) is easy to build, using pocket screws as clamps and to add strength.

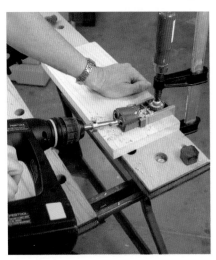

Drill the side panels. To use pocket screws to assist with panel glue-up, clamp the side pieces flat to your bench, and drill pocket holes to join the panel pieces. Here, I'm drilling the middle board with one hole 3" up from the bottom edge (it will get cut away when you cut the arc) and another hole 5¼" from the bottom edge.

the other at 11". Repeat with the second 20¼" piece. Now drill each 13¼" piece along the edges that will meet the short pieces. Locate one hole 3" from the bottom edge, the other at 5¼".

Next, it's time to glue up the side panels, and this is where the pocket screws come in handy — especially if you're short on clamps. Run a bead of wood glue along the edge of one of the 6¼" pieces, then line up that piece and a 13¼" piece flush across the bottom, and flat across the panel, then clamp across the two. Drive screws into the pockets

to join the two pieces together. Now that the screws are in place, you can unclamp and move on to joining the 20¼" to the 13¼" piece. Do the same with the other side panel.

Once your glue is dry, lay the panel screw-side up flat on your bench, and mark the center point across the bottom edge (it should be at 8¼"). Now, using an offcut as the base for the compass point, measure 2" down from the center point, place the compass point there, and draw the arc. Use a jigsaw to cut out the arc (you'll be cutting away the two bottom

# Parts List

| NO. | PART | STOCK | THICKNESS X WIDTH X LENGTH | |
|-----|------|-------|--------|--------|
| | | | INCHES | MILLIMETERS |
| 2 | Long panel piece | Poplar | $3/4 \times 5^{1}/2 \times 20^{1}/4$ | $19 \times 140 \times 514$ |
| 2 | Middle panel piece | Poplar | $3/4 \times 5^{1}/2 \times 13^{1}/4$ | $19 \times 140 \times 336$ |
| 2 | Short panel piece | Poplar | $3/4 \times 5^{1}/2 \times 6^{1}/4$ | $19 \times 140 \times 158$ |
| 3 | Step support | Poplar | $3/4 \times 1^{1}/2 \times 15^{3}/4$ | $19 \times 38 \times 400$ |
| 1 | Back brace | Poplar | $3/4 \times 1^{1}/2 \times 15^{3}/4$ | $19 \times 38 \times 400$ |
| 3 | Treads | Poplar | $3/4 \times 5^{7}/8 \times 18^{1}/4$ | $19 \times 149 \times 463$ |

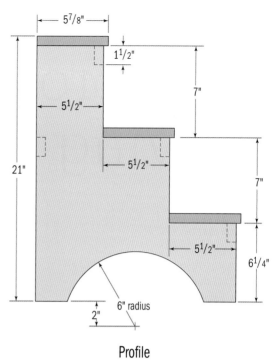

Profile

Panel glue-up. Use a clamp to hold your panel pieces together as you seat the pocket screws. Once the screws are in place, the clamp can be removed.

Quick and easy screwing jig. A scrap of 2x4 is clamped to the Workmate to serve as a guide and support for screwing the step supports and back brace in place on the side panels.

screws), then clean up the cut using a rasp and sandpaper.

Use a miter saw to cut the three step supports and back brace to 15¾" out of 1×2 (which actually measures ¾" × 1½"). Clamp each piece flat and drill one pocket hole into the center at either end. Set them aside.

Now, out of 1×8 (actually ¾" × 7½"), cut the three step treads to their final length of 18¼", then clamp a piece flat to your bench, with one long edge overhanging. Use your jigsaw to rip each tread to a width of 5⅞". (You'll get a straighter cut if you clamp a straightedge in place to guide the foot of the jigsaw.)

Now all the pieces are ready for assembly; this is a good time to sand (because as yet there are no corners to deal with). Sand over the panel joints to ensure the panels are flat. If you're planning to paint, sand to #120; if staining, you may want to sand to #180.

Joining the step supports and back brace to the sides is a bit tricky, involving some creative clamping and a scrap of 2×4. Separate the two halves of your Workmate so you can get clamps through the middle, then clamp the 2×4 scrap tight to the table. Butt the front edge of the bottom riser (the short piece in the panel) flush to the 2×4, and clamp the panel to the table. Hold the step support against the 2×4 flush with the top of the

riser, gripping firmly to keep it aligned, then drive the screw into the pocket to join the support to the panel (see picture at left). Reclamp the panel against the 2×4 to attach the center and top step supports, as well as the back brace.

Now attach the second side panel, using the same screwing jig. (If your drill is large, borrow a small one — or use a screwdriver — to more easily get inside the workpiece.)

Center each tread across the steps, drill pilot holes, then nail the treads in place with #6 finish nails. Use a nailset to sink the nails below the tread surface, then fill the holes with wood filler (or spackle), and let it dry.

Once the filler is dry, sand the joint edges and filler flush. Chamfer the front and side edges of the treads with a block plane to keep them from splintering, and break the back edge with sandpaper. Paint or stain as desired.

# Low-profile Serving Tray

**BY LINDA WATTS**

A shopping trip to the pre-cut moulding section at Lowe's was the beginning of my tray design. I had a general idea of what I wanted to make — a shallow tray without handles to transform my otto-man into a once-in-a-while coffee table. There were extra pieces of ½" plywood in the shop that would make a great tray base. All I needed was a way to cover the edges and a fancy profile to top it off. When I saw the corner moulding, I knew that the edge problem was solved. The cor-ner moulding profile would wrap around the top and side of the plywood perfectly, providing a base for fancier trim. I found the bead, cove and steps of the glass bead moulding to my liking for the top.

Moulding and miters. This combination pro-duced an elegant tray that was fairly easy to make, and involved only two power tools.

## Making the Tray

Cut the tray bottom from ½" Baltic birch plywood to size with a circular saw or jig-saw (a straightedge clamped in place will help guide a square cut). The finished size of the tray is 15" × 20". The corner moulding adds ¼" on each side, so the bottom is cut to 14½" × 19½".

Choose which side will be the top of the tray, and write "bottom" on the bot-tom side in pencil so there'll be no doubt about which side goes up.

## Mystifying Miters

Start with the corner moulding. With the miter saw, cut the pieces about 4" longer than you'll need — long sides about 24", and short sides about 19".

Fit one long side piece against the tray bottom with an inch or so extending be-yond the corner, and mark the inside of the moulding at the corner. Mark the direction for the miter on the top of the moulding.

At the miter saw, set the angle at 45° and make the cut at one end. Hold the corner moulding tight to the fence so your miter cut will be accurate. To avoid tear-out when the cut is made, release the handle switch as the cut is finished but leave the blade in place until it has stopped. Repeat this step for the other long side piece.

Take the moulding piece back to the tray bottom and fit it against the corner, leaving it just a little proud, and mark the other corner location on the moulding. Also make a mark on top to indicate the direction for the miter.

Back at the miter saw, move the blade to 45° in the other direction, and make the cut.

Cut a miter on a piece of scrap wood, and clamp it to the fence and table (long side against the fence) with the finished side moulding in place tight against the miter. This will ensure that the next side's end cut will be exactly the same as the first. Make the miter cut on the other long side piece.

Now make the miter cut on one of the short side pieces, following the same procedure.

With a long side piece in position against the tray side and corner, fit the mitered corner together and mark the inside of the short side at the other end. Again, mark the top direction for the miter cut. It's easy to get confused with the direction for the cut.

Make the cut at the miter saw on the other end of the short piece.

Take it back to the tray bottom and check your corners. If there's a little room for movement, that's OK. When you're satisfied with the fit, take the short piece back to the miter saw and adjust the stop

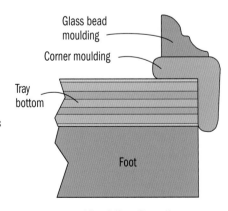

Glass bead moulding

Corner moulding

Tray bottom

Foot

**Moulding Detail**

Hold it right there. Make a 45° cut in a thick scrap to use as a stop. This will hold the moulding securely as you make the miter cuts.

to the short piece length. Make the cut to finish the second short side piece.

Now place all four sides of the moulding against the tray bottom and check the fit. Tape each corner (except one) tightly around the edge with packing tape to form the four-sided moulding frame. Then open the corners and lay the taped side down. It will be a long strip of wood with open taped joints.

Put a thin coat of glue on each of the miters and let it dry for about 10 minutes. The glue will soak into the short grain and form a slight coating. Add another thin coat of glue to the miters and press the first joint together, making sure it fits together as it should. If there's any squeeze-out, wipe it away with a wet rag.

Work your way around each joint, and when you've glued the last one, add tape to that joint as well.

Check for squareness, and when you're sure the joints are square, add another piece of tape across each corner to hold it square as it dries. Let it dry for a few hours. Remove the tape from the corners and clean up any squeeze-out on the bottom side of the frame so it will lay perfectly flat on the tray.

## Do It Again

This process is repeated for making the top moulding frame from the glass bead moulding. I chose the beaded edge to serve as the top edge, thinking that it would stand up to use better than the thinner coved edge. Again, cut the side pieces longer than needed, and cut the miter on one end of each of the long sides.

Line up the miter of the top moulding (with the beaded edge up) with the mitered corner of the corner moulding frame. The bead will be the top edge of the tray. It's important to remember that the bead is the top when making the miter cuts. It's easy to get confident about the cuts and forget which edge is up.

With the miters matched on the cut end, shift the bead moulding until its bottom edges are centered on the frame and make a pencil mark on both edges of the uncut end of the side piece to align it with the mitered corner. This will show you where to make the miter cut.

Make the cut (remember to keep the bead side up), and clamp the stop in position for the next side piece to be cut exactly the same size as the first.

Repeat the process for the short sides.

Now dry-fit the glass bead frame on top of the corner moulding frame. Hopefully it's a good fit and close to being centered.

Take the loose frame pieces and lay them on a flat surface in position for gluing. Put a light coating of glue on the miters and let them sit for 10 minutes. Then glue the joints together at opposite corners of the frame and tape the joints to hold them in place to dry for an hour or so.

Repeat the gluing process for the other two corners when the first two are dry, forming the completed frame.

I can see clearly now. Use clear packing tape to hold the glued mitered corners together. One piece of tape around the corner will hold the edges, then place another piece of tape underneath and pull the ends together above the joint to hold the corner in place.

## Build Up and Glue Up

Using a #120-grit sanding block and then #180-grit, sand all the surfaces smooth. Pay close attention to the mitered corners. They should be perfectly level. Always sand with the grain direction.

Place a couple thick scraps of wood under the tray bottom to raise it up enough to allow access. Run a small bead of glue near the inside corner of the corner moulding frame and put the frame in place on the tray bottom.

Run a small bead of glue centered on the bottom of the glass bead moulding and position it on top of the corner moulding frame. Use clear packing tape to hold it in place, then use small clamps on the corners and centers of the frame edges. Make sure there are no gaps between the mouldings and the tray bottom. Clean up any glue squeeze-out with a wet rag.

When the glue is dry, remove the clamps and tape.

## Finish Up

Using ¾"-thick scrap wood, cut four 2½" squares for the tray feet. Sand them smooth and round the corners with a rasp and sandpaper.

Glue and clamp the feet to the bottom of the tray, flush with the inside moulding corners. After a final once-over with a sanding block, paint or stain the tray, and apply a coat of spray lacquer to protect the surface.

## Parts List

| NO. | PART | STOCK | THICKNESS X WIDTH X LENGTH | |
| --- | --- | --- | --- | --- |
| | | | INCHES | MILLIMETERS |
| 1 | Tray bottom | Baltic birch plywood | ½ × 14½ × 19½ | 13 × 369 × 496 |
| 4 | Corner moulding frame | Pine | ¾ × ¾ × 24* | 19 × 19 × 610* |
| 4 | Glass bead moulding frame | Pine | ½ × 9/16 × 19* | 13 × 14 × 483* |
| 4 | Feet | Pine | ¾ × 2½ × 2½ | 19 × 64 × 64 |

* These measurements are longer than finished size. Cut miters to fit.

# Recycling Station

**BY MEGAN FITZPATRICK**

In some locations these days, recycling is mandatory; fines can result if recyclable materials are thrown out with your garbage. But at my local home center, there are few aesthetically pleasing options for sorting and storing recyclables until the weekly collection.

This project is sized to fit the cheerful green "party tubs" I found at the home center (just $8 each), which are 15½" deep, 21¼" wide and 11" high. Purchase your bins, buckets or baskets before buying your lumber, as you may need to adjust your sizes to fit whatever receptacles you plan to use.

## Overcome a Lumber Conundrum

If your bin sizes match mine, you'll need 60" or so of 18"-wide lumber for the sides, and 46" or so of 17¾"-wide lumber for the shelf and bottom (I've added a bit to the actual total necessary lengths to allow for saw kerfs). And you'll also need a ¾" × 18¼" × 25" piece for the top. You can't often purchase 18" or 18¼"-wide material off the rack, so you're going to have to glue up panels, or cut down premade panels. The less-expensive option (by far) is to glue up your own panels, at which point it's simpler to crosscut all your pieces to rough length first, then glue up each panel individually.

So, if you're buying off the rack at the home center, you may think that a 1×10 glued to a 1×8 will get you your 18" — but it won't. Remember that dimensional lumber is sold in nominal sizes, and widths greater than 6" are actually ¾" less than the nominal width (and ¼" less in thickness). So a 1×8 is actually ¾" × 7¼". It's confusing, but it's the industry standard. So, you'll be looking for nice,

Keep it neat. This handy piece helps you separate and store recyclable items.

straight, flat 1×10s, which will glue up into panels that are ¾" × 18½". From those, you can get all your panels.

After the glue dries, rip them to the necessary widths with a jigsaw or circular saw, guided by a straightedge. Then cut the sides, shelf and bottom to final length — hold off on cutting the top yet, as you may wish to adjust the overhang after the base is together.

## Pocket-screw Joinery

I chose clean, straight lines for the foot cutouts at the bottom to give the piece a contemporary look; refer to the illustrations for the layout.

The shelf and bottom are drilled for eight pocket screws, four at each end, spaced approximately 1½" and 5" in from each edge — avoid drilling directly on your glue line.

Now lay out the bottom and shelf locations, marking the top and bottom of each on both side pieces.

Next, clamp a wide, straight cutoff at the top edge of the shelf location. With the shelf pressed against the stop block and aligned at the front edge of the sides, sink the screw on one edge, then the other. These are wide pieces and you may have some cupping issues, but you should be able to pull the cup out as you screw the shelf in place, as long as you push each end tight to the stop block. Now sink the two middle screws. Place the second side flat on your work surface, align the shelf and bottom, and repeat.

## Top and Apron

Decide on the overhang for your top. I opted for a ¼" on the front to line up with the ¼"-thick screen moulding, and ½" on either side. Cut the top to final width, then align it to the case (the back edge is aligned with the back edge of the side pieces), mark a line from front to back ½" in from each end, and drill four or five holes for nails, then nail the top on. Use a nailset to sink the nailheads

Mark, then cut. After marking out the shape of the feet on one side piece, clamp the two sides together, make a relief cut or two, then cut away the waste. I use my thumb as a guide, but you could clamp a straightedge in place to guide your cuts if you're aiming for perfection.

below the surface, then fill the holes with wood filler or spackle.

Your apron is, in theory, 3" wide x 22½" — but things can change a bit during construction, so carefully measure from the inside face of each side to get the spot-on measurement, then cut it to length. The cutout is the same as on the side pieces and the apron is attached with two pocket screws on either end; pull it tight to the bottom as you sink the screws.

Grab an offcut that's about 1" wide, and measure and fit it ¼" in from the back edge of the top, aligned with the back edge of the sides, and nail it in place from underneath. You'll attach the back panel to this top rail, flush with the underside of the top.

## The Back Panel

For the back panel, I bought an inexpensive piece of ¼" × 3' × 3' piece of prefinished beadboard hardboard, and for

Plane to fit. If your apron and shelf aren't perfectly flush, a few passes with a block plane will even things up.

visual interest, ran it horizontally across the back. This piece must be cut carefully; it should fit tightly from side to side and top to bottom. Use a straightedge to guide your jigsaw or circular saw, use a sharp blade and cut slowly. Wait to nail in the back until after you've painted.

## The Finish

I applied two coats of semi-gloss latex paint to the carcase, back panel and

Square it up. Hang an adjustable square from the front edge of the carcase down the side to ensure you get the moulding installed at a perfect 90°.

screen moulding. After the paint dried, I installed the screen moulding around the edge of the bottom, cutting it at 45° angles at the miter saw. Align the moulding across the front, then mark the cuts directly from the carcase. Nail the moulding to the front.

Now head back to the miter saw and cut a 45° angle for the first side piece, leaving it over-long. Use a large adjustable square (as shown above) to ensure you have the moulding aligned properly. Fit the miter snug to the front moulding, and mark the back edge. Do the same with the other side moulding, then make 90° cuts at the back ends. If your piece is unpainted, apply glue to only the front 3" or so of the moulding, then nail it in place on each side. You have cross-grain construction here, so the glue will hold the moulding to the front edge, and any movement will occur toward the back, where the nails will move with the wood. (If it's painted, just glue the miters.)

Slip the backboard in place and nail it to the rail, shelf and bottom.

Now you're ready to break out a fresh case of Diet Coke.

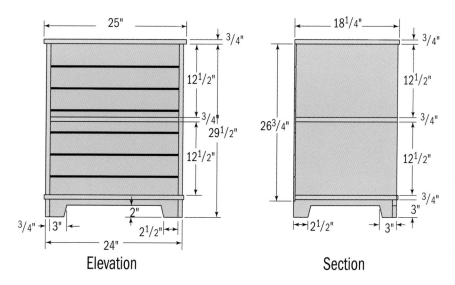

Elevation

Section

## Parts List

| NO. | PART | STOCK | THICKNESS X WIDTH X LENGTH | | |
|---|---|---|---|---|---|
| | | | INCHES | MILLIMETERS | COMMENTS |
| 2 | Sides | Poplar | ¾ × 18 × 29½ | 19 × 457 × 750 | |
| 1 | Shelf | Poplar | ¾ × 17¾ × 22½ | 19 × 451 × 572 | |
| 1 | Bottom | Poplar | ¾ × 17¾ × 22½ | 19 × 451 × 572 | |
| 1 | Top | Poplar | ¾ × 18¼ × 25 | 19 × 463 × 635 | |
| 1 | Apron | Poplar | ¾ × 3 × 22½ | 19 × 76 × 572 | |
| 1 | Screen moulding | Pine | ¼ × ¾ × 72 | 6 × 19 × 1829 | Wrap around sides |
| 1 | Top rail | Poplar | ¾ × 1 × 22½ | 19 × 25 × 572 | |
| 1 | Backboard | Hardboard | ¼ × 22½ × 26 | 6 × 572 × 660 | |

# Bi-fold Shutters

**BY CHRISTOPHER SCHWARZ**

After hobbit Frodo Baggins destroys the One Ring in epic film *The Return of the King*, there's an emotional reunion scene when Frodo wakes up in the city of Minas Tirith and is reunited with his long-lost friends.

While most viewers were transfixed by the hugging hobbits, all I could say was, "Look at those cool shutters on the windows."

After some design work with French curves, we produced this version of the shutters. They are astonishingly quick and easy to build with a minimum number of tools, off-the-rack pine and hinges. The most complex part of this project is in the planning.

Begin by measuring carefully the height and width of your window opening. Measure at the top, bottom, left and right. Now you need to figure out how wide your boards should be to do little or no ripping. All dimensional stock is undersized. You'll probably want to choose a combination of 1 × 4s (which are really 3½" wide), 1 × 6s (5½" wide) and 1 × 8s (7½" wide) to cover your window. Don't forget to allow for the gap created by the hinges. Each row of hinges will add about ³⁄₁₆" to the overall width of your shutters.

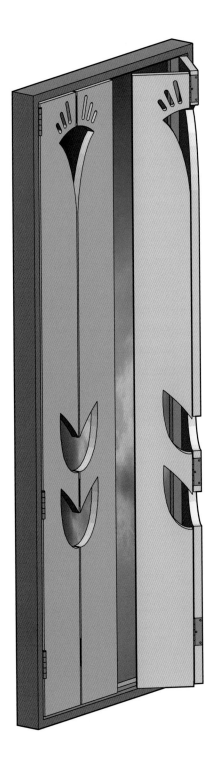

Cut your boards to width and length. If you are going to make more than a few of these, I would make a cardboard or wooden pattern of the designs for the leaves and the bloom. Lay out the bloom at the top of the shutter. Measure the remaining height on your shutter and position the leaves in the middle of that height. Make a few practice cuts on scraps first. Then, cut out the leaves and the large part of the bloom with your jigsaw.

The stamens of the bloom are easier than they look. With a nail or awl, prick the center of each hole shown on the illustrations. Drill a ⅜"-diameter hole with a brad-point bit at each location. Connect the two holes with pencil lines and jigsaw out the waste. Clean up all your jigsaw cuts with a file, rasp and sandpaper. Sand your shutters.

Join the mating pairs of shutters with your hinges. If your shutters are less than 48" high you can use two hinges. Bigger shutters need three hinges. Now add the hinges that will connect the shutters to the window. To hang the shutters, use commercial wooden shims to position the shutters in the opening and hold them there while you mark the location for the hinges on the window frame. You might have to tweak the edges with a block plane to get everything to fit. A magnetic catch at top and bottom does wonders to hold the shutters closed and in line with one another. Finish them to suit your castle's decor.

## Supplies

**Any Home Center/Hardware Store**

6 · Stanley utility hinges, 2 ½", zinc finish #819060, $2.59/pair

4 · 1 × 6 × 8' select white pine boards, $13.95 each. Choose No. 2 boards if you're going to paint them or want a more rustic look.

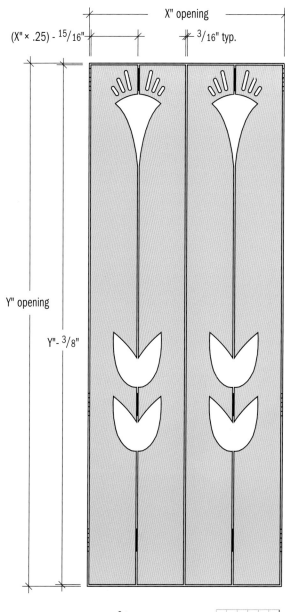

X" opening

(X" × .25) - $^{15}/_{16}$"

$^3/_{16}$" typ.

Y" opening

Y"- $^3/_8$"

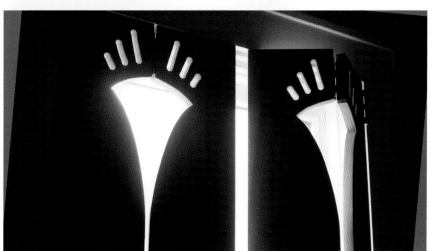

Drill $^3/_8$" holes, connect the tangents, and cut out the waste.

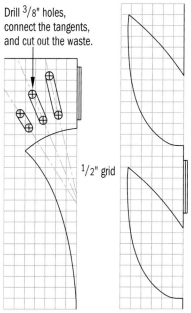

$^1/_2$" grid

# Magazine Rack

**BY CHRISTOPHER SCHWARZ**

Because you're holding this magazine, chances are you could use a magazine rack by your favorite chair to hold your current crop of periodicals and catalogs.

And because you like magazines, I suspect that you also like books, and you might have need for a stand to hold open your favorite reference book — whether that's a dictionary, "Baking Illustrated" or "Tage Frid Teaches Woodworking."

If you're nodding your head in agreement to either of the above statements, we have one project that can scratch both itches. This simple project has only two parts and they interlock: Slide them together one way and they make a magazine rack; slide them together the other way and they make a bookstand.

And here's the best part: You need only a handful of tools to make this project. Plus, it's a quick job; I built the version shown here in just a couple hours. It's the perfect "I Can Do That" project.

## Gather Your Materials

As with all "I Can Do That" projects, we buy all our materials from the local home center. So with a construction drawing in hand I hit the lumber section. I wasn't happy with the No. 2 pine in the racks. The poplar was an uninspiring purple. But there were a couple promising red oak 1 x 12s. These were expensive: $40 for a 6' length. But that was enough to make two racks, so I pulled the trigger.

## Make a Simple Jig

This project requires you to set the base of your jigsaw at 35° to the blade, sometimes tilted left and sometimes tilted right. To make these changes quickly and reliably, I made a little jig from a scrap. You don't have to make

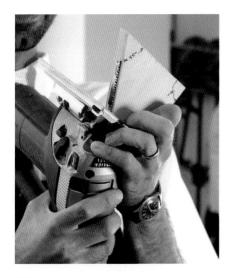

This scrap of wood acts as a reliable way to set your jigsaw's base to 35°. I found a protractor difficult to balance on the base and not nearly as accurate.

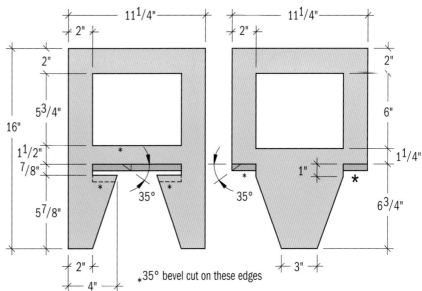

35° bevel cut on these edges

## Elevation

the jig for this project, but it sure makes life easy.

My blade-setting jig was made from a scrap piece of $3/4$"-thick plywood that was about 3" wide and 12" long. I cut one end at 90° on my miter saw. Then I set the saw to make a 35° miter and cut off about 3" of the plywood. The piece that falls off is the jig for setting the blade.

By placing the jig on the saw's base you can tilt the base to 35° left and right quickly. And you can use the square edge of the jig to return the saw's blade to 90°.

### Make Your Straight Cuts

Use the drawing to lay out all your cuts. Then, with the blade set at 90°, make the cuts that define the two feet on one piece and the single foot on the other piece.

Then make the square-shaped cutouts on each piece. Here's how: Drill a couple $3/8$"-diameter holes near the corners of the square-shaped cutout. Then use your jigsaw to remove the waste and square up the corners.

### Make Your Bevel Cuts

Tilt the jigsaw's base to 35° left and make all the cuts you can with the blade tilted this direction. Then tilt the blade the other direction and make the remainder of the cuts on the two pieces. In the end you'll have some waste hanging onto your work that needs to be removed with a coping saw. It's simple work. If you don't

have a coping saw, use a chisel and a mallet to pop out the waste.

Clean up all your cuts with a rasp, file and sandpaper. Then fit the two parts together — you might have to adjust a few edges with a rasp to get a good fit. If the part with the single leg is just a little too thick to fit through the slot in the other, reduce the thickness of the single leg with your block plane until everything fits. Sand all your parts and add a clear finish (or stain or paint).

In our office, we have far too many magazines for this project to be useful to us. So we're going to use it as a stand for our office dictionary, which settles our debates on word usage. But if we ever need a magazine stand, it's just a flip of the pieces away.

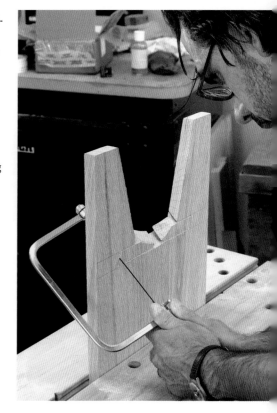

You can rotate the blade in its frame with a coping saw to make a tricky cut like this very easy.

## Parts List

| | | | THICKNESS X WIDTH X LENGTH | |
|---|---|---|---|---|
| NO. | PART | STOCK | INCHES | MILLIMETERS |
| 2 | interlocking slabs | red oak | $3/4 \times 11^1/4 \times 16$ | 19 × 286 × 406 |

# Lap Desk

**BY MAG RUFFMAN**

The glorious thing about being self-sufficient is that you can usually figure out ways to create what you need.

My latest need arose after a bad case of Burning Thighs Syndrome, a malady caused by sitting on the couch typing on a laptop computer. With my quadriceps performing as heat sinks for the laptop's toiling battery, I had the hottest legs in Canada.

I switched to writing longhand in a thick journal that never overheated. But to raise the book to a comfortable height for writing I'd have to pile up cushions on my lap, thereby creating a new thermal emergency.

My solution was this perky lap desk, a well-ventilated little unit that adjusts to serve the user's purpose and thigh thickness.

## Oaken-hearted

Start by cutting your desk surface to length with a circular saw (or Japanese-style handsaw if you want perky rear

deltoids). By the way, you might be tempted to use pine, but I learned the hard way that pine turns to mush around the insert nuts and the side pieces end up with hip dysplasia. Plus if you drop it on concrete, the side pieces shatter. Just sayin'.

Using a hole saw, create a grid of holes in the surface for ventilation. To accommodate a computer mouse, leave approximately one-third of the surface unviolated by the holey grid.

To make the desk surface appear thinner and more elegant, create a subtle (1/8") chamfer on the top and bottom edges of the desk using a block plane.

## Get Jiggy With It

Next, cut out the side pieces using a jigsaw fitted with a scrolling blade. If you don't like my curvy design, sketch your own version right on the wood. Once you've jigsawed one half of the side piece, you can use the offcut to trace a symmetrical match for the other half.

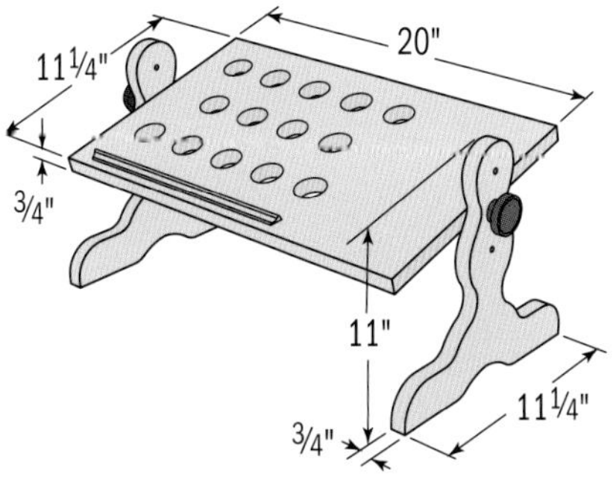
20"
11 1/4"
3/4"
11"
3/4"
11 1/4"

3D view

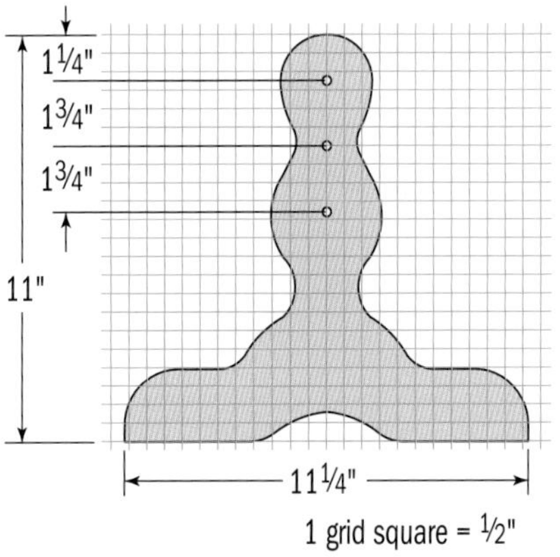
1 1/4"
1 3/4"
1 3/4"
11"
11 1/4"
1 grid square = 1/2"

Side Pattern

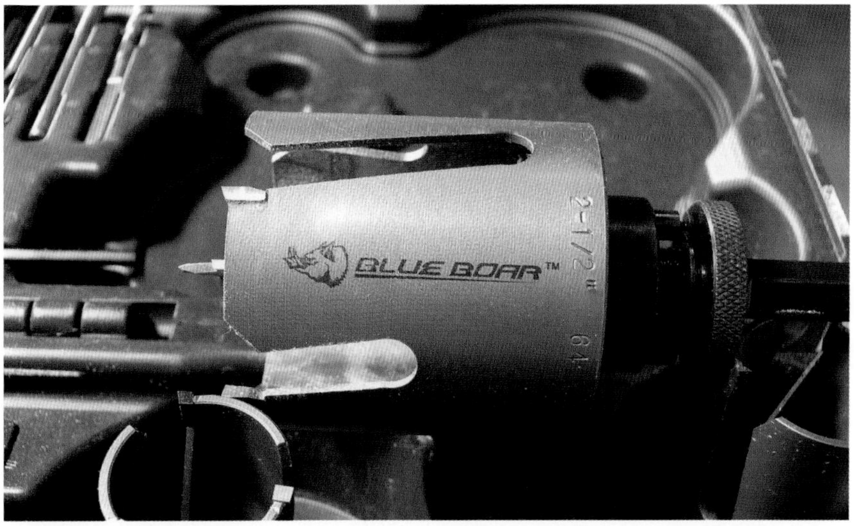
BLUE BOAR™
2-1/2"
64

Inexpensive hole saw kits are available at any home improvement store or hardware store.

Scrolling blades tend to scoff at perpendicularity so go slowly to prevent warbles and lumps in your finished side pieces. If you get them anyway, use a rasp to take out the wows. Or you can create The World's Cheapest Drum Sander by gluing sandpaper to one of the cutouts from the desktop holes, and mounting it on a bolt with lock nuts. Install the stem of the bolt in a drill press or a cordless drill and watch this small sanding cylinder erase your jigsawing sins.

Use a contour-sanding flap-wheel to quickly soften all of the edges on the side pieces. A simple sanding sponge works too if you enjoy the meditative aspects of corrective sanding.

Next, sand the desk surfaces lightly, along with the inside walls of the ventilation holes.

Then drill three height-adjustment holes in the side pieces using a drill bit that's just a hair bigger than the size of the post on your clamping knobs.

### Black to the Future

Ebonize the pieces, if desired. Ebonizing is fun, cheap and permanent. And because the stain penetrates the wood fibers and creates a chemical reaction with tannins in the wood cells, it doesn't wear as easily as a surface stain.

Oak has a naturally high tannin content but you can accelerate and deepen the effect by pre-treating the bare wood with a concentrated mixture of boiled black tea (for a greenish-black cast), or red wine (for a blue-black tint).

Once the liquid has penetrated and is fairly dry, add a coat of ebonizing "rusty nail" stain (drop a handful of old steel nails, bolts and assorted trail mix — the rustier the better — into a jar of white vinegar. Let it fester for at least two days with the lid off). Enjoy the drama of chemistry as the wood instantly turns deep black. For a deeper hue, add a second coat of beverage followed by more ebonizing stain.

While you're ebonizing, make sure to treat a piece of oak moulding that you'll glue onto the desk surface later to act as a ledge that keeps books and computers from slipping off. Sand the moulding before staining to remove any goop or tool marks from the mill.

When it dries the oak grain will be hairy and splintery, so lightly sand all surfaces with #150-grit sandpaper.

### Gloss-eyed

Next, give all pieces a clear coat. (I like acrylic driveway sealer because it's crazy-indestructible.)

The clear coat might raise the grain again, so lightly sand after the first coat dries then apply a top coat. (Acrylic driveway sealer dries a bit shiny so I rub it with #0000 steel wool after it's cured to bring down the gloss.)

**SUPPLIES**

Lee Valley
leevalley.com or 800-871-8158

1 1/4-20 insert nuts
#00M90.01, $7.50/10

2 1 3/4" clamping knobs (male)
#00M56.11, $2.50

Prices correct at time of publication.

## Parts List

| | | | THICKNESS X WIDTH X LENGTH | |
|---|---|---|---|---|
| NO. | PART | STOCK | INCHES | MILLIMETERS |
| 1 | top | oak | 3/4 × 11 1/4 × 20 | 19 × 286 × 508 |
| 2 | sides | oak | 3/4 × 11 1/4 × 11 | 19 × 286 × 279 |
| 1 | moulding strip | oak | 1/2 × 1/2 × 1/2 | 13 × 13 × 13 |

Glue a piece of sandpaper around a hole cutout, then mount it on a bolt with lock nuts – instant drum sander!

Now glue and clamp the moulding ledge onto the lower edge of the desk surface. If there's any glue squeeze-out, let it set up a bit before removing it with a scraper.

Finally, drill holes for the insert nuts using a bit diameter that matches the shaft of the insert nut (not including the threads). Drilling into end grain can be a cheek-sucking adventure in steering. Practice on scrap in a vise, attempting to keep the bit plumb. When you do it for real you might want a helper eyeballing the angle of your drill bit and screaming directional cues. Or not.

Finally, use a large slot-head screwdriver to screw each insert nut into the pilot hole until it's flush with the surface. Then assemble your lap desk with the clamping knobs.

You'll want to take your new lap desk everywhere including car trips, because most passenger seats lack tray tables – critical for navigational responsibilities and assembling snacks for the driver.

Use the offcut from the first half of your side piece to mark the matching shape on the remaining three cuts.

# Weekend Pot Rack

**BY MEGAN FITZPATRICK**

I like having the pots, pans and cooking utensils I use most often within easy reach of my stove, and this simple pot rack fits the bill (with a shelf on top for lids or what have you).

My original design of this piece hangs over the counter in my kitchen. That one has three sections (to span the counter-sink-counter span of my cabinet run) and is in hard maple, with two $3/4$"-diameter 304 stainless steel rods on either side of the sink.

The construction methods are basically the same as what I'm showing here, but to make this version more approachable, I used materials from a home center, including a $3/4$"-diameter wooden dowel. But there's no reason you couldn't get creative and use a copper rod or black steel pipe capped with matching metal bits on either end.

## The First Cut

This project is assembled using pocket screws, dimensional poplar and some maple Shaker pegs (because that's what the home center had available).

You'll need 4'-long pieces of 1x8 (the top) and 1x3 (the back), 2' of 1x6 (the sides) and a 4'-long dowel. (I considered using a smaller-diameter dowel, but had concerns about the weight of heavy cookware bowing it.)

One way I simplified this build from my original was to, as much as possible, use the actual widths of the dimensional lumber. But the 1x8 top simply has to be ripped — a $1^3/4$" overhang just looked bad.

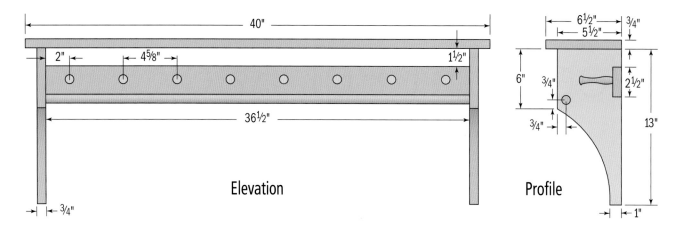

40"

2"  4⅝"  1½"

36½"

¾"

**Elevation**

6½"  ¾"
5½"

6"  ¾"  2½"

¾"  13"

1"

**Profile**

So the first task is to rip that 1x8 to 6½". For this, I used a circular saw with an edge guide (though you could also use a jigsaw), then cleaned off the saw marks with a block plane.

Next, cut the top and two side pieces to length at the miter saw. (It's best to hold off on cutting the back to length until you have the sides screwed to the top; that way, you can measure the actual rather than the theoretical distance.)

## Appealing Curves

Now set the top aside and work on the sides.

You have a couple options on laying out the curves. The easiest — if you have access to a printer with legal paper — is to download the SketchUp drawing from our web site (see popularwoodworking.com/feb15), print out the side piece full-size, then cut it out and use spray adhesive to stick it on the workpiece. Then, you can simply cut to the pattern.

But while I have access to a suitable printer, I prefer the "bendy stick" method. So, using a combination square, I measured 6" down from the top and made a mark on the front edge, then 1" in from the back and made another mark at the bottom edge. I tacked in a nail near each of those marks, then rooted through the trash for a thin offcut.

With the offcut registered against the nails, I can tweak the curve until I get something that looks right to my eye, then mark the curve with a pencil. Note that my curve might not exactly match the printout — and that's OK. What looks good to your eye is what matters.

Once you have the curve marked on one piece, cut it out using a jigsaw. And

the cleaner and more fluid your cuts are, the better — then there's less cleanup to make a fair curve.

If you've cut close to the line and have an almost-fair curve, go ahead and use the first piece to lay out the curve on the second, then cut it out, too. If you're not happy with the first cut, clean it up with a rasp until you're almost there, then mark and cut the second side.

Now clamp the two sides together (cut side up), and use a rasp and sandpaper to fair and smooth the curves on both at the same time; that way, they'll match. (But if they're a little off, don't fret. No one will notice when they're 36½" apart on your wall.)

The last bit of work on the two side pieces is to drill the holes for your dowel (or pipe). On my original, I used stopped

I often use two nails and a thin offcut to lay out curves. This approach allows me to tweak things to my liking rather than adhere to a strict pattern.

## Parts List

| | | | THICKNESS X WIDTH X LENGTH | |
| --- | --- | --- | --- | --- |
| NO. | PART | STOCK | INCHES | MILLIMETERS |
| 1 | top | poplar | ¾ × 6½ × 40 | 19 × 165 × 1016 |
| 2 | ends | poplar | ¾ × 5½ × 13 | 19 × 140 × 330 |
| 1 | back | poplar | ¾ × 2½ × 36½ | 19 × 64 × 927 |
| 1 | dowel | poplar | ¾ D × 29 | 19 D × 737    *cut to fit |

This jig's platform matches the width of the saw's shoe from the blade to the edge; the edge of the shoe rides against the fence. To use it, align the jig's bed with your cutline, then clamp it in place. Keep the saw tight against the fence as your cut.

To help with assembly, I clamp an offcut at my layout line, then use that to support the side and keep it aligned as I drive the screws.

A little glue and a light tap with a mallet to fully seat the pegs will keep things in place.

Along with clamping an assembly block in place, for this operation, I also inserted a 1$\frac{1}{2}$"-wide spacer block between the top and the back.

holes and captured the steel rod — but that makes the assembly a little trickier without a helper to hold things in place. So here I drilled through-holes.

To keep from getting blow-out on the backside, it's a good idea to drill in from both faces of the workpiece. First lay out the hole on the inside face of each piece, then drill a tiny hole right at the center. Now chuck a $\frac{3}{4}$"-diameter Forstner bit or spade bit in your drill and align the bit's point with the small hole. Drill halfway through, flip the piece, then repeat. (It's important that these holes be straight and at 90°, so grab a helper to spot you if necessary.)

## In the Pocket

Using a pocket screw jig, bore two holes on the inside faces at the top of each side piece. (I measured in 1$\frac{1}{4}$" from each long edge and struck a layout line...because I'm anal-retentive.)

Before getting started on the assembly, I recommend sanding the top and sides now. For painted work, I usually sand to #150-grit.

With the surfaces prepped, you're ready to attach the sides to the top. There's a 1" overhang on each end, so use your combination square to mark 1" in from both ends on the underside of the top. Clamp a straight block of wood at that line, and use that both to align the workpiece and help hold it in place as you screw the side to the top, flush at the back edge.

Repeat the process on the other end.

## Ready for Round Bits

Measure the distance between the two sides and transfer that length to the 1x3 (better yet, mark the length of the back by holding it up to those two pieces). Cut the back piece to length, drill two pocket holes on the back at either end, then sand up to #150 (it's awfully hard to sand after the pegs are installed).

Lay out the eight peg locations. On mine, the pegs are 2" in from either end, and 4$\frac{5}{8}$" apart on center. You can, of course, adjust this for your aesthetics and needs. Match your drill bit to the diameter of the tenons ($\frac{1}{2}$" on mine) and drill stopped holes a little deeper than the length of the tenon. You can drill through-holes, but then the glue will drip through.

Spread a little glue around the walls of each hole, then tap the pegs in place.

After the glue has sufficient time to set, screw the back to the sides.

Now insert the dowel rod through its holes, mark it to length, then cut it about $5/8$" overlong. Cut a $3/4$" deep kerf centered across each end, reinsert the dowel, then tap a wedge (with a little glue on it) into each kerf. This will spread the dowel just enough to lock it in its hole and keep it from sliding out.

After the glue dries, use a flush-cut saw to flush the dowel to the sides, then clean up the cut with sandpaper.

## Get Out Your Brush

Because of the pegs and the round dowel, I knew it would take me longer to paint this project than to build it, so I was sure to choose a good paint that included primer – I didn't want to have to apply more than two coats. In hindsight, it might have been easier to paint before assembly, then touch up where needed when done.

Of course, if you like the look of your wood, an oil/varnish blend or other clear coat would work nicely, too.

Once your chosen finish is dry, attach D-rings at the back on each side piece, hang your pot rack on the wall, buy a pack of S-hooks (mine are from Ikea) then decide which of your pots and pans to keep close at hand.

# Suppliers

**ADAMS & KENNEDY —**
**THE WOOD SOURCE**
6178 Mitch Owen Rd.
P.O. Box 700
Manotick, ON
Canada K4M 1A6
613-822-6800
www.wood-source.com
*Wood supply*

**PONY TOOLS**
404 N. Armour St.
Chicago, IL 60622
312-666-0640
www.ponytools.com
*Clamps and woodworking tools*

**B&Q**
Torrance House
Erskine Renfrewshire
PA8 6PA
0333 014 3098
www.diy.com
*Woodworking tools, supplies
and hardware*

**BUSY BEE TOOLS**
130 Great Gulf Dr.
Concord, ON
Canada L4K 5W1
1-800-461-2879
www.busybeetools.com
*Woodworking tools and supplies*

**CONSTANTINE'S WOOD CENTER**
**OF FLORIDA**
1040 E. Oakland Park Blvd.
Fort Lauderdale, FL 33334
954-561-1716
www.constantines.com
*Tools, woods, veneers, hardware*

**FRANK PAXTON LUMBER**
**COMPANY**
5701 W. 66th St.
Chicago, IL 60638
800-323-2203
www.paxtonwood.com
*Wood, hardware, tools, books*

**THE HOME DEPOT**
2455 Paces Ferry Rd. NW
Atlanta, GA 30339
800-466-3337
www.homedepot.com
*Woodworking tools, supplies
and hardware*

**KLINGSPOR ABRASIVES INC.**
2555 Tate Blvd. SE
Hickory, N.C. 28602
800-645-5555
www.klingspor.com
*Sandpaper of all kinds*

**LEE VALLEY TOOLS LTD.**
P.O. Box 1780
Ogdensburg, NY 13669-6780
800-871-8158 (U.S.)
613-596-0350 (International)
www.leevalley.com
*Woodworking tools and hardware*

**LOWE'S COMPANIES, INC.**
P.O. Box 1111
North Wilkesboro, NC 28656
800-445-6937
www.lowes.com
*Woodworking tools, supplies
and hardware*

**MICROPLANE**
1300 E. Upas Ave.
McAllen, TX 78501
800-555-2767
www.us.microplane.com
*Rotary shaper and other wood-
shaping tools*

**ESSENTRA COMPONENTS**
7400 West Industrial Dr.
Forest Park, IL 60130
800-847-0486
www.us.essentracomponents.
com
*Jig and fixture knobs and clamps*

**ROCKLER WOODWORKING AND**
**HARDWARE**
4365 Willow Dr.
Medina, MN 55340
800-279-4441
www.rockler.com
*Woodworking tools, hardware
and books*

**TOOL TREND LTD.**
140 Snow Blvd. Unit 1
Concord, ON
Canada L4K 4C1
416-663-8665
*Woodworking tools and hardware*

**TREND ROUTING TECHNOLOGY**
7351 West Friendly Ave.
Suite A
Greensboro, NC 27410
877-918-7363
www.trend-uk/com/en/US/
*Woodworking tools and hardware*

**VAUGHAN & BUSHNELL MFG. CO.**
11414 Maple Ave.
Hebron, IL 60034
800-435-6000
www.vaughanmfg.com
*Hammers and other tools*

**WATERLOX COATINGS**
9808 Meech Ave.
Cleveland, OH 44105
800-321-0377
www.waterlox.com
*Finishing supplies*

**WOODCRAFT SUPPLY LLC**
1177 Rosemar Rd.
P.O. Box 1686
Parkersburg, WV 26102
800-535-4482
www.woodcraft.com
*Woodworking hardware*

**WOODWORKER'S HARDWARE**
P.O. Box 180
Sauk Rapids, MN 56379-0180
800-383-0130
www.wwhardware.com
*Woodworking hardware*

**WOODWORKER'S SUPPLY**
1108 N. Glenn Rd.
Casper, WY 82601
800-645-9292
www.woodworker.com
*Woodworking tools and accessories,
finishing supplies, books and plans*

# Index

Awls, 20

Backsaw, 179
Band saw, 110
Bar clamp, 36
Batten, 85, 86
Benches
    hall bench, 52
    mud room bench, 70
    Skansen bench, 50
Bi-fold shutters, 192
Biscuit, 27-29, 73, 78, 80, 100-103
Biscuit joiner, 27-29
Blades
    circular saw, 16
    jigsaw, 12
Block plane, 9, 21, 25, 26
Bookcase, 144, 148, 158
Bookshelves, 164
Brad-point bit, 192
Butt joint, 28, 78, 130, 173

Carbide blades, 12, 13, 16
Chairs
    patio chair, 64
    simple side chair, 56
Chest, 110, 130
Chop saw, 12
Circular saw, 14–18
Clamps, 35–36
Climb-cut, 37, 41
Coffee table, 84, 90, 104
Collet, 38, 40
Combination square, 7
Compass jig, 152
Compound miter saw, 12
Coping saw, 72, 73, 112, 195
Crosscut, 9, 17
Cupboard, painted, 122

Dovetail, 27, 29, 39
Drills, 18–19

Edgebanding, 158-163
Egg crate shelves, 136
End table, 100

Fastening tools, 32
Fences, 14, 17
Files, 21, 22
Finishing tools
    basic strokes, 25, 26
    block plane, 9, 21, 25, 26
    files, 21, 22
    random-orbit sander, 22–24
    rasps, 21, 22
Folding Stool, 74
Forstner bit, 59, 61, 74, 201
Freehand cuts, 17
French curves, 192

Game table, 95
Guides, 17

Hall bench, 52
Hammer, 32
Hand plane, 16, 22, 86, 98, 122-127

Jigsaws, 9–12
Joints
    biscuit joiner, 27–29
    cutting, 43
    fitting, 43–44
    pocket-hole jig, 29–31

Knife block, 184

Lap desk, 196
Lumber, 45

Magazine rack, 194
Material selection, 45

MDF, 45
Measuring tools, 8, 9
Message center, 175
Metric conversion chart, 207
Miters, 9-14
Miter saw, 12–14
Mortise-and-tenon, 29, 50-51
Moulding, 12, 14
Mud room bench, 70

Nail set, 32

Ogee, 39
Open bookcase, 158

Painted cupboard, 122
Patio chair, 64
Piano hinges, 55
Pocket-hole jig, 29–31
Pot rack, 199

Rabbet, 39, 144-145
Radial-arm saw, 12
Random-orbit sander, 22–24
Rasp, 21–22
Recycling station, 190
Relief cuts, 12
Ripping, 42
Round taboret, 78
Router, 37–41
    router bits, 38
    bearing-guided bit, 37, 39
Ruler trick, 26
Rules for using the tools
    combination square, 7
    drills, 18
    fastening tools, 32
    finishing tools, 21–26
    joinery tools, 27–31
    measuring tools, 7, 8, 9
    tape measure, 8, 9

workholding, 36–37
Rust prevention, 6, 35, 36

Safety, 41
Sander, 22–24
Saws
    blades, 16
    circular saw, 14–18
    jigsaw, 9–12
    miter saw, 12–14
Screwdriver, 33, 34
Serving tray, 188
Shaker carry box, 133
Shaker shelves, 141, 150, 166
Shelves
    contemporary, 146, 164
    corner, 156
    egg crate, 136
    hanging, 172
    magazine rack, 154, 194
    open bookcase, 158
    shaker, 141, 150, 166
    simplified Stickley, 148
    stacking, 144
    whale tail, 141
Shutters, bi-fold, 192
Side table, 107
Simple side chair, 56
Sliding compound miter saw, 12
Square, combination, 7
Step stool, 180, 186
Straight miter saw, 12
Storage
    bench, 112
    cd/dvd rack, 116
    chest, 110, 130
    firewood box, 120
    painted cupboard, 122
    shoe rack, 114
    wall box, 120

Suppliers, 203

Tables
    coffee table, 84, 90
    game table, 95
    round taboret, 78
    tapered leg table, 92
    tiered end table, 100
    victorian side table, 82
Table saw, 4, 12
Taboret, 78
Tape measure, 8, 9
Techniques
    dimensional lumber, 45
    furniture lumber, 47
    material selection, 45
    ripping, 42
Tiered end table, 100
Tongue-and-groove, 123
Tool rack, 178
Tools
    awls, 20
    block plane, 25–26
    combination square, 7
    drills, 18–19
    files, 21–22
    hammer, 32
    joinery tools, 27
    measuring tools, 8
    nail set, 32
    random-orbit sander, 22–24
    rasps, 21, 22
    screwdriver, 33, 34
    tape measure, 8, 9
Trivet, 182

Veneer, 16, 23, 45

WD-40, 6, 12
Whale tail shelves, 141
Workmate, 35

# About the Authors

**Drew DePenning**
Drew is *Popular Woodworking Magazine*'s former associate editor for the web.

**Megan Fitzpatrick**
Megan is the editor of *Popular Woodworking Magazine*.

**Dave Griessman**
Dave builds reproduction furniture in his "free" time and lives and works in Cincinnati, Ohio.

**A.J. Hamler**
A.J. is the former editor of *Woodshop News* and the founding editor of *Woodcraft Magazine*. He is the author of numerous woodworking books including "Birdhouses & More" and "Build It With Dad."

**Glen D. Huey**
Glen is a former senior editor with *Popular Woodworking Magazine* and the author of several woodworking books.

**Robert W. Lang**
Robert is a former senior editor with *Popular Woodworking Magazine* and the author of several woodworking books.

**Mag Ruffman**
Mag is a Canadian woodworker, television producer, writer, comedian and actress. Read her blog at toolgirl.com.

**Christopher Schwarz**
Chris is a former editor of *Popular Woodworking Magazine* (now contributing editor) and is the editor at Lost Art Press.

**Steve Shanesy**
Steve is a former editor and publisher of *Popular Woodworking Magazine* and Popular Woodworking Books.

**Chad Stanton**
Chad Stanton has been a full-time licensed contractor and professional furniture maker for 20 years. He has written articles for *Popular Woodworking Magazine* and *American Woodworker* magazine, and teaches woodworking classes at Woodcraft stores. He also does demonstrations on hand-tool woodworking and home renovation at various shows and is the host of the "I Can Do That" video series.

**Linda Watts**
Linda Watts is the former art director for *Popular Woodworking Magazine*.

## READ THIS IMPORTANT SAFETY NOTICE

To prevent accidents, keep safety in mind while you work. Use the safety guards installed on power equipment; they are for your protection. When working on power equipment, keep fingers away from saw blades, wear safety goggles to prevent injuries from flying wood chips and sawdust, wear headphones to protect your hearing, and consider installing a dust vacuum to reduce the amount of airborne sawdust in your woodshop. Don't wear loose clothing, such as neckties or shirts with loose sleeves, or jewelry, such as rings, necklaces or bracelets, when working on power equipment. Tie back long hair to prevent it from getting caught in your equipment. People who are sensitive to certain chemicals should check the chemical content of any product before using it. The authors and editors who compiled this book have tried to make the contents as accurate and correct as possible. Plans, illustrations, photographs and text have been carefully checked. All instructions, plans and projects should be carefully read, studied and understood before beginning construction. Due to the variability of local conditions, construction materials, skill levels, etc., neither the author nor Popular Woodworking Books assumes any responsibility for any accidents, injuries, damages or other losses incurred resulting from the material presented in this book. Prices listed for supplies and equipment were current at the time of publication and are subject to change. Glass shelving should have all edges polished and must be tempered. Untempered glass shelves may shatter and can cause serious bodily injury. Tempered shelves are very strong and if they break will just crumble, minimizing personal injury.

## METRIC CONVERSION CHART

| to convert | to | multiply by |
|---|---|---|
| Inches | Centimeters | 2.54 |
| Centimeters | Inches | 0.4 |
| Feet | Centimeters | 30.5 |
| Centimeters | Feet | 0.03 |
| Yards | Meters | 0.9 |
| Meters | Yards | 1.1 |

Popular Woodworking Books
An imprint of Penguin Random House LLC
penguinrandomhouse.com

Copyright © 2016 by Popular Woodworking Books

Printed in China
10  9  8  7  6

ISBN 978-1-4403-4816-7

EDITOR: David Thiel & Scott Francis
DESIGNERS: Brian Roeth & Laura Spencer